Architecture Participation and Society

CW00820257

How can architects best increase their engagement with building users and wider social groups, and, as a result, improve the relationship between architecture and society while providing quality buildings?

Since the mid 1990s government policy has promoted greater social participation in the production and management of the built environment, including architecture. However, there has been limited direction given to the practising architect and no comprehensive review of the successes and failures of the past or of the conceptual bases for such participation.

Looking at the relationships between architecture and society, this book examines social participation in architecture from a number of standpoints. It bases its examination on a firm analytical foundation and draws from wider experience in related areas of work such as planning, wider governance and housing.

Reviewing international cases as well as past and contemporary experiences in the UK to analyse what lessons have been learnt, this book examines the scope for participation within architecture, and makes recommendations for architectural practices and other key actors.

Paul Jenkins is an architect by initial training, expanding this to work in urban planning, housing policy and a wide range of social research related to the built environment. His career has included extensive experience working with communities in the UK and overseas in Sub-Saharan Africa. He directs the Centre for Environment and Human Settlements (CEHS) research group at the School of the Built Environment, Heriot-Watt University and is Research Professor at the School of Architecture in Edinburgh College of Art.

Leslie Forsyth is an architect, planner and urban designer with experience in practice, consultancy, education and research in the UK and Germany. He currently is Head of the School of Architecture at Edinburgh College of Art where he also coordinates the postgraduate programmes in Urban Design.

Architecture,
Participation and
Society

Edited by Paul Jenkins and Leslie Forsyth

Routledge
Taylor & Francis Group

LONDON AND NEW YORK

First published 2010
by Routledge
2 Park Square, Milton Park, Abingdon, Oxon OX14 4RN

Simultaneously published in the USA and Canada
by Routledge
270 Madison Ave, New York, NY 10016

Routledge is an imprint of the Taylor & Francis Group, an informa business

© 2010 selection and editorial matter, Paul Jenkins and Leslie
Forsyth; individual chapters, the contributors

Typeset in Univers by Wearset Ltd, Boldon, Tyne and Wear
Printed and bound in Great Britain by TJ International Ltd, Padstow, Cornwall

All rights reserved. No part of this book may be reprinted or
reproduced or utilised in any form or by any electronic, mechanical,
or other means, now known or hereafter invented, including
photocopying and recording, or in any information storage or retrieval
system, without permission in writing from the publishers.

British Library Cataloguing in Publication Data
A catalogue record for this book is available from the British Library

Library of Congress Cataloging in Publication Data
Architecture, participation, and society / edited by Paul Jenkins and
Leslie Forsyth.
p. cm.
Includes bibliographical references and index.
1. Architecture and society. I. Jenkins, Paul, 1953- II. Forsyth, Leslie.
NA2543.S6A634 2009
720.1′03–dc22   2009013216

ISBN10: 0-415-54723-7 (hbk)
ISBN10: 0-415-54724-5 (pbk)
ISBN10: 0-203-86949-4 (ebk)

ISBN13: 978-0-415-54723-9 (hbk)
ISBN13: 978-0-415-54724-6 (pbk)
ISBN13: 978-0-203-86949-9 (ebk)

Contents

Contents

Contents

Contributors

Martin Edge is an independent consultant working in the area of people–environment studies. He has held research grants from the European Commission, UK Research Councils, central and local government and others in the areas of people, environment, affordable housing, technology in the home and disability, and has published extensively in these areas. For many years he led research in architecture and built environment at Robert Gordon University.

Leslie Forsyth is an architect, planner and urban designer with experience in practice, consultancy, education and research in the UK and Germany. He currently is Head of the School of Architecture at Edinburgh College of Art where he also coordinates the postgraduate programmes in Urban Design.

Paul Jenkins is an architect by initial training, expanding this to work in urban planning, housing policy and a wide range of social research related to the built environment. His career has included extensive experience working with communities in the UK and overseas in Sub-Saharan Africa. He directs the Centre for Environment and Human Settlements (CEHS) research group at the School of the Built Environment, Heriot-Watt University and is Research Professor at the School of Architecture in Edinburgh College of Art.

Joanne Milner is a lecturer in sociology at the University of Salford. Her research and teaching interests derive from an interdisciplinary socio-legal background, especially as it relates to regulatory frameworks, participatory housing design, and more recently intersectionality, identity politics and human rights with respect to EU and UK law.

Marcia Pereira is a qualified architect and experienced researcher with work informed and inspired by critical pedagogy and socio-cultural theories. She has been involved in a range of projects using participatory approaches in the design of real and virtual environments. Currently based in Edinburgh at Heriot-Watt University, she has lived and worked in Brazil and Switzerland as well as the UK.

Tim Sharpe is an architect with both practice and research experience in user participation and sustainability. His PhD and later practice experience at the

Technical Services Agency in Glasgow focused on user participation in design. He is now Head of Architectural Technology at the Mackintosh School of Architecture, and Co-Director of the Mackintosh Environmental Architecture Research Unit.

Leanne Townsend is a researcher working in the field of environmental psychology. As well as working on participation issues, she has a strong research interest in the connection between housing and identity. Other areas of research include market resistance to prefabrication and stress reduction in carers as a result of children's safety equipment.

Foreword

Jeremy Till

The key term in the title of this book, *Architecture, Participation and Society*, is society. It is important because it reminds us that architecture as product and process is always embedded in social dynamics. This may appear such an obvious statement that it really should not need repeating, but the evidence presented in this book suggests that architects, or more precisely architectural culture, have tended to avoid engagement with those dynamics. The reasons for this are multiple, but centre on the way that the complexity and strength of societal forces are seen to upset the purity of architectural values, conceived as they are on the false hopes of redemption through material and aesthetic matter alone. Too often, the result is the suppression of the voices of others in the production of architecture. Of course all architects do engage with others in the course of projects, most obviously with clients but also inevitably with users and the public as these two constituencies take on and then take over what the architect has left behind.

The question this book asks is: What could and should the nature of that engagement be, and how might it differ for the three different groups? Participation, as a nuanced mode of engagement, has in the past been treated as a form of intrusion into the idealised values of architectural culture, something that brings unwanted noise to an already complex process. Typically, it is at best tolerated, at worst played down, as much as is allowed. However, such tokenism in participation is increasingly unacceptable. What right does any profession have to determine the course of its own operation, and on what basis can the voice of the user possibly be denied? Regulatory frameworks in many countries now demand that professionals at least listen to, and preferably take on board, the views of others. Even if one might question the political expediency of these regulations and despair of their bureaucratisation, they do provide the opportunity to reconsider the operation of participation in architecture.

In particular, if participation is to become the norm rather than the exception, then we should be moving away from the polarisation that can be seen in the history of participation. Many of the main protagonists have started from a position in clear opposition to mainstream values and processes. The problem then becomes that a form of dialectic is set up, and the protagonists are moved to the margins, allowing the strength of the centre to evolve unchallenged. The challenge now is to understand participation not as 'either/or' but as 'both/and' within architecture. As the 'either' within architecture, participation has too often been treated as a worthy other, but not one that can deliver the core architectural values. Put simply, the classic participatory schemes mentioned in this book not only would never win architectural beauty contests but positively resist the siren calls of the traditional norms of beauty and tectonic delight.

The implication is that one can *either* have participation *or* Architecture (with a capital A) but not both. However, this implication only holds true if one accepts that the norms of Architecture are fixed. The real virtue of participation is that it brings another set of values to the table, and in so doing supplements the limited Vitruvian diet. Non-architects have different priorities and needs, and these have to be accepted as just as valid as the architectural ones. The issue therefore becomes not to dismiss normative architectural knowledge, and the values on which it is based, out of hand, but to see them as part of a much broader, socially oriented mix: *both* participation *and* architecture. Only then can participatory practice be moved from an oppositional, and potentially marginalised, position to something that can serve to revitalise the centre of the architectural profession.

Never has the need for this reformulation been more necessary than in the year of the publication of this book. Architecture played a key role in fuelling the binge of development in the early 2000s. In the rush to build, architecture was reduced to just one commodity among many, the stars delivering excesses of form and technique to sate the appetites of the high-end élite, and the rest left to meet the immediate demands of the debt-ridden marketplace. Now that the limitless trading of commodities has been staunched, and now that the very values on which that trade was founded are being called into question, architecture as a profession is left stranded. It needs to move fast to find another role. Surely the clue lies in the rediscovery of its connection with society (it is hardly as if it ever really went away), and surely the revitalisation of participatory practice as set out in the following pages is one way of achieving this.

Jeremy Till is Dean of Architecture and the Built Environment at the University of Westminster. His books include *Architecture and Participation, Flexible Housing* and *Architecture Depends*.

Preface

Paul Jenkins, Leslie Forsyth, Tim Sharpe and Martin Edge

This book is about the relationships between architecture and society and to this end examines social participation in architecture from a number of standpoints. These relationships are complex and rarely studied within architectural discourse, which tends to be self-referential. In addition, there are often quite different perspectives on these relationships within academic and professional discourses. The very definition of what constitutes architecture often isolates it from wider social engagement in the built environment through reference to elite values and/or professional exclusivity. Over time this has stimulated a sense of privileged isolation within many architects and a defensive relationship with wider society, excluding many buildings from the architectural discourse and ring-fencing what are inevitably élite professional values. The result is that many in wider society do not understand architectural output and discourse while architects decry philistinism in society. Not all societies and cultures have created such stand-off relations between wider society and architecture. However, this seems a common position in the UK, from which this book draws its core research. Through focusing specifically on wider social participation in the architectural process, this book aspires to contribute to a widening understanding of the social importance of architecture for society and architects.

The book is based on research undertaken by academics, who also have extensive relevant practice experience. However, it deliberately targets a wide readership and has specific recommendations arising from the analysis and conclusions for practices, the profession, policy-making institutions and others interested in this wider relationship.

The research was carried out by a core team based at the School of Architecture in Edinburgh College of Art (eca),[1] with participation from the Macintosh School of Architecture (MSA), Glasgow School of Art and Scott Sutherland School of Architecture (SSA), Robert Gordon University, Aberdeen – all in Scotland.[2] This team was created under the auspices of the eca architecture research centre ScotMARK.[3] The research was funded by a successful speculative research grant application to the UK Arts and Humanities Research Council (AHRC), and ran from March 2007 to May 2008.[4]

Although this core team had primary responsibility for the research, the investigation relied also on key inputs and guidance from a steering group made up of architecture practitioners, academics and representatives of relevant professional and policy bodies.[5] The main aim here was to avoid an overly academic focus and retain a strong link in the study between practice and 'theory', or analysis. While the research was not conceptualised as an 'action-research' project per se, it became one as the researchers widened the information collection process through involving key informants (through case studies and focus group meetings on initial findings), and ultimately through wider social discussion in participatory workshops. This underpinned the conclusions and provided a mechanism for recommendations from the research to be quite clearly targeted at relevant organizations, and as such the project evolved into one of research-action. Hopefully the book will assist in consolidating these initiatives to widen the social debate on participation in architecture, and through this reinforce the links between architecture and society.

Although the study focused on the UK, from its inception it endeavoured to widen its geographical scope to look at relevant experience elsewhere. It also set out to examine wider literature of relevance to the subject. However, this aspect was limited to 'scoping' out the 'field', as this is potentially extensive albeit under-represented in architecture literature, discourses and education. The research had finite funding and timescale, and as such a number of areas of potential research are not covered in great depth.[6] It was part of the initial conception to use the study to highlight gaps in information and research, and proposals for necessary research also form part of the conclusions. Readers are encouraged to build on this foundation and, to this end, a wider bibliographic and institutional resource is provided in two appendices.

While the book looks specifically at the role of social participation in the architectural process (i.e. participation by clients, users and wider society), it aims to stimulate a wider debate on the relationship between architecture and society. Reviewing this relationship is seen as crucial to the continued evolution of architecture as a discipline, practice and profession. Limited discussion on this includes Andrew Saint's *The Image of the Architect* (Yale University Press 1985); various chapters in Steven Harris and Deborah Berke's *The Architecture of the Everyday* (Princeton Architectural Press 1997); and Garry Stevens' *The Favoured Circle: The Social Foundations of Architectural Distinction* (MIT Press 2002). Although each of these is extremely different in approach and content, they explicitly or implicitly criticise the increasingly isolated position of architects.

While the Modern Movement advocated 'architecture as a social art' and this vision was perhaps most clearly implemented in the immediate post-World War II hegemony of state-led architecture in Europe and its international legacy,[7] the resulting approaches (in discourse and practice) were still largely élitist and in the tradition of the avant-garde. Avant-gardism was embedded in architecture prior to this of course, but arguably it has become increasingly detrimental to the practice of architecture and its potential engagement with social issues in the world of today.

In the contemporary context 'star' architects have become ever more decoupled from society; architectural activity is sidelined in large-scale 'building procurement' processes; and the many small local architectural practices struggle to survive in fluctuating economies. In parallel with these challenges to the discipline and profession, there are increasingly important challenges and opportunities for architecture to serve rapidly urbanising societies, and this is beginning to be raised in architectural discourse.[8]

While the book examines social participation in architecture in quite specific settings – historically in the UK and US from the 1960s and recent illustrative case studies in the UK – it goes beyond this with a wider reflection on contemporary practice in the US, Brazil and South Africa. The argument also goes beyond the presentation of the empirical to critically analyse the potential role of architects in social participation, drawing on experience in other disciplines and discourses. It thus sites itself within a critical studies tradition in architectural research and fundamentally queries why architects do not engage more effectively with social groups as a normal aspect of their professional role. This approach does not aspire to undermine professionalism, but argues that this needs to be the fundamental basis for professional practice in the evolving context in which architects find themselves in the twenty-first century. This needs to be different from the avant-gardist private or state-based approaches of the past century and the book recognises that such an evolution is as likely to emerge from other societies and cultures as from the UK or, more generally, the North.

This book raises fundamental challenges to how we perceive the discipline and practice of architecture and reinforces the key role architects can play in wider society by suggesting that 'architecture as a social art' is not a past concept, but one which needs to be reasserted. This needs to be through a change of focus in architectural education, practice, scholarship and research, founded on a clear analytical basis. As piloted in the book, such an analysis should critically embrace a wide range of intellectual thought, be adaptable to changing political, economic, social and cultural realities, engage in a mutually supportive role with policy, and express itself in practice and the professional ethos.

Edinburgh
March 2009

Notes

1 eca's Head of the School of Architecture Leslie Forsyth was nominated Principal Investigator and Paul Jenkins (at the time on secondment from his role as Professor of Architecture & Human Settlements at the School of the Built Environment, Heriot-Watt University, Edinburgh) was nominated Co-Investigator and acted as Project Manager, leading on all aspects of the research and the book. Research Associates employed by eca on the project were Joanne Milner (July to September 2007, now at the School of the Built Environment, University of Salford), Marcia Pereira (October 2007 to May 2008, now at the School of the Built Environment, Heriot-Watt University) and Leanne Townsend (September 2007 to March 2008, at the time on secondment from Robert Gordon University, Aberdeen). Marcia Pereira also contributed to book production in the May to September 2008 period.

2 Tim Sharpe, Research Developer and Head of Architectural Technology at MSA and Martin Edge, at that time Director of the Environments for People Research Centre at SSA (now an independent consultant), were also Co-Investigators, albeit with more limited advisory inputs to the project.

3 At the time of the research ScotMARK represented a network of Scottish Schools of Architecture/Built Environment. It reverted to its eca base in May 2008 at the end of this research project.

4 While acknowledging these multiple inputs to the research project, and the book chapters indicating specific authorship by various researchers, as usual the editors take final responsibility for the book content.

5 The following took part in the Steering Group: Les Brown, Partner, Fraser, Brown & Newman Architects; Anne Cunningham, Education Consultant, The Lighthouse; Edward Finch, Reader in Facilities Management, Heriot-Watt University; Pauline Gallagher, Board Member, Architecture + Design Scotland; John Gilbert, Chief Executive, John Gilbert Architecture; Ian Gilzean, Chief Architect, Scottish Government's Architecture Policy Unit; Jim Johnson, Former Director, ASSIST Architects; Richard Laing, Reader, Scott Sutherland School of Architecture & Built Environment; Andrew Leslie, Director of Education, Royal Incorporation of Architects in Scotland; Delia Lomax, Director of Housing Studies, Heriot-Watt University; Phil McCafferty, Director, ASSIST Architecture; Nigel Mellor, Chair, Comtechsa; Harry Smith, Lecturer in Architecture Engineering & Planning, Heriot-Watt University; Chris Stewart, Chief Executive, Collective Architecture; Jeremy Till, Director of Architectural Studies, University of Sheffield; Elanor Warwick, Head of Research & Futures, CABE; Nick Wates, Chief Executive, Nick Wates Associates Community Planners.

6 For instance, the case studies are predominantly illustrative of the different approaches to participation and claim neither to be representative nor exhaustive.

7 See, for example, Miles Glendenning's *Modern Architect: the Life and Times of Robert Matthew* (RIBA Publishing 2008) for a clear instance of an architectural career dedicated to this.

8 For example: Duivesteyn, *At Home in the City* (1996); 10th Venice Biennale, *Cities: People, Society, Architecture* (2006); Netherlands Architecture Institute, *Visionary Power: Producing the Contemporary City* (2007); Burdett and Sudjic, *The Endless City* (2008).

Acknowledgements

The editors gratefully acknowledge financial support from the Arts and Humanities Research Council for a speculative research grant (March 2007 to May 2008), which permitted the basic research for this book to be undertaken. In addition, the Edinburgh College of Art Research Board provided a small research grant to assist with final manuscript preparation.

Illustration credits

Alex de Rijke © 5.4, 5.5, 5.6, 5.7

Comtechsa © 5.8, 5.9, 5.10

Marcia Pereira © 1.1, 1.2, 1.3, 1.4, 1.5, 5.1, 5.2

Michael Mack © 5.3

Abbreviations

ABECs	Architecture and Built Environment Centres
ACD	Association for Community Design
ACSA	Association of Collegiate Schools of Architecture
ACTAC	Association of Community Technical Aid Centres
AHRC	Arts and Humanities Research Council
AIA	American Institute of Architects
AND	Asian Neighbourhood Design
ARB	Architects' Registration Board
ARC	Architects' Revolutionary Council
BDR	Bureau of Design Research
BNH	Banco Nacional da Habitacao – National Housing Bank in Brazil
BSF	Building Schools for the Future Programme
CABE	Commission for Architecture and the Built Environment
CAPP	Cornton Action Planning Partnership
CAS	Community Architecture Scotland
CAT	Centre for Alternative Technology, Wales
CDCs	Community Design Centres
CDCP	Community Design Center of Pittsburgh
CDG	Community Development Group
CETA	Comprehensive Employment and Training Act
COHABs	Cooperativas Habitacionais – municipality-based housing cooperatives in Brazil
CPD	Continuing professional development
CTA	Community technical aid
CTACs	Community technical aid centres
CUDE	Clients and users in design education
DCDC	Detroit Collaborative Design Center
DfES	Department for Children, Schools and Families
DoE	Department of the Environment
DQI	Design Quality Indicator
EAUFMG	School of Architecture of the Federal University of Minas Gerais
eca	Edinburgh College of Art
EDRA	Environmental Design Research Association
FLaT	Future Learning and Teaching

HAs	Housing associations
HE	Higher education
HEFCE	Higher Education Funding Council for England
HUD	Housing and Urban Development agency
IAPS	International Association of People–Environment Studies
IPS	Industrial and Provident Society
IPT	Identity Process Theory
KWMC	Knowles West Media Centre
LCC	Liverpool City Council
LMU	London Metropolitan University
MCD	Mass custom design
MDT	Minnesota Design Team
MSA	Macintosh School of Architecture
NAM	The New Architectural Movement
NHS	National Health Service
NHS	Neighbourhood Housing Services
NI	Neighbourhood Initiatives
NUBS	Neighbourhood Use of Building and Space
NVQs	National Vocational Qualifications
OSB	Oriented strand board
POE	Post-occupancy evaluation
PPPs	Public–private partnerships
PSSHAK	Primary support structures and housing assembly kits
PT	Partido dos Trabalhadores – Workers Party in Brazil
PV	Photovoltaic
RGU	Robert Gordon University, Aberdeen
RIAS	Royal Incorporation of Architects in Scotland
RIBA	Royal Institute of British Architects
RICS	Royal Institution of Chartered Surveyors
RSLs	Registered Social Landlords
RSV	Residential Serra Verde Project
SANCO	South African National Civic Organization
SFHA	Scottish Federation of Housing Associations
SHIs	Social housing institutions
SIP	Structured insulated panel
SNAP	Shelter's Neighbourhood Action Project
SRB	Single Regeneration Budget
SSA	Scott Sutherland School of Architecture
TIP	Tenement Improvement Project
TSA	Technical Services Agency
U-HAB	Urban Homesteading Assistance Board

Introduction

Paul Jenkins

This book examines the role of social participation in the architectural process with the objective of widening engagement between architects and society. While coming from an academic base, it is directed to architectural practices, relevant professional and other policy institutions as well as academics (in teaching and research). It covers a wide scope of historical, geographical, contemporary and conceptual contexts, including other relevant areas of practice and knowledge. It seeks to assist in transformation and ends with a series of recommendations which have been discussed in various venues as well as contemporary contextual review. As such, the editors hope the book will contribute to the evolution of architecture as a discipline, profession and practice within a wider debate on architecture and society.

The book is the result of a speculative research project funded by the UK Arts and Humanities Research Council entitled 'Scoping study as the basis for more detailed research into wider social participation in the architectural design process'.[1] The initial conception of the research, in 2005, was to respond to public policy concerning the promotion of participation by users in building design (mainly focused on public buildings such as health and education, but also residential design), and the promotion of wider social understanding of, and engagement with, architecture. It was also set up to investigate continuing interest in user participation in architectural practice. The aspiration was to provide a core source that examines a range of key issues concerning wider social participation in the architectural process and improve limited communication between researchers and practitioners on this issue in architecture. The project was created as a scoping project with limited resources and has evolved as 'action-research' through a wide range of discussion activities.

The main objectives of the project were to: map out the scope of existing knowledge of relevance to wider social participation in the architectural process and the key issues concerning this; explore existing methods of fostering forms of wider social participation and point to gaps in both knowledge and methods; and propose an agenda for further research.[2]

The project thus had an *inductive* focus, identifying key research issues and gaps in knowledge and assisting both in *theory-building* as well as encouraging *reflective practice* – i.e. aiming to achieve a balance between conceptual analysis and professional practice (and related policy).

The study was undertaken through the following. Initially it was a review of the existing (relatively limited) architecture literature of relevance, expanded by a scoping review of wider related literatures of relevance in associated disciplinary areas, including planning, housing, governance, facilities management and environmental psychology. This was followed by fieldwork through identifying institutions and good practice of relevance and, within these, identifying appropriate themes and developing illustrative case studies concerning these themes. The analysis of the findings from the literature and fieldwork (based on some conceptualisation at the start of the project) led to wide discussion on the conclusions. This was between researchers with significant relevant experience; with key informants within related disciplinary areas (through semi-structured interviews); in a steering group (with participants from practice, academia and professional/policy bodies); through focus group discussions with relevant stakeholder institutions (government, professional, civic, social and private sector), and eventually through dissemination and broader discussion in participatory workshops with a wider public.

In Part I, Chapter 1 outlines the initial conceptual framework which guided activities including: a focus on the architectural process rather than product; an understanding of different philosophical bases for participation; issues of 'supply' and 'demand' in social participation; the nature of 'value' in architecture and who and how this is created; which building typologies might be more or less likely to be open to participation in the architecture process; the balance between 'techniques' and 'tools' in participation; and the changing nature of the architecture process over time. An analytical framework was proposed based on three main types of (potential) participants: clients, users and the wider public; three phases of the architectural process when participation could take place (design, construction and post-completion) and three forms of participation (one-way information provision, two-way consultation and negotiated decision-making).

Chapter 2 outlines the growth and demise of the Community Architecture and Community Technical Aid movements which started in the 1960s, with an emphasis on the UK (but some reference to the US) experience. The US experience is examined in more detail, including more recent activity, in Chapter 3, which also looks at some experiences in wider social participation in architecture in the global 'South' (Brazil and South Africa). Chapter 4 then presents a scoping review of wider literatures of relevance as noted above.

Part II is based on sets of illustrative case studies focused on the following four different themes, each in a different chapter. The first set of case studies in Chapter 5 examines the *relationship between user participation and perceived quality in architectural design*, based on Kingsdale School in London, the Lee Valley Millennium Centre in Liverpool and Canmore Place Buildings in Aberdeenshire. These illustrate the complexity of the participatory process and the importance of clients' and architects' relationships and values vis-à-vis participation. These three examples have quite different types of participation and show overall that participation does not hinder quality in architecture, as defined by the architectural peer group. The second theme in Chapter 6 is the *institutional basis for community architectural practice/technical aid in the UK over time*, which examines Assist Architects in Glasgow and Comtechsa in Liverpool – organisations which survived the political and economic changes since the 1970s. Here important issues were found to be the role of key people (with a social ethos); the need for adaptation through financial and administrative restructuring with changing external circumstances; and diversification and cross-subsidisation from commercial activities (e.g. investment in property).

Chapter 7 has a third set of case studies which examine *inclusion of participation issues within architectural education*, based on the experience in Schools of Architecture at Sheffield University and London Metropolitan University. These case studies illustrate that it is possible to include 'participation' as part of the educational syllabus (both in live projects and modules). The fourth and final set of case studies in Chapter 8 investigates the *balance between social and technical mechanisms for participation in architectural design* through the experience of Cornton Housing Project, Stirling and 'the Glasgow Model'. Here it was clear that new technologies (e.g. computer-based visualisation) are helpful in facilitating the participatory process, but are not determinant for the quality of the participation, which relies more on social skills.

Based on the above documentary and illustrative evidence, Chapter 9 presents an analysis which responds to key research questions such as:

- Who gets involved in wider social participation in the architecture process, and how does this affect other roles and relationships?
- What activities in the architecture process are participated in and to what extent does the architect see this role as guiding the client/user/wider public as opposed to investigating their existing interests/awareness?
- How can social and technical tools for participation be used to communicate more openly in the process and how can this affect the use of resources?
- Which types of buildings might be more or less suited to participation of users and the general public in the design process?
- Why is there limited communication between research into, and practice of, wider social participation in the design process?

The analysis highlights the 'fuzzy' conceptual limits of the relevant scope for investigation, with the focus on the architectural design process inevitably to some extent being 'architect-centric'. As such it argues that there is a need for widening the issue of participation in the architectural process to a clearer understanding of the relationship between architecture and society – based on the inevitably multi-layered, interdisciplinary approach this needs to take. Essentially, widening social participation in the architectural process comes down to how value is created and who creates it, and how this is affected by power relations and played out in terms of knowledge. The application of the analytical framework mentioned above (and applied to the case studies) suggests that the 'normal architectural process' includes participation as shown in Table 0.1, whereas a 'participatory architectural process' typically widens this (Table 0.2), while a wider social participatory architectural process is as shown in Table 0.3.

Drawing from the analysis, the study presents conclusions in Chapter 10, which include action-oriented issues as well as proposed further research areas arising from the scoping exercise. The former is structured around resources, skills and attitudes. Resources are critical, with time for participation essentially being a financial resource. Here there is a key problem of fee competition and levels, and procurement processes. However, the lack of financial support for any post-completion feedback is also highlighted as an important issue. Another key aspect is the need to understand the balance of supply and demand for participation in any situation and when demand needs to be stimulated. Skills for effective and relevant participation are also an important area of issues, not only for architects (or other design process leaders) but for clients,

Table 0.1

	Client	User	Public
Design	Decision-making		
Post-completion	Information		

Table 0.2

	Client	User	Public
Design	Decision-making	Consultation	Information
Post-completion	Consultation		

Table 0.3

	Client	User	Public
Design	Decision-making	Consultation	Consultation
Post-completion	Decision-making	Consultation	Information

users and the wider public. Here social skills are emphasised as being more complicated than technical skills, such as IT skills, and need inclusion within educational programmes, continuing professional development and other 'supply-driven' programmes. Attitudes are seen as perhaps the most difficult to change, as these have developed over long periods but underpin action. Here the project identified the need to induce changes in attitude in the profession, but also users and wider society, to the possibility of realistic participation in architecture. As noted above, this cannot be approached within the architecture process alone, but requires a multi-disciplinary, multi-layered and multi-actor approach. Here there is a need to be proactive but also reactive – i.e. not only supply-driven, but stimulating demand at wider social and cultural levels.

The book concludes with a series of recommendations in Chapter 10, which are structured around target groups as follows. Academia is seen as playing a key role in changing attitudes on values in education, to emphasise the value of user and wider social engagement, as well as the value of generic knowledge as a means to indirect participation. Overall there is a need for more emphasis on the relationship between architecture and society in education and research, including engagement with wider literatures and interdisciplinary work. Academia may also play a key role in supporting wider social activities and developing a wider skill base. Academic teaching and learning needs to include a focus on social engagement, including practice, which can be a source of resources (e.g. pro bono work) for participatory activities (quite widespread in education in the US, for instance).

In the profession, professional organisations also play a key role in assisting in attitudinal change and skills development through regulation of education and continuing professional development (CPD), as well as general engagement on social issues with public bodies and policy-making institutions. There is a need for the profession (organisation and practices) to stress the importance of user and social participation in the brief development and design stages of the professional Plan of Work as well as an urgent need to review the impact of large-scale and/or public–private initiatives in the procurement and management of buildings on direct and indirect participation. The profession should consider the viability of reasserting the post-completion feedback stage within the Plan of Work (including engaging more with facilities management) and other mechanisms to encourage architects to engage with other generic forms of knowledge development and transfer. In addition, professional organisations and practices can play a key role in supporting wider social engagement with architecture through broadening the impact of current activities such as architecture centres, and promoting wider social engagement through, for example, competitions.

The book also makes recommendations for policy-making institutions to promote *skills* development through the regulation of professional training in academic schools/departments and inclusion of wider social aspects of architecture in curricula; and to assist with funding CPD activities, especially where these are directly relevant to large-scale public investment projects. They can also provide proactive support for dedicated research/teaching/training/information centre(s) to promote and stimulate wider social engagement in architecture (and related areas such as planning). They should also provide direct and indirect *resources* to support activities such as research funding (for specific practice-oriented and generic research); and support for civil society organisations in specific and generic participatory activities in architecture – i.e. a reactive programme. Finally, policy-making institutions play a key role in inducing changes in *attitude* across the wider public, private sector and profession through support for regulation of public and public–private procurement processes to ensure adequate social engagement and the promotion of wider social information/consultation processes such as through architecture centres and public involvement in architectural competitions.

Notes

1 While the research project was funded, this book is a separate production based on the research findings and is produced by the two editors with a range of authors who were part of the research team.
2 Areas for future research identified include: research that examines *the nature of direct participation in current architecture projects*, including community-based client bodies and urban regeneration projects, to understand the level and form of participation of users and wider social groups; research that focuses on *mechanisms for architecture practices to engage more actively in accessing generic information of relevance to practice*, post-completion feedback on practice and the development of other forms of relevant design inputs from practice as well as mechanisms for transfer of such knowledge; research into the *nature of participation in wider public engagement with architecture* such as architecture centres and architecture competitions (including experience in other parts of Europe) as a means to encourage wider public participation in architecture in the UK; research that focuses on the *changing processes for procurement of new buildings (including the planning process) and the impact this has on user and wider society participation.* Linked to this will be researching how corporate clients engage with their own building users in brief development; and finally, continued research to support *wider understanding of social participation in architecture through associated literatures* identified as relevant in the scoping study and investigating wider international experience. This could contribute to the possible new architectural training syllabus focus on architecture and society.

Part I

Background, context and analytical framework

Chapter 1

Concepts of social participation in architecture

Paul Jenkins

Introduction

As explained in the Preface, this book draws on an AHRC Speculative Research Project, and hence follows a structure to some extent dictated by the investigation. As such it is strongly research-based, but also – importantly – is speculative in its approach, specifically seen as a scoping exercise, and thus does not claim to be a final definitive treatment of the subject but aims to add to our existing knowledge and propose a conceptual framework for subsequent activity (research and practice) which is seen as rather weak to date in this subject area. While seen primarily as inductive in that it seeks to identify key concepts and an appropriate analytical basis derived from these concepts for further application, it is inevitably based on an existing set of concepts and issues largely drawn from the experience of the main investigators and book editors. This initial chapter thus aims to set out these – and the implications of the research methods – as a baseline to the research material presented in the book and the conclusions drawn from the research in the concluding sections. In this, the epistemological basis for the book is deliberately transformative as it seeks to draw from and enhance understanding and praxis.

Initial identification of key issues

Key issues and concepts with which the research initially engaged include the following.

The focus of the research activity

Potentially the research could be very wide ranging as architectural activity encompasses many different disciplinary and professional areas, as well as many different building typologies. Given its short-term, limited resource and speculative nature, the research had inevitably to be focused, and the key to this was the architectural process, more specifically the design process, albeit with inclusion of aspects of construction and post-completion of relevance.

The nature of the literature sources

There is a wide range of literature sources of possible relevance, with those of more direct relevance illustrated in Figure 1.1,[1] and again the research has needed to focus. This was undertaken in two ways in this initial speculative scoping exercise: first, targeted reviews of the specific literature perceived to be of relevance to participation in architecture and second, identification of key overview texts or concepts, in associated literatures through the research team's experience and that of key informants (e.g. Steering Group members). As to the international scope, other than the UK, this has focused in the first

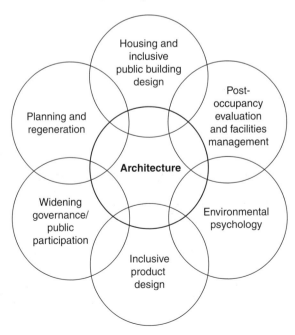

1.1
Areas of possible literatures of relevance

instance on the North American literature, although with some references to countries in the global South.[2] How such a wide scoping of literature is of relevance to the subject is described in more detail below.

The analytical framework

Research such as this, drawing on a wide range of disciplines with their different analytical and even epistemological bases, needs to define a clear analytical framework. This is also examined in more detail below, where other key issues of relevance are discussed. Essentially the research focuses on process rather than product and it acknowledges that the built products which are the outcomes of a more participatory process may be valued in different ways by different groups. In other words, an exclusively architectural peer group may apply different values to the end-product than a client or users, let alone the wider public. The research team wishes to avoid evaluating the products of more participatory architectural design in any narrow sense – such as their aesthetic value – and starts from the premise that engaging wider social groups in the architectural process can both produce better use values for buildings and assist with bridging a perceived widening gap between public perception of architecture and professional opinions. The evidence presented thus does not seek to prove this premise, as that could be tautological given the embedded values of the approach, but to demonstrate the potential validity of such claims.[3]

The nature of wider literature sources

How can the review of wider literatures noted above be of use to analysis of the architecture process? Figure 1.2 is an attempt to map out two broad

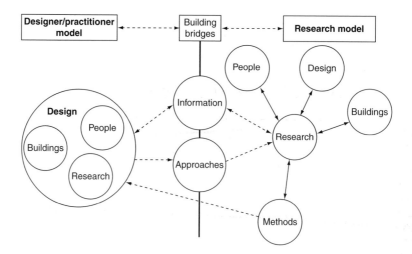

1.2
Models of
knowledge of
relevance

models of approaches to participation in this process.[4] On the left is the approach as it tends to exist in design practice. It is designer led and focused on the solution of specific issues by reference to the particular clients and people who will use or be affected by a building. Information on such approaches exists historically in the literature, in architectural practices which carry out such work and, in the academic domain, in the work of people like Henry Sanoff, as well as the recently revived interest in the sort of Design Charrettes carried out by organisations such as the Environmental Design Research Association (EDRA).

The research team recognises, however, that this is not the only sort of information relevant to the study and the research model represented in the right-hand side of Figure 1.2 shows how to draw on this wider set of information. Researchers investigate people, design processes and buildings, and produce information about specific building types, about the needs of specific groups of building users and about methods which may be used to engage in participation exercises. This information exists in sources like www.informedesign.com, the International Association of People–Environment Studies (IAPS) database of past papers, and increasingly in the work of organizations like the Commission for Architecture and the Built Environment (CABE).[5] It is in the nature of such academic work that it aims to generate conclusions from studies that can be generalised, albeit perhaps from particular buildings and/or processes, and thus can be applied to future design exercises. This sort of information includes work on disability and inclusive design, Post-Occupancy Evaluation (POE) and the effect of built environments on a whole range of human factors. These approaches also include a wide variety of methodological studies which may have relevance for an improved understanding and/or practice of wider social participation in the architecture process.[6]

In the light of the above perception of relevant information, this research identifies the gap between design practice and this wider set of information sources as often a barrier, represented in the diagram by a solid vertical line. Without bridging this barrier designers interested in participation continue to reinvent methods and spend a lot of time wastefully reproducing information which may already exist in domains with which they are less conversant. One role of the research project was thus to stimulate a flow of information from wider relevant research into design, to encourage the adoption of methods validated by research in participation exercises and, conversely perhaps, to ensure that research recognises the value of design itself as an approach to knowledge building – symbolised in Figure 1.2 by the dotted lines. In summary, the project identified a need to scope (inevitably in limited terms) a very wide-ranging literature concerning methods and approaches to, and information on, wider concepts and practices of participation in design.

Conceptual and analytical issues

In approaching the subject there is a necessity to define key concepts, and some form of analytical framework for structuring the study as well as any comparative work. These key concepts include:

- What is understood by participation, and more specifically the term 'wider' participation?
- How is this conceived of in the context of the architecture process, and more specifically the design process?

Participation is generally defined in the dictionary as 'taking part in' and typically three different 'participants' who take part in the architecture process, other than the architect and other design professionals, are: the client who commissions the building, the users of the building and the general public who are exposed to the building in some form or other. However, as virtually all architecture has some form of client, the participation of the client is assumed as normal, hence widening participation entails the participation of users and/or the wider public – and thus the term 'widening social participation'.

What form of participation is possible by these different participants? For the purposes of this study, the forms of participation can be seen in three broad categories:

1 Providing information, which is basically a one-way flow, from the professional to the client, user group or wider public.
2 Consultation, which is essentially a two-way flow between professionals and clients, users and the wider public.
3 Some form of negotiated/shared decision-making between professionals and clients, users and the wider public.

How can wider forms of social participation be envisaged within the architecture process? Although the process of commissioning, designing, constructing and reflecting on the process can be broken down into a series of detailed stage of work as defined in the Royal Institute of British Architects (RIBA) Plan of Work,[7] the processes can be simplified as:

- related to the design stages;
- related to the construction stage;
- related to the post-completion stage.

These initial definitions permit a form of analytical framework to be created which takes in three dimensions of participation in architecture: the nature of the participant (client, user and wider public); the form of participation (information, consultation and decision-making) and stages of the architectural process (design, construction and post-completion), as illustrated in Figure 1.3. While running the risk of at times being over-simplified, the analytical framework should permit a mapping of the nature/form and stage of participation in different situations and hence some form of comparative work.[8]

Other key conceptual issues which this study engages with include the following:

- different philosophical bases for participation as the basis for understanding value judgements;
- the role of 'supply' and 'demand' in participation (and temporal issues this raises);
- the relationship between process and product;
- the way value is determined;
- the link between participation and different building types;
- the differences between participatory 'techniques' and 'tools'.

There are two different philosophical bases for participation: the position which assumes that participation is a fundamental right for those who are affected in some way by a process such as architectural design, and the position which sees value in participation for instrumental reasons – i.e. it makes the process better in some way. The first does not exclude the second, but the second does not entail the first position. The first position may also be adhered to by

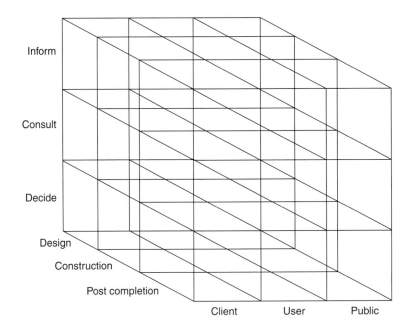

Inform

Consult

Decide

Design

Construction

Post completion

Client   User   Public

1.3
3D analytical
framework

widening the participatory process, but does not necessarily assume that any form of participation is more appropriate than any other – in other words, it may permit and/or promote wider participation to the extent that this is possible due to either demand/interest or other parameters such as what is possible given the relationship between the professional team and the client.[9]

This raises the issue of 'supply' and 'demand'. To what extent is wider participation demanded or of interest to the different types of participant? One may assume that clients are interested in information, being consulted and also in decision-making, although even here there can be degrees of interest and greater or lesser autonomy in decision-making for the architect and other built environment professionals. Clients may also not be much involved during the construction stage, and may not be directly involved in any form of post-completion review. Concerning users, can they always be expected to be interested in the architectural process for buildings they will be using? To what extent architects and clients might want this is of course another issue, as is what stages of the process are most of interest to users – possibly design and post-completion stages. The same may be said for the general public, who may be interested in information and even some form of consultation on new buildings – especially if directly affected as neighbours and also concerning key public buildings; however, they are probably less likely to have the opportunity to participate in any form of decision-making.

These 'demand'-side issues – assessing to what extent different potential participants may want to participate in the architectural process – is paralleled by 'supply'-side issues concerning to what extent clients and architects/other built environment professionals may want wider social participation, and the form this might take, as this may be seen as reducing their power of decision (see note 5). As well as issues of decision-making, as will be seen later, widening social participation has implications in terms of resources as well as the timing of the architectural process, and this can be an issue which constricts what is possible with limited funding, skills and/or time resources available. However, in certain circumstances clients and/or architects may promote wider social participation – such as in key urban regeneration projects. Here a supply-driven approach to participation can encounter limited interest or at least limited sustained interest.

Both supply- and demand-driven approaches to wider social participation in the architecture process are affected by temporal issues. The most simplistic of these is the time taken for wider engagement – whether information provision, consultation or negotiation on decisions. Linked to this is the issue of the nature of representation of 'stakeholder' groups – as it would be impossible to engage with all potential immediate users or the public on an individual basis, which represents the wider group. Thus, how does this representation take place (this of course is also relevant for clients where one hopes

the representatives and their decision-making remit would be clearly established at the start of the process). The temporal aspect has a strong effect here
– the immediate users may well not remain users for long, and how can such
representation and engagement represent more generic use values for future
users? This is also relevant for public opinion which changes over time – a currently much-loved building may have been very controversial in its early stages.
How can the architect thus deal with temporal change? One way to address
changing user needs is to build in flexibility, which may or may not be the
outcome of a participatory process.[10]

Concerning process and product, a key issue is the different links
between these, as mitigated by the philosophical positions noted above.
Hence, for those who believe wider social participation is a moral right, albeit
determined by the parameters of the 'supply' factors and 'demand' in practice,
the assumption is that the participatory process is something 'good' and to be
valued in its own right, whether it produces a better 'product' or not. However,
many although not all of the adherents to this position would probably also
assume that a more participatory process is likely to produce a 'better', more
highly valued, built product. This link between a valued participatory process
and a valued built product is more relevant for those who see participation as
less of an 'end' in itself, and more of a 'means' to an end, which assumes
some higher form of value in the built product – although this can be the value
of the 'supplier' (e.g. government agency) and not the 'demander' (e.g. a
community).

The nature of value is of course a difficult one to clearly define;
however, broadly speaking, architecture is seen as addressing issues of technical, functional and aesthetic values (otherwise Vitruvius' *firmitas, utilitas,
venustas*). There are issues in architecture concerning which of these is most
important, and hence more value-laden, and this is a complex area, as different
value systems are used in evaluating each of these issues – the first deriving to
a great extent from natural sciences, the second from social sciences, whereas
the third area is largely influenced by cultural issues. In that there are different
value systems that cross these disciplinary boundaries, there is little clarity as
to what is the balance between these values as applied to and in architecture.
This complicates the balance of valuing process and product. In short, a well-
designed product may or may not be the outcome of a participatory process,
and a participatory process may or may not produce a successful building as
valued in these different systems; however, participation would expect to be
valued in some way by some actor in the process (or else it would not be
promoted).

Another, not unrelated, issue is whether some building types potentially could or should have wider forms of social participation than others. There
has certainly been extensive debate concerning user participation in the design,

construction and – to a lesser extent – post-completion stages of housing. To what extent housing should be designed for its initial users or broader social needs is an area of continued debate with some advocating direct user engagement while others advocate a broader approach drawing on social research, and yet others see only the value of rather narrower market research referring largely to existing housing stock. There are obviously enormous differences between designing a housing programme and a one-off house. Similarly there has been a fairly long tradition of engaging with users in the production of other public buildings, especially educational and health buildings – including a recent policy approach which (similar to urban regeneration projects cited above) advocates a wider social engagement in the design process. However, although these areas are examined in the study, no specific typological emphasis was taken in the research approach, which aspires to study the opportunity and arguments for and against widening social participation in architectural processes more generally.

Finally, in terms of process, while the basis for values may differ between the 'ends' and 'means' approaches discussed above, in each approach there is a need to balance 'techniques' and 'tools' within any participatory process with clear objectives, assessment of demands and interests, and the nature of resources and other potential constraints or parameters. Here, techniques are seen as wider series of actions or activities, whereas tools are seen as specific actions or activities. There has been fairly extensive cataloguing of different potential tools and techniques for participation in the built environment (e.g. www.communityplanning.net), although arguably these need to be tailored to each context and situation. Most importantly the issue of power, as underlying how values will be defined and who will take decisions, is of the utmost importance before defining any participatory engagement. Too many participatory engagements have unclear and/or unrealistic aspirations which lead to adverse circumstances and reactions when they are not realised in practice. Thus – while it is very important to be aware of different tools and techniques, and to understand how these can be created and adapted in practice – most important is an understanding of the overall objectives of participation within a clear approach to the basics of which value system and which institutions/individuals are dominant and whether this is to be accepted or queried (and if so how and to what extent). These issues lead on to what is the 'forum' where participation takes place, what is the 'agenda' for participation, what 'languages' will this take place within, and who defines these.

The above introduces some key concepts and issues that the research aimed to investigate, and provide a framework for initial analysis of experience. On this basis, the book examines, first, how wider social participation in the architectural process has developed in the UK and internationally prior to an examination of contemporary case studies. Prior to this a short reflection on how the architecture process has changed is also important in understanding the structure of potential wider participation.

The changing architectural process

Historically most buildings have been primarily produced by either the users of these or more or less specialised builders, and this is still the dominant form of house production (see Oliver (1987) as representative of a wide literature on vernacular architecture worldwide). Monumental buildings have arguably always been conceived by specialists, however historically these were generally representatives of the political, military or religious élites. While architectural design as a distinctive role began to be perceived differently from other forms of plastic artistic creation in the Renaissance period, the specialised role of the architect as perceived today only began to develop with the rise of different, capitalist, forms of socio-economic interaction, predominantly in Northern Europe from the seventeenth century. This process was intensified with the increasing development of knowledge, and associated with this, of professions with some form of state-based licence, mainly in the nineteenth century. In this process architects defined professional boundaries with other professions such as surveyors and engineers as well as with builders and suppliers of building products. To a great extent this process was based on the increasing commodification of built form, specialisation in various areas of building production, and the resultant need for contractual interrelationships between actors in the building conception and production process. Associated processes were the development of drawings as a major form of (contractual) communication, the legal separation of the architect from the building construction process, and an increasing specialisation in building types.

In all of this evolutionary process the relationship between the architect, client, user of the building and wider public became ever more attenuated. From a starting point of direct and constant links between building users (often also client) and the builder (also often designer), with a fairly narrow socio-cultural set of parameters of what was considered appropriate (largely determined by élites but also the wider public) as in so-called 'vernacular' architecture, the situation at the beginning of the twentieth century was one of distinct clients (often separate from the users), a set of professionals (all working within the parameters of their professional organisations) and a set of builders and suppliers (usually acting through a general contractor), with an increasingly complex set of wide social and cultural parameters affecting the design process. In general terms, however, through the first half of the twentieth century the architect had a privileged position in coordinating these increasingly complex design and building processes and in determining the nature of the final form. By the beginning of the twenty-first century, however, the overall coordinating role of the architect became significantly reduced in many buildings to a subsidiary role dominated by regulatory bodies, surveyors, construction and facilities managers, as well as corporative funding organisations, as commodification increased its dominant role in the building design and production process, as professional monopolies were challenged, and as government regulation and guidance increased in scope and impact.

The main actors in producing the built environment in modern societies are clients, architects, other professions involved (surveyors, engineers, planners, landscape and urban designers), the construction industry (manufacturing, building and management), regulatory bodies (planning and building control in particular), the users and the general public.[11] Fairly typically, the design and building process is structured as illustrated in Figure 1.4, noting, however, that the central role of the architect is increasingly displaced by other professionals. The client consults the architect who refers to other professions and regulatory bodies in the design stage, including the construction industry in the construction stage, prior to handover to the client. As can be seen there is a very limited role for involvement of building users and the general public – if any – in this process.

Buildings should look good (aesthetics), function soundly (technology and structure), and also provide appropriate spaces (socially and economically). However, beyond this they are an extremely important part of a larger whole – physically and culturally – in their impact on the local and wider built environment. Throughout the past centuries, architects and their clients have come to expect to define what is appropriate in terms of aesthetics, function and space for any particular building, and architects have usually assumed they are the best qualified to define this also for the wider built environment. This social exclusivity in the design and production of the built environment has arguably serious failings, both for users and wider society and culture. This approach, however, is embedded in the training of architects, which focuses on aesthetics, space and function, with limited attention to cultural, and even less to social (and often economic) issues and hence builds this into professional exclusivity.

	The client	
Other professions	The architect	Regulatory bodies
Design stage		*Design stage*
Construction industry (and other professions)	The architect	Regulatory bodies
Construction stage		*Construction stage*
	Handover to the client	

1.4
The typical
architectural
process

Such wider socio-cultural exclusion in architecture has arguably led to increasing alienation of building users and a growing sense of alienation of the general public from specialist professions and clients, and thus from architecture and production of the wider built environment per se. The result has at times led to various explicit forms of protest, such as in the struggle against comprehensive redevelopment and for conservation in the 1960s and 1970s. However, perhaps more importantly, this underpins an implicit but widespread negative attitude to new architecture and a preference for a narrow set of 'traditional' aesthetic values in the built environment, for example, in the ubiquitous suburban house design.[12] The former explicit protests were in fact the basis for attempts to re-engage the users with the design process, as well as the general public on a broader scale, as described in the review of community/ social architecture in Chapter 2, but this has largely been surpassed as the social engagement function has also become professionalised (e.g. through conservation organisations as opposed to groups within civil society). Nevertheless, as the historical review shows, direct user participation in architecture has been retained in a number of forms: through continuation of 'community/social architecture' and through a certain re-emergence of 'self-build' activities in housing. In addition the tendency for widening direct participation in governance which is particularly evident in the UK since the 1996 election has led to an understanding that major government interventions in the built environment (such as urban regeneration and major educational and health building programmes, as well as social housing provision and management), need to engage with users and the wider public – often defined as forms of 'community'[13] – and this is increasingly linked to arguments about quality in the production of the built environment.

How can social groups such as users and the wider public engage in the process of producing the built environment? Basically in two stages: participating in some form in the design process and then in post-completion evaluation, with more limited possible engagement in the actual construction process. The first form of engagement may be prior to the definition of the brief/programme, during the design process itself (and even possibly adjusting this in the construction stage); whereas the second is after the construction process is complete (although could also possibly be before the end of this process). Here the client consults the architect who refers to other professions and regulatory bodies in the design stage – and also the building users. Following the handover to the client both building users and – where considered appropriate – a wider public can engage again with post-completion feedback. This is illustrated diagrammatically in Figure 1.5.

	The client	
Regulatory bodies	The architect and other professionals	Building users
Design stage		*Participation in the design process*
Construction industry and regulatory bodies	The architect and other professionals	
Construction stage		*Construction stage*
	Handover to the client	*Post-completion evaluation*
Regulatory bodies	Architect/client/other	Building users/ general public

1.5
A possible design-and-build process with wider social participation

Concluding remarks

The above are some of the issues and concepts that underpin the research and that are addressed in some form or other in the book, even if only to highlight the need for further investigation. In conclusion, the basic underlying positions of the investigators are reiterated as follows:

- widening social participation in the architectural process has an essential value in this process – whether philosophically or instrumentally based;
- study of past and current practice in this area can be enriched by a study of approaches in associated areas of activity, thus breaking down disciplinary barriers;
- the time is right for a (re-)assessment of the relationships between architects and other 'stakeholders', whether users or wider society, as architecture has an important social function which is often ignored by the profession; however,
- there are many parameters which condition the objectives, opportunity and praxis of widening social participation in architecture which need clarity in architectural thought and practice.

This book hopes to provide new focus for discussion and eventually the theory and practice of architecture through the scoping of these concepts and issues in this project.

Notes

1 The research team acknowledges that there are other potentially relevant literatures in such areas as wider sociology and/or development studies, which they draw on indirectly. Specific team expertise includes: architecture and participation/community architecture/

technical aid UK – Forsyth, Jenkins, Sharpe; housing and regeneration – Jenkins, Milner, Sharpe; governance and participation in planning – Jenkins; environmental psychology – Edge, Townsend; virtual environments – Pereira, Sharpe.

2 Ideally wider European experience could have examined; some of this documented in Blundell-Jones *et al.* (2005).

3 In essence the research is based on a social constructivist approach which depends on the validation of its findings through social groups – as is argued to be fundamentally necessary given the subject and is deliberatively built into the research method.

4 While this chapter has been prepared by Paul Jenkins, the section on Models of Relevant Knowledge, including Figure 1.2, was contributed by Martin Edge.

5 The Scottish Executive has also demonstrated commitment to this sort of research, for example by funding a 'mapping survey' of research on architecture (see: www.scotmark. eca.ac.uk/?research=64&school=5&content=2&parent=6).

6 For example, a recent study at Robert Gordon University for the Economic and Social Research Council looking at how people navigate through virtual built environments offers insights for practical participation exercises of that kind (see: www.scotmark.eca.ac.uk/? school=5&content=2&parent=6).

7 The RIBA Plan of Work includes: (A) Appraisal; (B) Strategic Brief; (C) Outline Proposals; (D) Detailed Proposals; (E) Final Proposals; (F) Production Information; (G) Tender documents; (H) Tender action; (J) Mobilisation; (K) Construction to Practical Completion; (L) After practical completion. For the purposes of this study the architectural design process incorporates stages (A) through to (F), construction (G) through to (K) and post-completion, stage (L).

8 This analytical framework emerged from discussions between the two editors based on the analysis put forward by the author of this chapter.

9 If participation is seen as some form of empowerment in wider decision-making, the relations of power between participants need also to be understood. Again this has different philosophical positions. One position is that power can be replicated without any theoretical end and hence empowerment is just a matter of getting a process right through good participation. An opposing position is that power is limited and – as a zero-sum game – if one person/group is to be empowered this entails taking power from another who has this power. These can be identified as 'top-down' and 'bottom-up' forms of empowerment. A contrasting position, however, argues that power infuses all relations and those with less power in any situation may accept the power relations and not necessarily desire changes, including 'empowerment'. This position argues for a contextual analysis of power relations in situations as the basis for deciding what is desirable, possible or acceptable in terms of power relations and such changes as empowerment, and hence defines the role of participation in any process. While this form of analysis has come from community development and planning literatures (and draws on Foucauldian analysis in the social sciences) it is also relevant to architecture.

10 See Schneider and Till (2007) for a review of flexible housing.

11 Increasingly corporative funding organisations bring together a set of professionals, including the architect, in complex speculative contractual procurement and management processes as in Public–Private Partnerships (PPPs) – however predominantly for large, complex building programmes such as in state-funded education and health sectors.

12 This negativity is both individual culturally channelled choice (where the 'traditional' is more highly valued) as well as anxiety about wider social acceptability (i.e. through impacts on sale value).

13 In these there is usually an assumption of a territorially bounded 'community', although in reality these often have a wide and potentially conflicting range of 'communities of interest', which can undermine simplistic approaches to participation.

Chapter 2

A brief historical review of community technical aid and community architecture

Paul Jenkins, Joanne Milner and Tim Sharpe

Introduction

As noted in the introduction to this book, part of the interest of the investigators in researching the scope of wider social participation in the architectural process is their previous involvement in what has been loosely termed 'Community Technical Aid' and 'Community Architecture'. In the United Kingdom this largely developed in the 1970s but became eclipsed by the mid-1980s, surviving for longer in the US (the experience of some in more international activities as described in Chapter 3). The history of the UK movement has been written up in a number of key texts (Blundell-Jones *et al.* 2005; O'Sullivan 1988; Towers 1995; Wates and Knevitt 1987), but the literature dries up in the latter part of the 1980s. Thus, as an entry point for the research the study reviewed previous experience with the intention of identifying what happened to these movements. The objective of this chapter is to examine the origins, activities and experience of some of the community technical aid and architecture movement actors in the UK and from this review draw issues of relevance for the contemporary context.[1]

Origins of community technical aid and architecture

Longer-term antecedents to wider social participation in architecture may be identified in concepts of 'indigenous' knowledge, 'Rapid Urban Appraisal' and sociological investigation of 'slum' communities,[2] as well as the concept of the 'everyday' as applied to architecture, contemporarily interpreted through, for instance, Venturi and Scott Brown's work.[3] However, more explicitly, in the early 1960s some practising architects/planners began to write specifically about the role of community in the built environment development process. One of the most influential in the UK was John Turner, a British architect working in Peru in squatter settlements. Turner's articles in *Architectural Design* (1963, 1968) fitted in with radical intellectual themes of the mid- to late 1960s. Another writer and practitioner, more influential in continental Europe, was Dutch architect John Habraken, whose flexible design approach to housing, *Supports*, was published in 1961 (first published in English in 1972). While these two approaches were from very different geographical and eco-nomic worlds, and their approaches derived from different perspectives (Turner emphasising the role of households vis-à-vis the state and Habraken criticising the role of the state vis-à-vis households), there was a lot of convergence in their ideas.

Turner went on to develop his ideas through a considerable number of publications, including a celebrated debate with neo-Marxist structuralist Rod Burgess on the nature of self-help housing in the so-called 'developing world'.[4] While he was influenced by a number of Latin American and sociological/anthropological sources which were not clearly acknowledged, Turner developed a coherent and influential approach which moved from the role of the state vis-à-vis the household in so-called 'self-help' housing to the role of the community and the 'Third Sector'.[5] A generation of architects/planners active, in what was generally termed the 'developing world', based its profes-sional activity on this approach, and one of the most powerful international aid agencies (the World Bank) went on to adopt key elements of this between 1970 and 1985, with varying degrees of success (Jenkins *et al.* 2006). One UK architect who developed a system for self-build was Walter Segal in the 1970s. This was based on timber-frame prefabricated panelling and was used in a project supported by Lewisham Borough Council in London from 1981. Segal's technique was adapted by Rod Hackney (see below) for a self-build housing association in Stirling in the late 1980s. Habraken developed his initial ideas in the mid-1960s in a number of projects developed at the Technical University of Eindhoven which demonstrated his approach to family-controlled house con-struction in practice. This was subsequently developed in Adelaide Road, Camden, London by Nabel Hamdi and Nicholas Wilkinson in the mid-1970s in a public housing project for the Greater London Council (Primary Support Structures and Housing Assembly Kits (PSSHAK)).

While intellectually influential, the practical application of the 'supports approach' was never really taken up by the major investors in housing in Europe, whether state, private or voluntary sector. However, it later influenced international housing approaches after the 'self-help' era as an element of the United Nations supported 'enabling strategies' approach. Hamdi also moved into academia and continued to practise in the field of 'development' and publish within the 'self-help' tradition (e.g. Hamdi 2004). In addition, in the late 1990s there was a resurgence of interest in self-build in the global North (especially in the UK as this continued strongly in the US), partly due to economic, but also ecological pressures, with various examples of 'green housing'.

Other, less well-known pioneers of participatory architecture in Europe in this period were Belgian architect Lucien Kroll who incorporated Habraken's ideas in public buildings such as the Louvain Medical School extension (begun 1969); Anglo-Swedish architect-planner Ralph Erskine's late 1960s development of the 'Byker' public housing estate in Newcastle, with intensive community participation; and British writer Colin Ward, whose most influential book *Housing – An Anarchist Approach* (1976) dealt mainly with participation of tenants in public housing management.

A different strand of community engagement in the built environment came from the United States and was more allied to the wider social protest movements of the mid- to late 1960s. This strand was the advocacy planning approach where professionals represented poor communities in resistance to comprehensive redevelopment (Davidoff 1995). In the 1970s this approach was often based on Community Design Centres providing local-level technical assistance within communities on a number of issues, architecture as well as planning, forerunners of such centres in the UK. To a great extent these came to depend on government funds, which initially flowed from federal agencies such as the Housing and Urban Development agency (HUD). One of the lasting conceptual impacts of these activities was the 1969 analysis of community participation by Sherry Arnstein, the Chief Adviser on Citizen Participation to HUD, whose 'ladder of participation' is still constantly used as a reference for community participation, despite critiques.[6]

The urban unrest in the US was paralleled with increasing public disaffection in the UK from the mid-1960s of the central and local government policy towards increasingly large-scale, post-war urban slum clearance and renewal programmes, and the wholesale replacement of older properties in poor condition with what were seen as featureless system-built multi-storey flats. Local authority architecture and planning departments were largely viewed as monolithic and unresponsive to the social upheaval, dispersal and breakdown of traditional communities attributed to their redevelopment plans.

In the light of this, UK groups developed community engagement activities including the organisation Support (1976) in London, which coordinated planning assistance to communities such as those resisting redevelopment in Covent Garden, as well as supporting the squatter movement – where squatters inhabited unused buildings in areas blighted for redevelopment as well as upmarket housing and office areas (Anning *et al.* 1980). Squatting had existed after each of the world wars but became fairly widespread in the UK and continental Europe again in the late 1960s and through the 1970s, particularly in Holland, but also in Denmark where the 'Free city of Copenhagen' (Kristiania) was created, still existing today in a much modified form. In some cases squatters' activities led to the creation of formal housing associations, such as in Bristol (Ospina 1987).

These early community architecture and planning movements to a great extent depended initially on students and radical architects and planners working with communities on a voluntary basis. However, with the growing realisation that the social movements these organisations serviced were significant, government agencies began to support these activities. They also began to include participation as an element in policy, with (in the UK) the publication of the Skeffington Report on Public Participation (*People and Planning*) in 1969. This led to a growth of local pressure groups which were to be included in the statutory planning process. The Housing Act of 1969 also introduced General Improvement Areas and later (1974 Act) Housing Action Areas and Priority Neighbourhoods, signalling a reversal of the comprehensive redevelopment approach to one of rehabilitation. In addition, the formation of the Planning Aid Scheme in 1973 by the (then) Town and Country Planning Association consolidated the US advocacy planning approach in the UK.

What is community architecture and how does it differ from community technical aid?

The term 'community architecture' can be traced back to the early 1970s when the then President of the RIBA, Fred Pooley, used it to refer to the provision of architecture for the community by local authorities (Wates and Knevitt 1987). This definition was contested (e.g. Wates and Knevitt 1987: 32) and in fact was greatly expanded over the next two decades to refer to the provision of a wide number of related built environment professional services, which included not only architecture but also planning, landscape, surveying and even graphic design, to enable local groups to actively participate in the (re)development of their environment (Towers 1995). Wates and Knevitt (1987: 119) argued that as 'the built environment is too complex and inter-dependent to be fragmented ... it has to be treated as a whole system'. To this end they place a greater emphasis on 'the process of development than ... the end product', noting that the most appropriate solution to a local group's problems may not even necessitate an architectural input.

This greater focus on process rather than end-product, however, not only blurs the boundaries between community architecture, broader community technical aid and wider forms of community development, rendering it more difficult to identify and trace historically, but it also encapsulates the fundamental tension between process and product inherent within community-oriented architecture/technical aid. This tension is captured in Table 2.1, where Wates and Knevitt contrasted a process-led community architecture with an end-product-led conventional architecture in an attempt to offer a polarised overview showing the clear advantages of the former and the clear disadvantages of the latter. Till (2005: 25) argues that such an approach, however, leads to a 'simplistic dialectic: inclusive/exclusive, democratic/authoritarian, bottom up/top down', which leaves 'the original terms unscathed and the new terms unanalysed'.

The Wates and Knevitt definition of community architecture does not allow for any difficulties which may arise from emphasising process over end-product. As such, the problems outlined by Comerio (1987) below would fail to be identified and addressed. Comerio (1987: 16), when outlining the development of community design centres in North America in the 1970s, pointed out that some of the problems arising from an undue emphasis on process meant that 'unfortunately a large percentage of the designs and plans produced in the 1960's and 1970's were never implemented', as:

> most Community Design Centres were staffed by young inexperienced professionals whose ideology was stronger than their technical skills. Their rebellion against the system was as much a rebellion against the sterility of modern planning and design, and they looked to participatory techniques to give them a new way to approach design. As such they focused more on process than product.

An essential difference, however, between pioneering community architects in Europe and advocacy planners in the US was the tendency for the former to look upon participation as a means to produce good design, whereas the latter were interested in community empowerment itself. Thus, while community architecture and planning began to become more acceptable and mainstream, it also represented very different political and professional approaches. Comerio (1987: 26) emphasised the need for community architecture to also pay heed to the end-product and cautioned that design is just as fundamental as the politics of participation. 'We should recognise that the social motivation behind community design does not, and should not, preclude good design.' Yet how

Table 2.1 What makes community architecture different?

	Conventional architecture	Community architecture
Status of user	Users are passive recipients of an environment conceived, executed, managed and evaluated by others: corporate, public or private sector landowners and developers with professional 'experts'.	Users are – or are treated as – the clients. They are offered (or take) control of commissioning, designing, developing, managing and evaluating their environment, and may sometimes be physically involved in construction.
User/expert relationship	Remote, arm's length. Little if any direct contact. Experts – commissioned by landowners and developers – occasionally make superficial attempts to define and consult end-users, but their attitudes are mostly paternalistic and patronising.	Creative alliance and working partnership. Experts are commissioned by, and accountable to, users, or behave as if they are.
Expert's role	Provider, neutral bureaucrat, élitist, 'one of them', manipulator of people to fit the system, a professional in the institutional sense. Remote and inaccessible.	Enabler, facilitator and 'social entrepreneur', educator, 'one of us', manipulator of the system to fit the people and challenger of the status quo: a professional as a competent and efficient adviser. Locally based and accessible.
Scale of project	Generally large and often cumbersome. Determined by pattern of land ownership and the need for efficient mass production and simple management.	Generally small, responsive and determined by the nature of the project, the local building industry and the participants. Large sites generally broken down into manageable packages.
Location of project	Fashionable and wealthy existing residential, commercial and industrial areas preferred. Otherwise a greenfield site with infrastructure (roads, power, water supply and drainage): i.e. no constraints.	Anywhere, but most likely to be urban, or periphery of urban areas; area of single or multiple deprivation; derelict or decaying environment.

Table 2.1 continued

	Conventional architecture	Community architecture
Use of project	Likely to be a single function or two or three complementary activities (e.g. commercial, housing or industrial).	Likely to be multi-functional.
Design style	Self-conscious about style; most likely 'international' or 'modern movement'. Increasingly one of the other fashionable and identifiable styles: postmodern, hi-tech, neo-vernacular or classical revival. Restrained and sometimes frigid; utilitarian.	Unselfconscious about style. Any 'style' may be adopted as appropriate. Most likely to be 'contextual', 'regional' (place-specific) with concern for identity. Loose and sometimes exuberant; often highly decorative, using local artists.
Technology/resources	Tendency towards: mass production, prefabrication, repetition, global supply of materials, machine-friendly technology, 'clean sweep' and new-build, machine-intensive, capital-intensive.	Tendency towards: small-scale production, on-site construction, individuality, local supply of materials, user-friendly (convivial) technology, reuse, recycling and conservation, labour- and time-intensive.
End-product	Static, slowly deteriorates, hard to manage and maintain, high-energy consumption.	Flexible, slowly improving, easy to manage and maintain, low-energy consumption.
Primary motivation	Private sector: return on investment (usually short-term) and narrow self-interest. Public sector: social welfare and party political opportunism. Experts: esteem from professional peers. Response to general national or regional gap in market, or social needs and opportunities.	Improvement of quality of life for individuals and communities. Better use of local resources. Social investment. Response to specific localised needs and opportunities.

Table 2.1 continued

	Conventional architecture	*Community architecture*
Method of operation	Top-down, emphasis on product rather than process, bureaucratic, centralised with specialisms, compartmentalised, stop–go, impersonal, anonymous, paper management, avoid setting a precedent, secretive.	Bottom-up, emphasis on process rather than product, flexible, localised, holistic and multidisciplinary, evolutionary, continuous, personal, familiar, people management, setting precedents, open.
Ideology	Totalitarian, technocratic and doctrinaire (Left or Right); big is beautiful, competition, survival of the fittest.	Pragmatic, humanitarian, responsive and flexible, small is beautiful, collaboration, mutual aid.

Source: Wates and Knevitt 1987: (24–25).

can this inherent tension be reconciled – for as Till (2005: 25) observes 'partici-pation presents a fundamental threat to normative architectural values' which rest on a belief that the architect as technical and aesthetic expert must have full control of the drawing-board.

Community architecture was really only a movement in the sense that it promoted a range of activities within the profession which incorporated some form of wider social participation in developing the built environment. As such, arguably Community Technical Aid (CTA) encompassed community archi-tecture, as is highlighted below. A key issue concerning the emergence of these movements and their consolidation (and eventual demise) was the changing policy context that led to the growing professionalisation of community-oriented activities, both of the activists and other professionals, as well as the growth of more general engagement with individuals and commun-ity groups through Citizens Advice Bureaux from the 1970s.

Community architecture and community technical aid in the 1970s and 1980s

Community architecture

Ralph Erskine's success at Byker paved the way for Rod Hackney, who was to become the community architecture movement's leader and one of its most celebrated champions. Hackney started out in 1972 in Black Road, Maccles-field, Cheshire as an architectural student who lived in a two-up-two-down terrace which lacked an inside toilet. On applying to the local authority for a grant to renovate the property, he found that the area was designated for clearance in five years' time. He founded the Black Road Action Group and led a successful campaign on the grounds that the housing was sound and suitable for rehabilitation, a cheaper and more sustainable option than large-scale redevelopment. Under the 1969 Housing Act, Hackney was able to claim that the area was eligible for a general improvement grant, and thus qualified for upgrading rather than clearance. Hackney became the lead architect for the project and engaged the tenants in the construction process, which was the first general improvement area to be proposed, developed and managed by the residents themselves.

Throughout the 1970s the practice of community architecture remained a relatively fringe activity, but by the early 1980s it had proliferated to the point where the Prince of Wales used the occasion of an RIBA gala dinner to, on the one hand condemn the practices of conventional architects for their apparent lack of regard for the needs of people while, on the other hand, praising community architects, especially Rod Hackney (Sim 1993). The movement further consolidated its influence on the profession when in 1987 Rod Hackney became president of the RIBA.

Another influence on the profession which led to this incorporation of the movement was the Architects' Revolutionary Council (ARC), set up by architect Brian Anson who had worked on the Covent Garden project. This was predominantly a pressure group targeting the RIBA, seen as a bastion of corporate interests that did not adequately reflect those held by a growing number of architects. By 1975 the group had a growing membership of a 100-plus architects and had expanded into the New Architectural Movement (NAM), which circulated a newsletter emphasising the merits of understanding user need. The RIBA responded in 1976 by setting up the Community Architecture Working Group answerable to a newly created Community and Working Affairs Committee and led by Hackney from 1977. This was later led by architect Ian Finlay who instigated the development of a National Community Partnership of approximately 20 voluntary organisations with the aim of securing funding more effectively. Both groups led to an increased focus on the need for architects to develop closer ties with the community, and in 1982 the RIBA set up the Architectural Aid Fund to offer resources to community groups to pay fees for professional services. This was financed from the Department of the Environment's Special Grants Programme, to fund feasibility studies for community projects.

The process of institutionalising community architecture was continued through the first international conference on community architecture ('Building Communities') and the creation of the National Community Aid Fund and the Prince's Inner City Trust. Increasingly, the approach was used predominantly by government as a component within its inner-city renewal policy – partly as its housing policies cut back drastically on aid to housing associations. The peak of the community architecture movement was celebrated in 1987 by the book *Community Architecture: How People are Creating Their Own Environment* (Wates and Knevitt 1987).

Community technical aid

By the early 1980s the concept of providing technical aid direct to the public – similar to the US Community Design Centres – was developed in the UK through Community Technical Aid Centres (CTACs). These benefited from a favourable political climate, as the Conservative government was supportive of the voluntary sector, preferring local initiative to local authorities. However, CTACs were generally funded either through local authorities or the government's urban programme which permitted them to support organisations at the early stage of a project and allow them to apply for funding with a professionally prepared feasibility study. An Association of Community Technical Aid Centres (ACTAC) was set up in 1983 to provide a forum and resources and advice to CTACs. While the Association began with only 15 member organisations, within two years this number had grown to over 50.

The experience in England

The first Community Technical Aid Centre had been developed in London by an American, Ed Berman, who had been involved in the Community Design Centres Movement in North America. Although this did not include architecture until 1975, it comprised a cooperative of community workers, teachers and artists with the aim of enhancing environmental awareness, and supporting groups to set up related educational and/or arts projects. By the mid-1970s this CTAC was housed in a purpose-built office in Camden, and founded Neighbourhood Use of Building and Space (NUBS), which developed to fulfil a community need for a free architectural service (Towers 1995). By 1979 NUBS had worked on three projects, including one which aimed to preserve and convert the Victorian public baths in North Kensington, which had attracted support from the Ancient Monuments Society, albeit not implemented. The original aim of NUBS to provide a free service seems to have been curtailed by the architects' Code of Professional Conduct which prevented them from doing so. It did, however, succeed in harnessing public support for preserving buildings deemed of architectural heritage via change of use (Towers 1995).

In 1976 Tom Woolley and a group of students at the Architectural Association in London set up Support Community Building Design which aimed to provide an architectural service along the same lines as NUBS. Support was a cooperative based on the premise that it would only assist groups which undertook their own building work and it worked within the boundaries of the Professional Code of Conduct. That is, it offered services for a minimum fee to voluntary groups who had managed to secure funding.

In Liverpool the council sought the help of housing advocacy organisation Shelter to promote ways of rehabilitating the Granby area of Toxteth in 1969, leading to Shelter's Neighbourhood Action Project (SNAP). SNAP set up a neighbourhood office with planners, architects and social workers who provided a wide range of technical advice. Among its recommendations when it completed its short period of work was that the redevelopment of areas like Granby needs to be undertaken by an agency with powers akin to a new town development corporation to cut through the complex bureaucracy, and also to have the funds to meet the high costs involved. Another of the products of this pilot project was the creation of a housing cooperative, which eventually, together with other co-ops, created a new specialised service organisation – Neighbourhood Housing Services (NHS) – to provide professional advice to new housing cooperative ventures. NHS pioneered two key approaches: first, that of architects working with local residents in a community; and second, the promotion of the co-op concept. It was very successful, and by 1997 it was supporting eight co-ops with over 20 staff. This eventually led to the creation of the first new-build housing cooperative in the UK – the Weller Street Co-op.

In the late 1970s and early 1980s such positive experiences with tenant cooperatives within state stock led to their replication, and various local authorities supported these, including Glasgow, where the best-known co-op is the Calvay Housing Cooperative (see below). By 1981, the Labour Party, via the Greater London Council, supported and funded the development of a number of community-led co-ops in London, including the Matrix Feminist Architectural Co-op. This offered a design service aimed at women's needs.

In Manchester in 1979 the Town and Country Planning Association, as a 'Planning Aid' service, set up a Community Technical Aid Centre (CTAC), which focused initially on planning before evolving into a design cooperative. This was recently subsumed into Trafford Council. In 1979, just a few months after the first CTAC was set up in Manchester, the first such user-managed organisation was set up in Liverpool, the 'Community Technical Services Agency' (Comtechsa) Limited (registered as an Industrial and Provident Society). This was funded through Liverpool City Council's Inner City Partnership Programme. Now, it operates as a Society for the Benefit of the Community, with a membership comprising largely community and residents' groups. The membership has grown to over 600 community and voluntary groups.[7]

The RIBA Community Architecture Group offered support and funding to set up an 'urban workshop' in Newcastle-on-Tyne, which ran an environmental education service and advice centre in the city centre. This was staffed by three architects and Newcastle University architecture students, and later evolved into 'the Newcastle Architecture Workshop', a CTAC. However, in 1999 the CTAC workshop resource closed due to lack of funding, and has now been replaced by Northern Architecture, an Architecture Centre funded by CABE and the Arts Council of England. Although not part of the English experience, a Community Technical Aid Centre was also set up as a voluntary organisation in Belfast in 1984 by community groups to assist develop projects benefiting disadvantaged communities. It has been partially funded by the Department of the Environment, this funding being used to provide free services to community groups deemed most in need.[8]

The experience in Scotland

In Glasgow, Raymond Young, a student in the Department of Architecture at Strathclyde University, wrote his thesis on the topic of public participation in housing rehabilitation. The Tenement Improvement Project (TIP) was an outcome of the thesis, which demonstrated the economic and social viability of in-situ tenement housing rehabilitation, was grant funded for three years and led to the development of a Housing Research Unit in the Strathclyde University Department of Architecture and Building Science. Jim Johnson and Raymond Young were joint founders of the TIP, which developed along similar lines to the Architecture Department-based Community Design Centres (CDCs) in the US and ran for three years.

On this basis, ASSIST was set up in 1972 by a group of architects and students from the Department of Architecture at the University of Strathclyde, with the aim of offering a free technical aid service for the rehabilitation of tenements. To this end, they set up an office in an old bicycle shop in Taransey Street, Govan, which led to the development in 1973 of the 'Crombie' Central Govan Housing Association. ASSIST directly supported the creation of community-based housing associations as project managers and clients and worked through locally based 'architectural shops'. The project developed both innovative technical solutions and its professional services went considerably beyond the traditional architectural professional remit to include accessing government finance, negotiating with lawyers and assisting with the initial managerial institution building. ASSIST was funded by Glasgow City Council through fees for improvement grants. The Govan Housing Association moved to Dennistoun in 1976, and ASSIST then opened another office in Govanhill.[9]

The demand for technical advice by a well-established urban network of tenant and community groups in Glasgow led to the formation of the Technical Services Agency (TSA) in 1983, a community-controlled technical aid centre. Originally funded by the Gulbenkian Foundation and Glasgow City Council, and latterly Urban Aid, TSA offered free advice to over 200 member groups and organisations, and was able to undertake projects that were not viable commercially, completing several refurbishment and new-build projects.[10] Aware that criticism of housing and repairs policy was leading to antipathy from the City Council, TSA was instrumental in setting up Community Architecture Scotland (CAS), which aimed to generate funding as a trading subsidiary. CAS lasted until 1990, when the departure of a number of key individuals, along with the change in housing funding through the establishment of the direct government housing agency Scottish Homes, which changed the landscape of tenant organisations.

In the 1980s, dissatisfaction with council approaches, and limitations on budgets and strategies resulted in many of Glasgow District Council's projects being unsuccessful. As a result the Council became more directly active in encouraging housing associations as a vehicle for local tenants and users to become involved in the processes of design, management and maintenance. As well as refurbishing older tenement properties, associations were also set up to address the considerable problems in the social housing of the post-war peripheral estates. Early examples of such Associations were Calvay Cooperative in Easterhouse and Castlemilk East, and by the mid-1980s there were over 30 Associations in Glasgow.

The rise in popularity of community-based housing associations in Scotland reached a significant cusp in the late 1980s when the provisions for housing procurement underwent a radical change. The new Conservative Party central government altered the arrangements for funding of housing through the Housing (Scotland) Act 1988. This legislation aimed to revitalise the private sector in housing but also had the effect of reducing finance available to local authorities. Instead, spending on social housing was provided through a new government-funded agency, Scottish Homes, that directly grant-aided developments by Associations.

The fact that these Associations were formed as a result of community activism by people attempting to improve their housing and environment has led to them being closely associated with participation in design and management. This is supported by a structure based on association membership, with the activities of Associations directed by an elected management committee. Members of community-based housing associations are drawn from the geographical area served by the association, and in cooperatives only tenants can be members. This form of participation in housing is now supported by groups such as the Scottish Federation of Housing Associations (SFHA) and SHARE (Training for Housing Associations), and is identified in performance standards for housing associations.

Through the late 1980s and early 1990s a great deal of refurbishment and new-build housing was produced by housing associations, and this has been repeated in other areas throughout Scotland. However, the housing association movement has changed over this time, as has the political and economic framework within which HAs operate. Although able to draw on the engagement with participation by particular architectural practices and technical aid centres during the 1980s, housing associations have increasingly used mainstream architectural practices to meet their demand. Although the high profile of participation has meant that many were both able and willing to adopt this approach, there have always been concerns that for some practices participation was a token gesture nearer to consultation than genuine negotiated decision-making. Recent cost constraints, increase in competition and tight timescales have also affected the provision of participation in design, as highlighted later in the book.

An analysis of the UK experience of community engagement in architecture

Before examining why much of the above initiative dissipated in the 1980s, it is important to highlight the essential differences, in terms of advantages and potential benefits, between community architecture and community technical aid. Community architecture emphasised the relationship between the architect and the client and sought to strengthen this to increase the relevance and appropriateness of the design approach and solution for the client who would quite often be a community organisation or voluntary group. The Community Architecture Fund (established by the RIBA) enabled willing architects to meet the costs of one-off feasibility study assignments with such organisations. Further work on the full technical design stage would be met from fees payable when the job went ahead. As such, much – but certainly not all – activity under the banner of community architecture was strictly focused on early inputs into design.

Community technical aid services, however, offered a greater variety of assistance, more user control and wider benefits from their continuing presence and accrued experience gained through working with an increasing number and variety of organisations as clients over the years. Community technical aid centres also sought to maximise opportunities for members of the organisation to become involved in the architectural process from initial concept through to implementation stage. Their involvement was arguably also more attuned to the financial situation of client groups, and the use of local or voluntary labour. They also emphasised the demystification of technical jargon to promote better understanding of the architectural and/or planning process. As they increased their knowledge of the needs of their client groups, some extended the services which they provided to be able to respond more effectively to wider social needs. Resource centres, managed workspaces, more generic training programmes, business planning and funding services were provided. This range of activities contrasts with the more individualised client approach generally taken in the community architecture movement.

Max Hutchinson took over from Rod Hackney as President of the RIBA in 1989 and promptly declared that community architecture was 'dead': 'It was not simply killed, it was over killed. It was a PR exercise masquerading as a crusade' (cited in Towers 1995: 217). Towers responded to Hutchinson's observations almost a decade later (1995: 218):

> Community architecture may be dormant but it is not dead. Properly pro-
> moted, its revival could do much to stimulate the development of altern-
> ative values. For the inner cities still characterised by social disintegration
> and physical decay, the revival of community architecture has never been
> more urgent.

Arguably, community architecture came to be seen as a potential new area for earning fees by the RIBA and hence the professionals supported this – espe-cially to fund feasibility studies so that projects could attract funding for design and implementation. When the funding sources for such activity dried up the RIBA lost interest and this may be a key reason for community architecture's announced demise. Some community technical aid centres and community-oriented architectural firms survived, however, and how they managed this in an increasingly competitive and economically strapped context is examined in two case studies later in the book of ASSIST (Glasgow) and Comtechsa (Liverpool).

Two key issues arising from the above partial history are related to concepts highlighted in Chapter 1. While some individual architects and architec-tural firms within the community architecture movement no doubt adhered to a philosophical position of participation as a right and not as an instrumental mech-anism, particularly in earlier phases, the consolidation of the movement within the profession seems to have essentially undermined this and led to a dominant attitude of user participation being seen as a means to an end – whether to bring in further work and fees (as through the RIBA support) or to ensure less criticism of housing provision (as in local government support). In contrast, while again no doubt some individual architects or other members of CTACs may have been interested in instrumental issues, the focus of these organisations was both more socially oriented (in providing wider support for clients) and more comprehensive in terms of engagement through the architectural process. This essentially entailed caveats on the power of decision-making of the professional in the design and related support activities, and indeed in the creation and man-agement of the organisations themselves, which grew in response to demands and initiatives in the voluntary sector. Thus it could be argued that to some extent wider social participation through community architecture was more supply-driven, whereas that through CTACs was more demand-driven.

Again, as the later case studies highlight more clearly, the changing political and economic circumstances affected both movements, but were adapted to in very different manners. The coming to power of a right-wing Conservative government in 1980 serially undermined local authority power as well as seeking to reduce government roles in the economy, promoting private sector and individual initiative (including to some extent through associations). This changed funding possibilities for the consolidating movements in a radical way, and over time, while stimulating some community-based activity initially, longer-term funding and development funding became focused on specific perceived 'problems' such as inner-urban areas and away from wider state support for housing provision and/or renewal. For many architectural practices this led to a simple reversion to 'business as usual' vis-à-vis clients with communities becoming less a necessary option than in the relative scarcity of work in the 1970s. The architectural firms that retained a more philosophical commitment then had to change their approach and become more entrepreneurial. Local authorities cut community-oriented programmes and CTACs also had to become more entrepreneurial in accessing funding, but with a wider activity span and thus funding arena. This reinforces the necessity for a clear understanding of the political and economic context for engaging with wider social participation, a theme the book will return to later.

Notes

1 While attempting to provide a wide overview, this is inevitably constrained by available sources – literature and contacts – and as such it is stressed that this is not an attempt at a comprehensive history, but argues that its partial nature does not detract from its conclusions concerning key issues for later deeper investigation – see case studies.
2 See e.g. Lewis 1961; Mangin 1970; Perlman 1976.
3 Venturi and Scott Brown are less known for their advocacy planning work, which more directly engaged with communities and participation.
4 See Burgess 1978, 1982, 1985, 1987, 1992; Turner 1976, 1978, 1982, 1986; Turner and Fichter 1972.
5 This position was advocated in Turner (1988), and later further developed in Turner (1992).
6 See Chapter 3 for more on the US.
7 Members each have a £1 share in the organisation and elect a voluntary committee of management from their representatives to run the organisation on their behalf. For more information, see the Comtechsa case study (Chapter 6).
8 Where groups are able to pay fees these are used to offset costs for those unable to pay – the principle of all CTACs.
9 ASSIST Architects Ltd is now a cooperatively run architectural practice. For more information see the ASSIST case study (Chapter 6).
10 TSA also played a central role in the HEATFEST event which led to Glasgow's first European-funded solar demonstration project (Easthall Solar Demonstration Project).

Chapter 3

International experience

Paul Jenkins and Marcia Pereira

Introduction

This chapter examines some international experiences in wider social participation in the architectural process, with the main intent to, first, illustrate important parallels to the UK experience in the global North (mainly in the US), and second, to illustrate some alternatives to this experience in countries in the South (Brazil and South Africa).[1] The objective is not to be comprehensive in describing international experience but to highlight the relevance of some of the key concepts and issues identified in Chapter 1. To this end the three international 'snapshots' of experience in this chapter focus on some different aspects of wider social participation in the architectural process: institutions in North America and typologies (housing in Brazil and community buildings in South Africa).

USA

As mentioned in the previous chapter, a different strand of community engagement in the built environment to that developing in the UK in the 1970s took place in the United States of America, which was more allied to the wider social protest movements of the mid- to late 1960s. This strand was based on the advocacy planning approach where professionals represented poor communities in resisting comprehensive redevelopment and gentrification (Blake 2003). In the 1970s this approach was often focused on community design centres (CDCs) providing local-level technical assistance within communities on a number of issues, not only planning but also architecture. To a significant extent these CDCs depended on government funds which started to flow from federal agencies such as the Housing and Urban Development agency (HUD), and one of the lasting conceptual impacts of this was Arnstein's 'ladder of participation' (Arnstein 1969). In 1968, in a similar vein concerning institutions, the Executive Director of the Urban League spoke out for more direct accountability by architects to the public at the 100th Convention of the American Institute of Architects (AIA).

The community-based struggles of the 1950s and 1960s – e.g. the civil rights and women's liberation movements – changed the legal context for public participation[2] as well as leading to government-sponsored programmes focused on community development (e.g. community action agencies and Office of Neighbourhood Development). The Model Cities Program of 1964 to 1973 provided grants and technical assistance to communities to participate in the planning and implementation of urban development activities which were influenced by the neighbourhood organiser and sociologist Saul Alinsky and Davidoff's advocacy approach in planning and urban renewal was another major stimulus (Davidoff 1995). Participatory approaches were thus embedded in a range of planning, architecture and related urban development activities by civic organisations and not-for-profit community-based development corporations working with community design centres, which were often linked to academic institutions.

One of the first community design centres was the Architectural Renewal Committee in Harlem, which in 1964 opposed a new freeway through the northern part of Manhattan. It was typical of its time in having a fairly radical political objective of empowerment as well as urban development per se. Community design centres flourished in the 1970s with some 80 existing across the whole of the US. These were at first staffed by young inexperienced professionals with a strong ideological orientation and, despite the technical assistance given to hundreds of neighbourhoods, the successful projects and programmes were usually small, local and non-replicable (Comerio 1987: 16); however, some have evolved to be significant influences. For example, the Community Development Group (CDG), founded in 1969 at the School of Design of North Carolina State University, has provided design and planning assistance to communities in the state of North Carolina for three decades. As director of CDG, Henry Sanoff accumulated a rich experience in participatory design, which he has shared via numerous publications.[3]

US–Europe cross-inspiration

Although North American community designers influenced community design in the UK, they were also inspired by European designers and projects, such as

Giancarlo De Carlo (University of Urbino), Lucian Kroll (Medical Dormitories at Louvain La Neuve in Belgium), Ralph Erskine and Vernon Gracie (Byker Housing in Newcastle), Nicholas Habraken (flexible designs for housing in the Netherlands) – see Chapter 2 (Comerio 1987: 19). According to Comerio, although the young US community architects had such European participatory architects as heroes, 'their political heroes were the rebellious and self/reliant Third World squatters' (Comerio 1987: 19).[4] The impact of many of them, however, whether European or in the US, was mostly local and non-replicable. Comerio argues that the basic differences between the US and UK community design projects were as shown in Table 3.1.

Whether this is an accurate perception or not, it is important to note that, despite causing limited impact, the US grassroots movement of the 1960s and 1970s dramatically affected the way decision-making about the built environment took place within society. Citizen Design Review Boards were established in the 1960s in every municipality and government-funded projects were scrutinised by the Human Rights Commission to ensure that minority and/or women's enterprises were also considered. The consequences of these effects may not always have been positive, however, and the institutionalisation of citizen participation through Design Review Boards and citizens' committees was not always effective in improving the quality of life (Comerio 1987: 26).

By the late 1970s the political (and linked academic) basis for community participation – focusing on preliminary design options for programme-wide social regeneration – had been overtaken by the instrumental (and professional) basis in community design centres (CDCs) – focusing on a complete design service for project implementation, largely through the influence and nature of government funding. This trend continued in the 1980s as CDCs adapted to a new, more conservative, political and economic regime with many of those that survived being transformed into private practices, or retaining only intermittent activities related to particular 'crises' (Toker 2007). In the 1970s

Table 3.1 Comparison between early community design in the US and in Europe (after Comerio 1987)

US early community design experience smaller projects	European early community design experience larger projects
Young and relatively inexperienced architects	Well-established architects
Participation as fruit of grassroots movement aiming at empowering users	Participation is sanctioned and made part of an institutional building programme
Small amounts of federal funding	Large amounts of funding (which continue)

there were still some 50 to 80 CDCs in the US but by 1987 only 16 remained, 12 of which were from the earlier period. CDCs were forced to become more entrepreneurial, accessing finance from government programmes but also charitable foundations, private philanthropists, universities and the American Institute of Architects (AIA) chapters and corporations with social responsibilities activities. Pressures from the profession were also a factor in their demise (Blake 2003).

In this changed political economic context the politically oriented model of empowerment was replaced by an economically oriented model and community design started to be replaced by community development (Comerio 1987: 20). As such, the focus went from working with community groups in rehabilitation projects to helping residents in these areas own their houses. However, several different creative initiatives were generated at this time, as may be seen in the experience of the Urban Homesteading Assistance Board (U-HAB) in New York and the Asian Neighbourhood Design (AND) in San Francisco (see below).

Community design centres have retained their activities in the US through the 1990s into the new century, with some 46 university-affiliated programmes and 26 independent design centres registered with ACSA (Association of Collegiate Schools of Architecture).[5] In recent years various new CDCs have been formed as new government and other charitable foundation funding becomes available and architecture schools increasingly recognise the value of such engagement as part of education (Blake 2003).[6]

The Association for Community Design (ACD) was formed in 1977 and holds an annual conference as well as an Internet site and forum, supporting CDCs in capacity building in architecture and planning across a range of base organisations such as universities, NGOs and other 'not-for-profits'.[7] These represent the three main institutional bases for CDCs. Most are based in large cities across the US, although serving both urban and rural populations at need. While most focus on planning and architectural design, others specialise in education and training. Most have a predominance of architects in comparison to planners (Blake 2003), but there is also a wide range of other professions represented (engineers, landscape architects, interior designers and others). Budgets range enormously from thousands to millions of dollars. The legal basis is either independent non-profit, volunteer or university affiliated and they vary extensively in the detail of their mission and objectives as well as staff and activities, as described in some brief case studies below (which draw mainly on Blake 2003).

University-affiliated CDCs

University-affiliated CDCs include non-profit organisations that provide training for students as well as university departments, some with outreach/extension services. They may act pro bono or adjust fees to suit the funding available. Most such activities are based initially on an individual staff member's interest, although many have evolved into wider programmes. The Pratt Center for Community Development (www.prattcenter.net) in Brooklyn, New York is one of the oldest and longest running of such CDCs. It was founded in 1963 and engages in technical assistance, education and policy advocacy (Curry 2004). The Pratt Planning and Architectural Collaborative, a division of the Pratt Center, was established in 1975 to provide design, development and planning services based on community organisation and mainly within affordable housing. The Pratt Center is linked to the architectural graduate programme of the Pratt Institute, with its teaching staff and students working in the centre. In 2003 there were some 20 full-time staff, including five architects and a number of planners, as well as an operating budget of around US$2 million (Blake 2003).

Detroit Collaborative Design Center (DCDC), on the other hand, is much more recent – having been established in 1994 as a non-profit subsidiary of the School of Architecture at the University of Detroit-Mercy. It focuses on education in an undergraduate neighbourhood design studio, providing internships for students. The Center provides services to non-profit organisations at neighbourhood level (www.arch.udmercy.edu). The focus is on organisational capacity-building and education collaborative design processes, bringing together the main stakeholders in architectural design (e.g. funding organisations, community organisations and residents). The design work has won a range of awards from local to national level. DCDC has five full-time employees, including two design fellows and one student intern (a rotating position). The annual operating budget is US$300,000.

Independent non-profit CDCs

Independent non-profit CDCs are seen as more stable than some of the university-based organisations (Blake 2003) and rely more on direct fee income. An example is Asian Neighbourhood Design (AND), founded in 1973 by Asian architecture students at Berkeley, California. They started using the Comprehensive Employment and Training Act (CETA) to teach cabinetry to high school drop-outs and also used federal grants to help with housing rehabilitations in Chinatown. With the federal funding almost at its end in 1981, they decided to sell their architectural design and furniture-building services, becoming the architects of choice for most of the housing rehabilitation projects undertaken by non-profit organisations, due to their past experience with communities. Their work evolved over time to provide a wider set of community development services such as family and youth (including employment creation), community planning and development, and construction management services (www.andnet.org). A key role for AND is prior to selection of the architect, and the organisation works through the whole building programme with the client/ user. AND now has a regional operation with a staff of some 120, including nine architects and a budget of several million US dollars (Blake 2003).

Another independent non-profit CDC, from 1987, is the Community Design Center of Pittsburgh (CDCP) – originally called Pittsburgh Architects Workshop in the late 1960s. CDCP both provides architectural services and brokers' funding for other service provision through a design fund – used for a range of projects including housing, commercial and mixed-use building as well as community planning. It also links volunteer architects with individuals needing advice through a renovation information network and offers a wide range of educational resources (www.cdcp.org). It has five full-time staff including one registered and one intern architect, with an annual operational budget of some US$385,000.

The Urban Homesteading Assistance Board (U-HAB) in New York is yet another example of an independent non-profit CDC. Created in 1974 by architects inspired by squatters in Latin America and Asia, U-HAB provided technical assistance to gang members and ex-offenders, promoting self-help labour, and facilitating the rehabilitation of abandoned houses by their own inhabitants. With time, the provision of technical assistance for rehabilitation became part of a much larger process of cooperative ownership of affordable housing in Manhattan. By 2002 U-HAB had turned into New York City's largest non-profit developer of affordable housing co-ops, supporting community organisation, development, management training, technical assistance and emergency support programmes (www.uhab.org). An important aspect of their work is the need to balance the tension between organising communities (via courses and support) and actual development, and U-HAB strives to combine both (Carlson 2006: 12).

Volunteer organisations

Volunteer organisations usually link service providers with community organisations and coordinate service provision. An example is the Minnesota Design Team (MDT), existing from the 1980s, which works across a range of activities vis-à-vis the built environment from regional planning to interior design, as well as economic development, tourism and so on (www.minnesotadesignteam. org). Volunteer teams engage in action research with communities (expenses being partly paid by the community) and in 'charrette'-type community design processes with a focus on implementation methods. They also provide follow-up progress monitoring.

An issue that has been discussed in the US concerning pro bono or reduced fee work is that of 'unfair' competition by voluntary bodies. These claims – generally from the private sector – have been met by highlighting that non-profits bring in funding that might otherwise not be accessed, often rely on existing architectural practices through networking for implementation (with the CDC taking a support role (e.g. through education)), and also the fact that most professions have some form of voluntary work ethos.

Other forms of architecture participation

Recent research (Toker 2007) highlights the diversity of contemporary community design practice across the US, also focussing on sustainability and design of the public realm. Although this indicates that there is significant coherence around the ideal of participation by communities in the design of their built environment, there is a lesser ideal of empowerment for lower-income communities – representing the changed political, economic, social and cultural context for such community design. Toker (2007) suggests that there has been a change from an idealistic community design towards a more pragmatic one, where 'pseudo-participation' takes place. He cites Wulz (1986), whose landmark study showed the shift of participation from an advocacy approach, within a continuum, from participation moving from a position of 'maximum-say' to a minimum: self-decision, co-decision, alternative, dialogue, regionalism, questionnaire and representation. This shift started in the late 1970s due to the conservative political climate of that time, and its pace increased with the economic pressure of the 1980s (Comerio 1984; Curry 2000; Sachner 1983). Collaborative decision-making overtook advocacy approaches within community design by the mid-1990s according to Toker, who, however, acknowledges that the change has been in the area of focus rather than in the nature of the field, as community design continues to be about people being in control of decision-making processes related to their communities.

Although community designers who are committed to genuine participation and design decision-making are seen as still being in the forefront, a new group has emerged along with the new uses of the terms 'community design' and 'participation' (Toker and Toker 2006). Through this, community design has been pushed into the mainstream in some ways and new lines of thought have appeared, as shown by the later study (Toker 2007). Thus, while Henry Sanoff (e.g. Sanoff 2000), Rex Curry (e.g. Curry 2000) and Michael Pyatok are still considered to be key community design leaders in the US, new names have appeared, such as Andres Duany, Elizabeth Plater-Zyberk and Peter Calthorpe. These latter names represent a new development in community and participatory design through the new urbanism movement – although this has been critiqued as spatial determinism disguised as community design, with queries as to the nature of such 'community'. According to Toker, community design acquires a new meaning within the new urbanism approach, where it does not include genuine participation of a local community or 'efforts of actual community building', but merely means community involvement in 'the design of a physical environment'. Within this approach 'charrettes', mostly designed as showpieces, are primarily information sessions but are referred to as 'participatory meetings' (Toker and Toker 2006).[8]

Another practitioner, based in the United States but working internationally and promoting 'user participation' is the architect Christopher Alexander. Professor Emeritus at the University of California, Berkeley, his book *A Pattern Language: Towns, Buildings, Construction* has been influential since the late 1970s. In this and his subsequent more theoretical work, Alexander proposed to empower any human being to design and build at different scales (Alexander 1979; Alexander *et al.* 1977).

An example of the application of Alexander's approach is the design of the Eishin School, in Japan (Davis 2006). The process of participation in the development of the programme for the school resulted in a programme that reflected a strong, collective architectural vision. Alexander had intensive discussions with the clients, and involved students, teachers, gardeners and parents in the process, which lasted for six months. The process generated a strong overall vision, which guided the development of the design that began in its actual site, with flags marking the corners of buildings. The physical design helped bring together the school community's vision and the features of the site. Davis argues that this is an example of how, within contemporary society and techniques, a careful design and building process can recover traditional values of craftsmanship, requiring 'a professional instance of great sensitivity and immediate response to subtle hints from people about things that are close to their hearts and to the felt aspects of the site' (Davis 2006: 249), resulting in a more harmonic solution. Alexander's ideas have also been influential in software design and he has been responsible for more than 200 building projects in the UK, US, Japan and Mexico, among others.

Despite Comerio's analysis of differences, cited above, the experience in the US is not dissimilar to that in the UK concerning the transformation of more politically motivated community design activity into that co-opted by established institutions and then the impact of neo-liberalism in the availability of funding. The essential difference is the closer link between CDCs in the US and academia, which has arguably provided a mechanism for these to survive in more economically tight periods. In addition – or probably because of this –

there is a more firmly established contemporary tradition of community-oriented design in architecture across the US. However, despite the impressive number of higher education institutions with their outreach programmes in the US, this is still a minority activity for architecture and arguably fills part of the gap in state-funded welfare activity through the reliance on charitable institutions and social responsibility of the corporate sector. As such, wider social participation in architecture is not necessarily achieved, since the majority remain excluded from engaging with the dominant architectural realm – reinforced in this case by the strong tradition of individual house building in the US. Nevertheless, the strong emphasis on such activity in many architectural schools is something that can be an inspiration for the UK.

Brazil

Historical development

As in most parts of the world, low-income households in Brazil have been historically involved in the construction of their own dwellings, and this remains the situation today. However, throughout time this direct participation has taken different forms, from the rural vernacular types of construction to 'self-build' in informal settlements in the city (*favelas*) or in poorer neighbourhoods in the periphery of cities (*loteamentos irregulars*). This form of participation has been incorporated within government-created housing systems based on self-management, and this is still evolving in nature.

The beginning of the 1960s was a time of rich political debate in Brazil, with several active social movements. It was in this period that the 'Arquitetura Nova' (new architecture) movement was launched by young architects (Sérgio Ferro, Flávio Império and Rodrigo Lefèvre). This was inspired by the Cinema Novo (new cinema) movement which aimed at exposing underdevelopment, and Arquitetura Nova criticised the 'positive and uncritical attitude towards Brazilian modernisation' (Arantes 2004: 179) shown by most of the architects at the time, unconcerned with the exploitation taking place in the process of architectural production – this criticism originating particularly from the situation of workers during the construction of Brasilia, the new capital city.

The 'Arquitetura Nova' group urged architects to acknowledge the conflict between labour and capital and to take a position on the side of the workers. They were critical not only of new modernist architecture, but also of the 'popular' or 'vernacular' forms of architecture, which they saw as repressive and populist. They were thus also against 'self-build' as experienced by the great majority of the Brazilian population, due to its poverty of resources and its urgent nature, not providing opportunities for learning new techniques. A key element of their approach was the use of a vaulted roof as a contemporary and creative solution which expressed the 'poetics of economy', allowing flexibility in the organisation of rooms. It also allowed the creation of a 'method of learning' on the building site, where the vaulted roof would be used as a workshop for a collective decision-making process among users, workers and architects, 'dispensing with a priori design and placing greater value on individual contributions' (Arantes 2004: 183). Their objective was the democratisation of architecture, proposing not only a change in working relationships, which affected the whole production process, but also a change in consumption trends, increasing the supply of adequate housing.

In 1964, however, a coup d'état installed a military dictatorship in the country, on the pretext of protecting against communism, but in fact aiming at consolidating conservative politics to boost capitalism (Arantes 2004: 186). The country erupted in turmoil, with protests and violent repression, ending up with many people being imprisoned, exiled or killed, and organisations being outlawed. Ferro joined the armed resistance in 1967 and was captured and imprisoned. When released he emigrated to France and became a professor in Grenoble, while Lefèvre and Império stayed in Brazil, limiting their activities to academia. It was within this context that the government took a renewed interest in housing, as a way of 'soothing the civic wounds' of the majority, and created the National Housing Bank (Banco Nacional da Habitacao (BNH) as the main component in a national housing finance system. However, instead of solving the housing problems of the majority, the BNH served mainly as a way of enriching the increasingly powerful Brazilian developers, financing large government housing schemes with resources from the new Severance Indemnity Fund for employees on which the bank was based.

A new development took place from the 1970s when Lefèvre wrote a Master's thesis based on his experience, entitled 'The building site and design', published in 1976, proposing a policy of mass construction by mutirão (collective construction) and drawing on the work of the Brazilian educator Paulo Freire, who regards education as a means of awareness development, empowerment and liberation (Freire 1970). To understand the relevance of this requires some background. Until 1980, the great majority of low-income housing in Brazil was basically self-built in informal settlements, or built by commercial companies normally financed by the BNH government-based programme, with implementation via state- or municipality-based housing cooperatives (Cooperativas Habitacionais COHABs) (Malard et al. 2006). While the informal settlements in the cities are normally self-built on invaded land, at the urban periphery self-built houses are normally on the proprietor's own land, albeit not through approved subdivision and sometimes without an appropriate infrastructure – as well as without any official building permission. Self-built houses are normally built by the owners and their direct family, together with the help of friends, or via informal contract with an independent tradesman with more practical experience. The word 'mutirão' is used to describe this collective effort in building a house among the lower-income population in Brazil. People get together on weekends and holidays and help each other to construct their houses. This can be a long process, as the construction stages take place according to the availability of resources. In these cases, the owner/s of the house manage(s) the construction and take(s) responsibility for the decision-making during the whole construction process, using own resources – and hence is more 'self-managed' than 'self-built'.

In contrast, the houses constructed by the COHABs involved three main agents: the state- or municipality-based cooperative (COHAB), which provided the land and selected the buyers; the National Housing Bank (BNH), which managed the finance and passed this to the banks (also federal) which would be in charge of administering the mortgages; and the private construction companies which produced the housing. Malard *et al.* (2006) describe this as an enterprise management house model (modelo habitacional de gestão empresarial), where there is no user participation in any stage of the process, be it in the design or the construction phase (Bonduki 1992; Conti 1999; Maricato 1979, 1994, 1997; Valadares 1978, 1980).

In the 1980s social movements, which had been developed as a mechanism for protest during the years of military dictatorship, became an important force in Brazil. A strong and skilled working class was created by the fast industrialisation, based to a great extent on labour exploitation, giving rise to a form of 'new syndicalism', as well as strong social organisations in the bigger cities, where women played an important role in demanding better housing, crèches, sanitation and transport. These movements were also largely supported by the progressive Brazilian Catholic Church within the context of the 'Theology of Liberation'. Members of grassroots movements, new syndicalists and dissident intellectuals, with the support of the progressive church, funded the Partido dos Trabalhadores (PT) – Workers' Party – in 1980. In the early 1980s, after nearly 20 years of dictatorship, a period of transition between the military and a civil government was eventually established and elections were planned. The Workers' Party experienced rapid growth, becoming the largest left-wing party in ten years, and the party won several municipal elections, permitting innovative responses to the demands of social movements. In this context some of the experiments of the 'militant architects' could become public policy.

The exclusion of user participation in the housing process articulated by the government was one of the main reasons for protests by social movements, which developed the idea of a wider community-based 'housing self-management process' in the early 1980s. The proposal of these movements involved the creation of entities that would represent community organisations, managing all the stages of housing development, which would take place on land obtained from the government at zero cost. Construction material to build a 40 m² house would be financed for those with a household income of a minimum wage and the construction would incorporate the workforce of the local community via the process of 'mutirão'. One of the main difficulties encountered in the execution of this idea, however, consisted in the legal basis for these independent housing production cooperatives. It was only in 2005 that the federal government (then under the administration of the Workers' Party) created a 'Common-interest Credit Programme' operated by the Federal Economic Bank with the explicit objective of financing low-income citizens organised in cooperatives or housing associations. Within this programme, low-income families form an association to obtain credit and the associations then manage the design and construction of the houses themselves via self-construction or direct management, contracting professionals or firms to execute specialised services as needed. As such, 'mutirās' have become a more significant part of the wider state-supported housing system for lower-income communities.

The Residential Serra Verde Project

An example of wider social participation in architecture within this programme is that led by Professor Maria Lucia Malard and her research group at the School of Architecture of the Federal University of Minas Gerais (EAUFMG). EAUFMG is part of an interdisciplinary group made up of academics, the City Council of Belo Horizonte and the Association of Homeless People of Belo Horizonte, which is developing a pilot housing project with the aim of creating a model for implementing the new collective housing loan system in Brazil, developing strategies for design, self-management and sustainability in low-income housing. Funded by the federal government, the research aims to generate a model to enable the construction of social housing through self-management, incorporating principles of a common-interest economy, community participation, digital inclusion, and environmental, social and economic sustainability through job and income creation (Baltazar dos Santos and Malard 2006). The proposed model is being applied in the Residential Serra Verde (RSV) project, to house 76 homeless families. User participation started with an early community consultation to identify the community members' habits and vocations as well as their readiness for the implementation of strategic sustainability measures (e.g. the reuse of water and waste); included community training in understanding spatial design and in expressing themselves comfortably within the design arena; and went on to include community acquisition of computer and construction skills. Within the project, education has been seen as vital to empower the community and break the self-perpetuating and vicious circle generated by a governmental tutelage as well as by users' lack of formal knowledge. Moreover, the education of participants is also seen as pivotal in avoiding manipulation via technical assistance during the decision-making process. The pilot opted for a combination of educational action with the development of new participatory processes in the housing design and execution using computer technology. This allowed participants to acquire new skills as well as to be able to better participate and manage the design and production of their own houses.

The participatory process took place in several stages. In a first stage, participative design strategies which generated digital inclusion were undertaken where users took part in a series of workshops applying techniques to familiarise them with discussion about space as well as the use of computers. This stage was based on a digital inclusion strategy developed by Ballerine and Cabral Filho (see Ballerine 2002), which was further developed by the project team for this work. Comparing the use of traditional visualisation methods, such as physical models and printed drawings with the use of digital models, the researchers found that, due to the lack of fixed scale of the latter, people tend to see them not as fixed but as abstract representations which can be changed. Having more time to 'play alone' with the digital model, users got more involved and brought more ideas into the discussion process.

A second stage consisted in the participative design of dwelling units via collective and individual decision-making. For this stage the design team developed a strategy based on their specific constraints: in order to apply for a loan, the design has to be previously approved by the city council, which means that they did not know if those taking part in the exercises would definitely be the final dwellers – and despite its common 'low-income' nature, the community had different demands and expectations. The project therefore opted for an 'open design' approach, a term borrowed from 'product design' based on the Open Source principles of software design (Kadushin 2008), which is participative by nature. In this it aimed to achieve a 'partial participation', according to Carole Pateman's classification of pseudo, partial and full participation (Pateman 1970). It was argued that, although ideal, full participation where each individual member of a decision-making body has equal power to determine the outcome of the decisions could not take place in architecture, as this effectively does not acknowledge that architects have the monopoly of power through their technical knowledge. On the contrary, this approach regards such power as an instrument which may be used to facilitate a participative design, in helping people to understand their lived spaces and to better interpret their demands, without imposition of the architect's values per se. Inspired by John Habraken's ideas of support and in-fill and also by Walter Segal's self-building processes as well as Cedric Price's idea of flexible spaces open to users' appropriation, the researchers have developed the approach, which also takes the local building regulations and the low budget available (around US$10,000 for each dwelling unit) into consideration.

Within this approach, a series of design proposals ranging from 40 m² to 50 m², with different articulations of internal space, were discussed with the community within small focus groups (12 to 20 participants) and wider social meetings (over 20 participants). Digital 3D models produced with the software Sketch-Up were used to show proposals for large groups and then discussed in smaller groups where participants proposed changes to the models. A combination of 3D physical models and 2D printed drawings, which could be modified by users (i.e. drawn over), was used in both large and small groups. After the first round of discussion groups, common options (e.g. separate wet area, one master bedroom) were identified as well as the non-consensual points (e.g. number of bedrooms, size of bedrooms and living room). The team decided to define as 'collective' not only what Habraken called 'support', but also the common demands (including most of the infill – wet area), and defined the living spaces as 'individual', allowing each family to decide upon their organisation. The community also opted for having an overall apartment area of 50 m², even if this means they will not have their flats completely finished given financial constraints.

The third step of the process was the participative design of the housing scheme itself. Part of the decision-making in this stage was undertaken by the architects based on results of previous research. In response to existing demand for a safe overlooked area for children's play identified previously, they opted for terraced housing in a horseshoe format with a large internal collective area. The building develops from two-storey height on the steepest part of the terrain to five-storey height at the lowest part. The units have one façade with the main entrance towards the internal courtyard and across the whole width of the building to the external façade on the exterior of the horseshoe shape. The length and depth of the units, as well as the positioning and articulation of the rooms, was defined with the users. Given the principle of open design, the team opted for an open structural system, enabling different choices of materials and components (likely to be driven by the large variation in building material prices locally), without losing the core spatial quality of the scheme.

In order to prepare users to understand and make informed decisions regarding the construction of the building, as well as to carry out construction work themselves, a game strategy was adopted. Using the experience of video games associated with Paulo Freire's educational approach to adult education, a series of games where users are involved in different situations within a building site, from its initial organisation to carrying out construction tasks, was developed.

All the results of this pilot project are considered to be 'open source', and can be freely used by others – from the design solution, the interfaces for digital inclusion, to the training games – and the team hopes this will encourage other low-income housing collectives to make use of these tools in their own participative processes.

Concluding remarks on the Brazilian experience

Important conclusions may be drawn from this experience, which evidently reflect the context where it takes place, but could also be useful elsewhere. First, it is clear that participation needs to start from the beginning of the design process, recognising it as cumulative, and users continuously improve their ability to understand the process and thus become able to better participate at subsequent stages. Second, easily changeable 3D digital models were the best medium to facilitate visualisation and negotiation of space (e.g. Sketch-Up models) in comparison to other media, such as drawings, physical models and 3D still images of digital models. The researchers indicate that 'the discussion process becomes less a matter of speech and leadership, and more a matter of action (people acting on the representation of space)' (Baltazar dos Santos and Malard 2006: 45). Third, the actual participative process allowed the design team to learn from users and identify collective and individual demands, generating a design project responsive to these; however, there was still a key role for architects in the design process. Fourth, the use of an 'open design' approach proved appropriate within the context of a less stable economy, allowing for different structural systems and materials to be used, yet retaining a guarantee of spatial quality, flexibility and low cost. Finally, the important role of academic institutions is noted; however, this is just one resource with other strong social institutions – and the wider impact is only possible within a supportive government environment.

South Africa

Different forms of social participation in architecture in South Africa

South Africa is fairly unique in the Sub-Saharan subcontinent in being a middle-income developing country (in international agency terminology) in a global macro-region with marked social and economic challenges such as very high levels of poverty and accelerating urbanisation among other challenges to political and general stability. In this context, the country has a relatively strong professional and academic infrastructure based on British and North American concepts and practices. It is also unique in having undergone an exaggerated form of racially based segregated development ('apartheid') for almost half a century during the period when most African countries were becoming independent from colonial rule and related segregated forms of development and

exploitation. As such, during the last decade and a half of democratic government, South Africa has faced enormous challenges of (largely reactive) political
and economic restructuring allied to (largely proactive) social and cultural
change. Reflection on how to approach architecture and how to work within
this context has become widespread with debates on the nature of a 'relevant'
architecture. These range from the pragmatic, which

> holds that architecture, particularly public architecture, should be socially
> relevant and empowering by generating employment, providing training
> opportunities, building capacity by engaging and involving people in various
> ways, and creating structures that serve the community's needs more
> than the architect's image.
>
> (Marschall and Kearney 2000: 2)

to more complex discussions of reframing architecture within a post-colonial
discourse (e.g. Murray 2006).

The role of participation in architecture in such a situation ranges
from the local engagement with regionally widespread development-oriented
approaches to 'self-help' (or more rightly 'self-managed') housing,[9] through to
various forms of public engagement with culturally significant iconic buildings
and public areas which aim to highlight past socio-cultural dominance and
support new urban space formation (Deckler *et al.* 2006; SAIA 2005/2006).
Concerning the former, several non-governmental and civic organisations have
been involved in assisting with 'self-help' housing projects across South Africa,
especially the NGOs in the (now defunct) Urban Sector Network and the South
African Homeless Peoples Federation/Utshani Fund. These involve participation
in planning and service delivery as well as different forms of participation in
housing design and delivery.[10] In addition, various planning practices are
engaged in assisting to develop municipal integrated development plans, which
have a statutory requirement for participative processes. However, while social
participation in the planning process is thus required by the state, the opposite
is true for most social housing projects.

'Self-help' housing is limited in scope due to resistance at government level to integrating this form of housing delivery with the state-subsidised
and generally private sector delivered housing policy for low-income groups. As
such, the continued proliferation of 'informal' settlements produced by people
with their own resources seems here to stay (Huchzemeyer and Karam 2006)
and is increasing in scope as the state subsidy deepens in standards and cost
in relation to its breadth of application, and housing need continues to increase
– and this needs to be recognised by the government and architecture profession (Low 1998). However, this form of participation in architecture is not
strongly promoted by the state-supported low-income housing system and

architects only occasionally work for social housing clients (e.g. through the, as yet relatively small, Social Housing Foundation, which is modelled on the UK and Dutch housing association movements).[11]

The other end of the spectrum includes some wider social engagement in iconic buildings – whether directly through public consultation or indirectly through competition. Here a range of new commemorative buildings and spaces as well as government buildings have aimed at both redressing past imbalances in political and economic advantage as well as socio-cultural representation. Most of these have not, however, been engaged with indirectly by wider society (e.g. through public competitions) or directly through participative design processes, and time will thus tell to what extent the architects and clients have managed to capture wider national and social values. Key examples of such buildings include the new national Constitutional Court complex in Johannesburg[12] (Law-Viljoen 2006), new Provincial Legislature buildings in the Northern Cape and Mpumalanga[13] and a series of museums (Deckler *et al.* 2006).[14] Closely associated with this approach is that of new public spaces designed in urban situations often with both commemorative/civic and practical (e.g. transport interchange/market) functions. Examples include the Baragwanath public transport interchange and traders' market, Soweto; the Farady market and transport interchange, Johannesburg; Khayelitsha services centres and pay points, Cape Town; Philippi public transport interchange, Cape Town.[15] Other urban design projects include the Gugulethu urban upgrade projects in Cape Town by a variety of firms (SAIA 2005/2006).

Within the above two extremes, 'community participation' in architecture has been promoted through forms of representation on client bodies – and typically used for the design of community buildings as the new government redresses past imbalances in social facilities (e.g. schools, clinics, community centres, sports facilities) and public spaces. Here the emphasis is on empowering the community through the design and construction processes, with this seen as a key element of human capacity development. This architecture inevitably emphasises process over product, while in no way diminishing the value of the product – but celebrating community values in this through widening social engagement in the process. Examples of this approach based on community engagement are the Maskhanye Isibane Sakho Multipurpose Centre in Nyanga township in Cape Town, designed by Carin Smuts – CS Studio (Marschall 2000); the Mbazwane Resources Centre in rural KwaZulu/Natal designed by Rodney Harber (Slessor 1995) and the Lakeside Community Creche and Pre-School in Evaton south of Johannesburg, designed by Mphethi Morojele Architects (Morojele 1998).

The latter project was begun within the government public works programme[16] for a new residential area of 1000 houses, and the local civic organisation affiliated to the national South African National Civic Organisation

(SANCO) network was the main client. When the architects were engaged the community had already drawn up some ideas for what they wanted as a part of the public works business plan. They organised visits to existing facilities to challenge the preconceived traditional designs, although with limited success, as no women participated in the visits. This was followed by extensive consultation meetings where the architects focused on setting up a framework for the community participants to make appropriate design decisions. Some of the most difficult discussions related to the nature of spaces and their management, local authority requirements not considered culturally or socially appropriate by the community and the nature of finishes which while low-cost should not be seen as 'inferior' given the historical legacy of disadvantage. The construction process opted for was one where small local contractors/tradespeople were to supply labour while the community took responsibility for procuring and storing the materials. While this proved successful, there were problems of satisfying competing local pressures for contracts. In the end some 40 per cent of the labour was provided by local women and young people, also seen as a success in terms of the participatory construction objectives. The architects in their paper on this experience highlight the need to recognise the higher time-consuming nature of their inputs in such projects as well as the need for better coordination between architects and construction managers on site as many decisions had to be taken in situ (Morojele 1998).

This involvement of the community entails explaining typical professional roles (architect, engineer and quantity surveyor), how tendering and contracts work, and the nature of architectural drawings. The construction process is also at times an opportunity for further skills training and employment, as well as promoting small and/or local entrepreneurs and local material production as described above. The architect may also become involved in assisting with funding applications, financial management and raising capital for small local businesses (Beni and Callaghan 1997; Coppola 1995). All of this entails a significant input of time and hence hidden costs to the architect – who may feel frustrated with the nature of the decisions and quality of the final product that the more participatory process throws up, not to mention the emergence of latent or submerged power struggles within communities (Lyons and Smuts 1999). To top this, the building produced may not be any more treasured by parts of the community through the participation process and hence no less prone to vandalism and violence for other social or political reasons. All of these reasons may well be behind the tendency for this form of work to more typically (but certainly not always) be undertaken by recent architecture practices (Marschall 2000) and in public sector projects (Morojele 1998). While the former is commendable, at least some of these generally young and enthusiastic architects may not have had any real exposure to the contextual reality of the sociocultural group with which they need to engage and/or to participatory approaches – and as such probably needs to feature in the education process. As to the latter, there are some questions whether such objectives as small entrepreneurial development is sustainable and has success in the longer term.

Concluding remarks on the South African experience

The South African experience is interesting as there is both a link with the traditions of 'self-build' in the housing sector, as in Brazil and many countries of the South (although not strongly supported currently by the state), but also a perceived need to (re-)engage with wider society in architectural endeavour, especially for buildings and spaces with public significance. This, however, is being dealt with in what seems to be generally a rather exclusive manner, with limited competitions and public opportunity to engage. Whether the emerging architectural forms and discourse will achieve wider social recognition and become iconic in a national cultural sense – as it was in Brazil (Jenkins 2009) – remains to be seen. The experience of 'community architecture' has a shorter history in South Africa than in Brazil, the US or UK; however, it was a feature of engagement between 'progressive' professionals and civic movements in the late 1980s and early 1990s, rather as noted in the above contexts. In South Africa this has not, however, been coopted into the mainstream in any significant way and widening social participation in architecture education would appear to be very limited. There thus seems to be a potential role within the architecture schools to reassess the role of the architect vis-à-vis society, as has been embedded in Brazil.

Conclusions

The above brief – and rather different – 'snapshots' of international experience illustrate a broader range of engagement with user groups and wider society in architecture than in the UK, with the nature of this being fairly similar in the US, but rather different in Brazil and South Africa. In institutional and funding terms, the US relies on both government funding schemes and – particularly – not-for-profit organisational forms for architecture services, and the relatively high level of engagement of academic-based organisations is noted (compared to the UK). In Brazil and South Africa funding tends to be from the government, but rather differently targeted, with this having a strong focus on housing in Brazil, less so in South Africa where the housing policy is based more on private sector delivery (perhaps similar to Brazil in previous periods). The institutions involved in Brazil are also not-for-profit and academic, whereas in South Africa it seems small private architecture practices, especially recently formed ones, have more engagement – this being predominantly for community buildings.

While non-governmental organisations are involved in participation in planning and services issues in South Africa (as in Brazil), this does not have a strong architectural component (if any) and hence is not illustrated in detail here.

In summary, the US experience focuses on architecture design and development, with some engagement with wider social development goals (such as employment generation), and has become (like the UK) more entrepreneurial over time, yet remaining very much based in the not-for-profit sector. In South Africa there is also a (much more limited) focus on participation in architecture design and development – with participation in the construction as well as the design process – whereas in Brazil, the focus is less on architecture and more on housing; however, participation again takes place in design and construction. A possible observation is that the nature of the participation is related to levels of general 'development', but in fact much of what takes place in the US is in 'underdeveloped' communities. Of interest is the importance of not-for-profit organisations and academic institutions across very different contexts. The nature of the available literature does not allow more profound conclusions (e.g. whether there is participation of users in architecture for higher income groups (such as corporate clients) or whether there is any systematic post-completion feedback processes in operation in any of the countries), and this is potentially an area for further enquiry.

Notes

1 The US is chosen as there was substantial interchange between the experience there – at least in the past – and the UK, and Brazil and South Africa have been chosen as these middle-income 'developing' countries have established architectural traditions but significant political, social, economic and cultural differences from the UK (or US). Furthermore, the chapter authors have personal experience here of architecture and participation.
2 Through laws such as the Civil Rights Act (1957), Economic Opportunity Act (1964) and Demonstration Cities and Metropolitan Development Act (1966). See References.
3 See Appendix III Bibliographic resources for list.
4 As noted in Chapter 2, other younger and less famous community architects in Europe were also politically influenced by similar sources.
5 See https://www.acsaarch.org/home.aspx.
6 According to Rios (2004) over 30 per cent of architecture departments in North America now run university-based community design centres and research centres.
7 See www.communitydesign.org/.
8 This view is confirmed by a report from the Mackintosh Environmental Research Unit (MEARU 2007), which evaluated a charrette exercise facilitated by Andres Duany in Scotland.
9 For an overview of the development of 'self-help' housing internationally, see Jenkins et al. (2006).
10 For individual NGO links see: www.sangonet.org.za/portal/index.php?option=com_content& task=section&id=43&Itemid=326.
11 See www.shf.org.za/.
12 Designed by OMM Design Workshop & Urban Solutions Architects and Urban Designers.

13 Designed by Luis Ferreira da Silva Architects and Meyer Pienaar Tayob Schnepal Architects & Urban Designers.

14 These include: The Hector Pieterson Memorial Museum, Soweto (Mashebane Rose Architects); the Apartheid Museum, Johannesburg (Gapp Architects and Urban Designers, Mashebane Rose Architects, Britz Roodt Association, Linda Mvusi Architecture & Design); Red Location Museum, Port Elizabeth (Noero Wolf Architects) and the Nelson Mandela.

15 Designed respectively by Urban Solutions Architects and Urban Designers; Albonica + Sack Architects and Urban Designers with MMA Architects; Piet Louw Architects; and Du Toit & Perrin in Association.

16 The national community-based Public Works Programme promotes job creation through such public investment projects.

Chapter 4

Wider scoping of relevant literature

Paul Jenkins, Marcia Pereira and Leanne Townsend

Introduction

This chapter presents an initial investigation into participation across a number of disciplines and subject areas as a means to identify other possible concepts of relevance to wider social participation in architecture. The areas of Environmental Psychology; Widening Governance; Housing; Planning and Regeneration; Facilities Management and Post Occupancy Evaluation; and Product Design were considered relevant for this study, as identified in Chapter 1. The scope of potential literature relating to participation within these fields is extensive and hence this chapter needs to be seen as a 'scoping' exercise to identify key issues for possible further investigation.

The key method by which this wider scoping of relevant literature was approached was through the experience of the investigators and that of the members of the Steering Group which guided the deliberations of the research project from which this book originated. Based on the identification of this wider scoping as conceptually necessary (see Chapter 1), the Steering Group was made deliberately broad in its professional, policy-making and disciplinary composition with members having relevant experience across most of the above fields of relevance to the core subject. As such, in the first instance, the researchers opted to interview a number of 'champions' from the Steering Group and some others indicated by them for each relevant field noted above. These informal interviews focused on identifying relevant concepts, key literature, important institutions and possible case studies across the areas mentioned above. To the extent possible, given the limitations of resources, this was followed up later by the chapter authors, widening the initial literature review.[1] This broad scoping exercise showed that in fact a number of key issues identified in the different areas are of common interest across disciplines.

Identification of key issues

Environmental psychology

Environmental psychology is a discipline which has an ambiguous definition in the sense that academics from a number of disciplines (e.g. psychology, geography and architecture) contribute to its main streams of literature, particularly to journals such as *Environment and Behaviour* and *Journal of Environmental Psychology*. In this, the discipline concerns itself with all aspects of the built and natural environments in terms of the way people feel, behave and interact in those environments. The field is therefore of great relevance to architecture and architects, as well as the wider built environment.

Place identity is an important concept within this field. The concept of place identity theory, which was proposed by Proshansky *et al.* (1983), argues for a psychological aspect of identity relating to the inhabited environment. They assert that place identity can affect self-evaluation at a number of levels. Uzzell *et al.* (2002) further argue that place identity is a component of social identity. In this sense, 'place identification would reflect membership in a group that is defined by location' (Uzzell *et al.* 2002: 29). Drawing on this basis, Identity Process Theory, (IPT) (Breakwell 1986), provides a hypothetical model of identity processes within the individual. This model considers the role of motivational aspects such as a need for distinctiveness and self-esteem, as well as suggesting ways in which identities are created or maintained. Importantly for the current study, this model includes the physical environment as an important factor in identity processes. The theory argues that identity processes are driven by four key principles – a need for distinctiveness, continuity, self-esteem and self-efficacy (Breakwell 1986; Twigger-Ross *et al.* 2003).

The central concepts in the identity theories discussed here are of relevance to participation in architecture because they support the role of users in the design process in aiding group memberships in an environment (thereby enhancing social cohesion) – as has been argued as fundamental in some of the international experience in housing and other community facilities in Chapter 3. Falke and Balatti also conceive of place identity as a construct 'that people create together through talk' (Falke and Balatti 2004: 5). Such participation facilitates 'talk' between members of a community, and can therefore potentially enhance aspects of identity in the individual and the group – which is often an argument for social participation in urban regeneration. Here participatory processes are often seen to enable building users to identify problems and needs. The process of achieving this potentially enhances both the overall well-being in individuals and the community as a whole. This approach essentially underpins wider social development programmes such as those undertaken by Community Technical Aid Centres (UK) and Community Design/Development Centers (US) as described above.

A number of other key issues in environmental psychology are of relevance to participation in architecture. One is the study of which factors laypeople consider important when assessing the built environment (see e.g. Gifford 1980; Nasar 1988; Stamps 2000). This line of research considers the different perceptions and evaluations made by laypeople, for example, inhabitants of residential environments. Other related research looks at the differences between how laypeople and architects undertake assessments of the built environment (see Gifford *et al.* 2002; Hubbard 1994; Wilson 1996). Such research has the potential to query existing positions concerning the ability of laypeople to make quality assessments of the built environment. Bonnes *et al.* (2007) argue that a more congruent understanding of the built environment between laypeople and architects is desirable – especially a better understanding of what factors matter to laypeople in terms of quality in the environment. This is not least because 'policymakers' resistance to more inclusive and participatory processes in environmental governance is sometimes based on their assumption that laypersons do not always have the capacity or the knowledge necessary to assess environmental quality in an "objective" or reliable fashion' (Bonnes *et al.* 2007: 63). Hence architects carrying out a participatory exercise need to be concerned with the fact that users may not understand the specialised languages they use (technical, aesthetic, spatial, etc.), thereby rendering the exercise limited in effect. However, architects who are aware of the problem often try to find ways around this issue (see e.g. Blundell-Jones *et al.* 2005).

More specific theories have been suggested within environmental psychology which can be useful in participatory exercises. For example, Gibson (1979) argued that the purpose of perception is to determine possible actions on the environment. The term Gibson used for the perceived qualities in terms of such actions held by physical objects or aspects of the environment was 'affordances'. An object thus *affords* different actions to different types of people. For example, therefore, a door handle affords the ability to pull the door open, a chair affords sitting and a path affords walking. Affordances can thus be a useful way in which to examine findings from a participatory exercise. Once participants have outlined the aspects that are important to them in a built environment context, sense can be made of the various themes by applying the theoretical model of affordances to these (e.g. how a building can 'afford' or provide these aspects). Another theoretical area is that of 'contextual compatibility', proposed as being of potential relevance to participation in architecture (see Groat 1988). Contextual compatibility refers to the degree to which components within the environment are perceived as 'fitting' with the other components within that environment. Thus, for example, a building which is being proposed in a consultation workshop involving the local community may be perceived as either being of a good or a bad fit within the existing perception of environmental context.

Space syntax is yet another area cited as of relevance to participation, used in environmental psychology and overlapping with planning. It was developed by Professor Bill Hillier and his colleagues at The Bartlett, UCL, in the 1980s.[2] Space syntax is a technique through which space is used as a basis for methodically analysing relationships between different areas of a city or building and may be used as a basis for examining the way in which people perceive and interact with these areas. For example, space syntax may be used to determine which urban areas people are most likely to use prior to knowing anything about the people of a town or city. Although space syntax analysis could thus be seen as detracting from the need to talk to users directly, its use in wider social participation is that it can lead the designer to focus on the most important spatial issues.

Also of potential interest within the scope of environmental psychology is the more specific field of 'design against crime'. Design against crime research focuses on design features which may detract from or encourage criminal behaviour such as vandalism, burglary, theft from shops and so on. Landman and Liebermann (2005) outline how participation can be linked to crime reduction through actively involving community members in discussions on this issue. Such activity can reduce the fear of crime, which can itself perpetuate the use of barriers and other environmental symbols which in turn create hostility in an environment. Landman and Liebermann discuss two very different approaches in this respect – that of creating hostile barriers which emphasises exclusion and, in contrast, that of encouraging a participatory approach to urban design which emphasises inclusion. This latter approach is based on the belief that members of a community are best informed on the local problems and disadvantages of an area.

Other similar fields of proactive research in the built environment drawing on environmental psychology include the concept of 'restorative spaces'. This focuses on the potential for different kinds of natural and built environments to provide restorative psychological benefits to those inhabiting the space (e.g. Gesler *et al.* 2004). Given that people differ in what they will find restorative, it seems likely that different communities may have different desires and needs in relation to restorative qualities of their environments. Literature and research findings in this field again may be used in setting up and unravelling findings from participatory exercises where these refer to restorative or therapeutic qualities of an environment. Another proactive area of research looks at the ability of children to contribute to participatory exercises.

The subject of children and participation was a popular research theme in the 1970s, vanishing in the 1980s and re-emerging in the 1990s (Horelli 1997), then becoming more popular worldwide again recently (e.g. Chawla and Heft 2002). More recent studies have shown that when participation is well structured, younger participants are very competent at making quality contributions to the discussion, both in terms of identifying local problems and needs, and in the formulation of good ideas (Horelli 1997; Horelli and Kaaja 2002). What is more, involving children in participatory exercises not only empowers them in that particular context, it can also contribute positively to perceived control and therefore psychological well-being and confidence in the long term (Chawla and Heft 2002).[3]

Environmental psychology and related fields have a lot to offer architects; however, ways to directly (or even indirectly) identify detailed user needs are usually not made a priority in the education of architects. Social issues are typically brought in at a later stage of architectural education and while some schools of architecture do offer a module in environmental psychology, understanding how to engage with users and their real and perceived needs potentially should be put much higher on the agenda.

Widening governance

This area promotes wider social participation as being valuable to all actors in the built environment production process – clients, developers, private and public sectors, local authorities and architects. Apart from valuing wider social participatory processes, how participation takes place is also seen as an important issue, with the need for appropriate procedures being put in place at the right time, and with dedicated time and effort being invested. The participation of individuals who are representative of their communities is considered important for widening governance, highlighting a critique of the practice of participation in various current community-based housing associations, where despite community roots, representatives may have limited connection with their base communities and be influenced by developers. Investment in 'social entrepreneurship' is also considered to be necessary, such as in urban regeneration where creativity in communities can be encouraged and resources used to develop a sense of identity, there is no dominant 'top-down' approach and communities can address sustainability with their own resources and ideas in collaboration with professionals (echoing issues noted above).

Widening governance of course is not limited to the fields of architecture or other activities in creating and sustaining the built environment (such as planning). There has been a general re-emphasis on the importance of engaging directly with electorates in recent debates on representative political democracy, with a widening range of techniques being advocated, as well as earlier engagement. As more clearly enunciated in the planning discourse, this comes to some extent from a reaction to, yet continued emphasis on, key issues in the neo-liberalist government approaches of the 1980s and early 1990s in both the UK and US. There has been a reaction to the push within these approaches to 'slimmed-down' government and 'withdrawal of the state', through widening the concept from government to governance, recognising the importance of processes of interaction – formal and informal – between actors in the act or manner of decision-making. Governance thus assumes that real authority, leadership and/or power does not lie exclusively with the formal or legal structures which it is deemed to lie within, and focuses on the sphere of relations between government and other actors in civil society or non-governmental sectors as well as the private sector.

As an example of this area of wider governance, recently the Scottish government commissioned research on the public value of participation, entitled *Public Value and Participation: A Literature Review for the Scottish Government*.[4] This argues that 'public value' offers a new framework for thinking about public services and the role of public managers. Public participation, they argue, is a tool for allowing public managers to identify the objectives that the public genuinely value and to engage in an ongoing process of listening, debating and responding to their interests – what is called 'refining public preferences'. Within a definition of 'public participation' as 'all activities by which members of the public contribute to shaping the decisions taken by public organizations', the report states that a substantial amount of participatory activity is taking place across Scotland, at government level and within local public service providers. However, traditional forms of engagement such as written consultations are still the preferred approach, despite being also used in conjunction with newer approaches such as focus groups and opinion polling.

The report also highlights that there is mixed evidence of a 'public appetite' for participation (or 'demand' as argued in Chapter 1), which is dependent on several factors, such as whether the issue is local or national; how much input from the public is required; and proof that participation will make a difference. The authors argue that successful public participation relies on both the belief from those in power that the process is valuable and the willingness of members of the public to engage. Barriers to public participation are: lack of clarity of purpose; inconsistent use of terminology; risk of participation overload; difficulties of getting organisational backing; and accountability issues. The publication stresses the importance of engaging 'hard-to-reach' groups through choosing approaches which are best for the specific context, and in a transparent manner. Finally, they conclude by saying that to achieve the full benefits generated by public participation fundamental issues need to be addressed, such as: evidence needs to be provided to demonstrate the link between public participation, actions and outcomes; the aims of consultation need to be clearly communicated both to participants and internally (within governmental institutions); ongoing sustainability of such participatory processes has to be built; and there is a need to ensure that new processes are integrated into existing governance structures so that deliberative and representative forms of governance are not in conflict (e.g. internal cultures and processes need to be re-evaluated).

While seen as a way to rejuvenate democracy, on the other hand, many such wider governance approaches still focus on individual as opposed to collective engagement through taking on board much of the management praxis of the neo-liberal period where individuals are seen as 'clients' and government as 'service provider'. This potentially defuses collective action and as such some of the political dimension of participation. Nevertheless, the post-neo-liberal and centre left approaches which underpin the new wider governance emphasis on renewing government do provide some spaces for negotiation and wider (collective) social participation. Whether there is the social and political will to engage is a key issue (related to 'supply' and 'demand' issues of participation noted in Chapter 1) but also the economics of participation is important, as this has become increasingly professionalised.

A key issue is thus the availability of funds for participatory design processes. As has been highlighted in Chapter 2, positive past experiences with for example, technical services agencies and community technical aid have become difficult to sustain, as core government-sourced funding tends to be limited. In the context of the above overview of widening governance, the architecture participation debate of the 1970s and 1980s has moved on and most professionals in general have become less interested. This has also taken place within a certain devolution of authority from central to local government with a stress on quicker service provision, and greater involvement with the private sector as public sector resources are cut back. Within this context new government procurement processes for social housing, education and health buildings potentially reduce the possibility for direct participation by users and the wider public (see Appendix I for more discussion).

Despite such potentially negative changes, the relatively recent advent of architecture centres is a positive change within the broader field of widening civic engagement in architecture. Apart from their public exhibition activities these provide an important range of particular programmes, such as work in the field of general education, developing a range of educational materials, ideas and case studies based around the built environment, which can enrich learning and teaching. Such activities have played an important role in guidance for new building, drawing on generic research. Examples include *From Consultation to Design – Design for Learning: 21st Century Schools* (2004) and *Designs on My Learning. A Guide to Involving Young People in*

School Design, both published by The Lighthouse in 2005. Such publications contain resources intended to support local authorities, schools and architects and to help them develop their own strategies for designing future learning and teaching environments.

Organisations working within widening governance issues of relevance to architecture include the Architecture Centre Network (www.architecturecentre.net), which plays an important role in supporting the work of the 23 architecture centres across the UK, acting as their central development and advocacy organisation. The network encourages good practice as well as innovation, emphasising the importance of architecture and the built environment in improving public engagement with the physical space; and involving a wide range of stakeholders, including government, in their projects. In addition, the UK-wide independent Commission for Architecture and the Built Environment (CABE)[5] is the government's adviser on architecture, urban design and public space, aiming to improve people's quality of life through good design and via its work with the principal stakeholder groups: policy-makers; planners and councillors; developers and designers; clients; and the public. CABE supports all of these 'stakeholders', and aspires to get the public involved in the design process, as well as documenting, evaluating and disseminating the experiences. An extensive set of case studies, teaching resources, as well as articles and other policy and practice guidance publications related to the built environment may be accessed via their website (www.cabe.org.uk). A similar, although smaller, organisation exists in Scotland: Architecture and Design Scotland.

Housing

Within the field of housing there is a rich history of user participation, with the 1970s and 1980s generally seen as the phase of highest engagement by communities and professionals in the participatory design process within the UK (see e.g. Sim 1993). Housing associations are considered to have worked closest to users and to have had more legitimate participatory activity at that time. The political shift of the mid-1980s, with the change towards a conservative government, is said to have eventually broken the power of the participatory movement resulting eventually in the re-emergence of participation in more institutionalised and top-down approaches.[6] As access to funds became more difficult in the mid-1980s, organisations which promoted participation in housing and building design struggled to survive and hence professionals moved their interest elsewhere. A few organisations, such as Comtechsa in Liverpool and ASSIST in Glasgow, have survived by successfully restructuring their organisation and access to funding (see Chapter 6). More recently, as noted below, there is an increasing degree of formal requirement for participation within social housing management, with this being included in legislation as opposed to taking place as a result of demand from users.

Housing associations are often claimed to empower tenants through extensive participation (Docherty *et al.* 2001); however, this depends on the nature of the participatory process within the association. Housing associations with limited participation can be dominated by developers and the participants in such exercises may well not be considered representative of the wider users/residents. Within this context, there is the need to make a clear distinction between the various participatory process actors (clients, developers, owners, end-users) and where their respective inputs are suitable/possible. A critical review of how participation takes place is a potentially important follow-up research project, as it can help clarify to what extent there is a demand for such participation.

On the 'supply' side of participation in housing, the Housing (Scotland) Act 2001 introduced statutory duties for local authorities and Registered Social Landlords (RSLs) to involve tenants in all aspects of housing. To assist landlords in implementing the tenant participation provision of the act, Communities Scotland (an executive agency of the Scottish government responsible for housing, homelessness, communities and regeneration throughout Scotland until 1 April 2008[7]) published a report entitled *A Good Practice Framework for Tenant Participation in Scotland* in 2004.[8] The researchers identified considerable variation in quality and levels of tenant participation across Scotland, with some areas at the very early stages of implementation, and others with well-organised tenants' groups which are proactively working with landlords to improve housing services and standards. The study identified issues landlords face when implementing participation, such as the need for resources and time, challenges in involving excluded groups (e.g. youngsters, ethnic minorities) and rural areas (geographical isolation, dispersed tenants and consequent higher costs of facilitating participation), among others. Case studies as well as a review of literature on good practice were carried out, and a framework for good practice was proposed. This framework sets out a series of key principles, checklists and examples for landlords and tenants in developing tenant participation in three key stages: 'involving tenants', 'strategy for effective participation', and 'monitoring and evaluation'.

While the above focused on housing management, how participation takes place and the appropriate use of techniques at the right stage of the process are significant issues in direct participation in housing design (see e.g. Sanoff 2000). Participants need to be well prepared and a common language between all stakeholders needs to be developed and used (as argued in Blundell-Jones *et al.* 2005). This requires a considerable amount of time and tends to make the participatory design process longer than a non-participatory design process. The need to allow users to experience real buildings, as well as the use of relevant techniques which facilitate inclusion such as the DQI (Design Quality Indicator), Spaceshaper (CABE), 'Planning for Real' and 'urban initiatives' are crucial. Some new techniques, such as 3D visualisation, are argued to be potentially useful in this regard, but in fact are used in many cases to sell projects instead of facilitating participation (see Al-Kodmany (1999) for a review of the use of visualisation in enhancing participation). The attitude of architects towards participation is considered to be the major issue in housing design, and architects are said to have difficulties in working with other professionals and with communities. Moreover, architectural education is blamed for promoting this attitude (for a discussion relating to educational approach in architecture see Nicol and Pilling 2000).

Another issue arising in relation to housing design – also mentioned in Chapter 1 more generically – is the idea of using literature-based knowledge as a form of indirect 'third-party' participation; that is, engaging with available generic knowledge stemming from research relating to user needs and the things that users consider important in their built environments. Extensive literature exists on housing design for different communities, including demand studies, and engaging with such knowledge might alter the need for direct participation in some cases, or be used to clarify findings from specific participation exercises and as a means of finding the key issues to focus on in a specific participation exercise. Related to this is the problem of making such generic knowledge more available to architects. Although this research exists in the public domain and is thus potentially available to architects, those carrying out housing research are often not very proficient in disseminating the information they produce to those who could benefit from it. Instead, potentially useful research findings often remain in the realm of academia – in journals and books largely read by academics.

Planning and regeneration

There is substantial literature on wider social participation in planning – not surprising, since this is the only professional activity where some form of wider social participation is statutorily required. The origins of participation in planning go back historically to developments in land and subsequent planning legislation, and are largely seen as developing particularly in the 1960s in the UK and North America as a reaction to 'top-down' planning decisions of large-scale, state-led postwar redevelopment. The definition of the form and levels of participation are considered key for those involved in planning and regeneration, with Arnstein's 'ladder of participation' (1969) and Davidson's 'wheel of participation' (1998) as fundamental models in defining participation mechanisms/ 'levels' and links to power. Overall it is perhaps in the planning literature that the importance of power relations in participation is most discussed, drawing on theorists such as Foucault and Habermas. Within this theme, the relationship between participant and practitioner is also highlighted, where Davidoff's 'advocacy planning' (1995) is an important concept. In advocacy planning the planner acts for the interests of a particular group or community, via a participatory process, in opposition to plans being prepared by the official planning authority. The planner is then responsible to the group rather than to the authority.

The way knowledge and discourse are handled during the process is also seen as fundamental in critiques and promotion of participation in planning – or participatory planning (the former seen as more passive, the latter more active). Theoretically based positions such as Friedmann's 'transactive planning' (1987), Forester's 'deliberative practitioner' (1999), Healey's 'collaborative planning' (1997) and Chambers' work on 'participatory appraisal'[9] provide an important basis to understand how knowledge and discourse are taken into consideration in participatory planning. Robert Chambers, one of the icons in participatory planning in social and economic development, defines it as the 'handing over the stick' process, where the planner acts as a facilitator, allowing local people to generate outcomes by themselves. The attitude of the practitioner her/himself should be one of self-critical awareness and personal responsibility.

This concept is taken on board in a review of different approaches to participation in planning in Sandercock (1998). Sandercock, with an emphasis on the US experience, identified four approaches as follows. A radical political economy approach was promoted mainly in the 1980s, where Marxist analysis saw planning as a function of the capitalist state in rationalisation and legitimation, negotiation and mediation between different fractions of capital, and as a regulator of pressures and protest of dominated classes. This was a primarily theoretical position of urban political economy and was based in academic departments of geography, sociology and urban studies; hence its lasting value is at the level of critique (which cannot be ignored) rather than action – which is also its weakness. A parallel approach was the equity planning approach which was promoted through the 1980s and 1990s, and still has active practitioners today. Equity planners work within the political system in a (self-defined) progressive way, with the objective of redistribution of power and resources from local élites to the poor. They do not see the state's role as structurally determined, but as a terrain of political struggle and agency. In this the planner still has a specialist role, but focuses on communication as well as researching (gathering and analysing information) and formulating issues. While still arguably 'top-down', this approach is much more inclusive and proactive while retaining a critical stance.

A social learning model of participation in planning was promoted in the 1990s recognising the validity of personal/experiential knowledge as well as processed/expert knowledge, and stressing the growing distance between experts such as planners and their 'clients'. This led to a 'transactive' style of planning where both were involved in mutual learning, which required skills of resolving conflicts as well as recognising the non-verbal. The Habermasian concept of 'communicative action' underpinned the main strand of this approach which entitled itself 'communicative planning'. While recognising power relations, it hoped to overcome these through open dialogue – and has been criticised for some naivety in this respect (Hague and Jenkins 2004). Another 1990s' approach is the radical planning model where planners focus on existing unequal relations and distribution of power, opportunity and resources, with the goal to work towards structural transformation of these inequalities through empowerment. Many such planners are involved in social transformation through community organisation and urban social movements as opposed to working with the state or the private sector. Part of the problem in this approach is how to understand the role of the professional, with some planners renouncing professional and expert status to identify themselves with the participants offering their expertise on a more equal footing to other inputs.

Determining the right stages of participation is also seen as a key issue in participatory planning. Generally, people's involvement in the planning process takes place after the plan is ready, which has been the statutory position until recently.[10] There is recognition that earlier involvement is better, partially to promote ownership, but also to avoid objections. In line with widening governance issues at a broader scale, there has thus been a change in legislation in recent years in the UK to promote earlier involvement; however, this does not guarantee the quality of participation. While this is fundamentally based on issues of 'demand' and 'supply' of participatory opportunities, it also requires different techniques for information provision, consultation and/or negotiation in decision-making. A range of tools and techniques have been developed for use in planning, with a pedigree stretching back to the 1960s' investigations of indigenous knowledge, participatory rural appraisal and so on, and increasingly published in the public domain.

In practice, apart from a tendency in recent years for government to promote earlier engagement in local planning with communities, and more proactive approaches developing and being disseminated, there has been a growing requirement for government-funded regeneration projects to incorporate some form of wider social participation. This, however, can lead to such activities being rather 'top-down' and 'supply-led' rather than 'bottom-up' and 'demand-driven'. In general, however, planning deals with wide social impacts and hence probably emphasises wider social participation rather than architecture – although planning (through development control) also incorporates something more akin to user participation within architecture design. The relatively longterm experience in participation in planning and regeneration has produced a rich set of practices and techniques well summarised in manuals such as *The Community Planning Handbook* (Wates 2000)[11] (see also Appendices II and III).

Facilities management and post-occupancy evaluation

Within facilities management, relative to participation, the areas of importance relate mainly to workplaces, schools and healthcare facilities. For some time it has been acknowledged that employees of workplaces should be involved in the design briefing and facilities planning processes (e.g. Becker 1990). Becker argues that the level to which users are involved in a design or planning process can greatly influence their acceptance of changes to come. Traditionally, facilities management may have focused on physical aspects of a building, but recently a more holistic approach is being implemented. As a result, workers and users of buildings are being involved in decisions relating to other aspects and functions of the building (e.g. services such as cleaning, security and reception).

Reminiscent of approaches within environmental psychology dealt with above, Kernohan *et al.* (1992) argue that people constantly assess and evaluate a building they are in, in terms of its ability to meet their current needs. They describe a phenomenon called 'user knowledge' which refers to deeply embedded knowledge held by a user relating to the various components of a building they have become familiar with, such as how to navigate the building, or how a building supports users' needs and activities. According to Kernohan *et al.* (1992), there is a large discrepancy between identification of needs and mechanisms of provision in buildings which appropriate facilities management can reduce. Users and building providers may be seen as equating to demand and to supply, with a potential clash of interests existing between the two. Furthermore, users tend to accept what is provided to them even when it does not meet their expectations, owing to an embedded confidence in the 'expertise' of the providers (Kernohan *et al.* 1992). Users more recently have been involved in decisions relating, for example, to furniture choices, personalisation and room layouts. However, professionals can be concerned that giving too much control to users can result in negative outcomes, for example, in terms of health and safety. This is reflected in the work of Becker (1990) who argues that all employees of a workplace should be given some input into some of the decision-making processes, but not every employee should be involved at every level, some of these decisions being best left to technical experts. In general there has been an opening to wider and earlier engagement with users in facilities management, driven partly by the increasing importance of environmental issues such as energy use, and the role of centralised versus user controls of environments.

Post-occupancy evaluation (POE) has a potentially much wider scope of application across architectural types and is 'an assessment process that can be applied to any type or size of environment or facility' (Sanoff 2000). POE attempts to identify areas of success and good practice, and likewise, areas of failure or bad practice for future use in design. However, it seems there is a general reluctance to having a design or building evaluated after the completion stage of a project in architecture – even for designers who encourage participation in the design stages. Where post-occupancy evaluation is used, there can also be problems in that they may play down negative feedback, or the POEs are so simplistic that any value is minimised. While this may be potentially true for POEs that enter the public domain, concerns about legal responsibility may still exist for more confidential evaluations. Another issue is how a transitory user group such as library users can be represented in such evaluations. This is also a common concern in participative design processes (e.g. housing users who may well move on).

According to Joiner and Ellis (1989), most post-occupancy evaluation tends to be based on physical rather than use-based analysis. Joiner and Ellis describe alternative techniques such as 'Walkthroughs' or 'Touring Interviews' in which users of buildings and facilities (as well as other concerned parties) walk through the building 'observing, commenting and evaluating'. Another technique they describe is the Focus Study – similar in description to the well-known focus group method of qualitative data collection. Another option, differing from the main model of POE (Preiser *et al.* 1988), is where this is turned on its head and seen as a 'pre-occupancy evaluation'. In this approach similar existing buildings are evaluated by future occupants of a new facility and the findings are used to add to the new design.

Key to the potential of post-completion feedback – as a broader form including more specific post-occupancy evaluation – is the provision of adequate resources to underpin this. While this can be of use to the client of a building, the evaluation is also of potential importance to the architecture firm, particularly if the building has entailed the generation of new knowledge in its design. In a recent knowledge transfer publication on architecture research in practice (ScotMARK/gm+ad 2008) a range of possible mechanisms to capture such experiential knowledge developed in architecture firms has been reviewed, including both hindsight and foresight reviews. These can permit knowledge developed within a firm, usually around specific projects, to be captured within the firm and – importantly – disseminated to other practices and those involved in the built environment, and as such contribute to generic knowledge of use for architecture in general, as mentioned above. To date much of this research and development activity in architecture practices has been lost and this leads to 'reinventing the wheel'; a more coherent and accessible body of such knowledge can thus be an important source for the profession and of use in indirect participation activities.

Product design

Within the field of design there is a growing concern with user satisfaction, which benefits from technological innovation in order to identify users' needs and facilitate user participation in the design process. New movements such as 'Open Design' (Kadushin 2008), inspired by the Open Source Software movement, are taking place, allowing for design co-authorship and reuse. In this, a global network of digital manufacturing hardware allows users to co-create individualised products and send them to be produced via the Internet, for example.[12] Within this field, creativity and technology have been put together to allow individualisation, but also collaboration. The developments in user participation within two specific product design areas are particularly relevant to our discussion and are presented here: software design and mass customisation in housing.

Software design

A famous call to bring people into the design of software is made by Mitchell Kapor in 'A software design manifesto', where he says:

> The most important social evolution within the computing professions would be to create a role for the software designer as a champion of the user experience.... What is design? ... It's where you stand with a foot in two worlds – the world of technology and the world of people and human purposes – and you try to bring the two together.
>
> (Kapor 1996: 1)

User participation in information technology started in the 1970s in Norway via the liaison between computer experts and union leaders (Iron and Metalworkers Union) to enable workers to have more influence on the introduction of computerised systems in the workplace. At the time there was a high demand for software applications and these were more typically systematically designed from formal specifications – especially in the US. However, as software solutions multiplied the focus moved to 'usability' of software in the 1980s – or 'human-centred computing' (Carroll and Rosson 2007). While initially also seen as rational approaches to user needs and demand through systematic observation and measurement, by the 1990s the Scandinavian approach to user engagement in the design process had come to the fore. By 2000 computing and information science and engineering had taken such participation in software design on board, albeit still with different approaches across the Atlantic.

Different participation techniques are normally used, incorporating the more traditional social sciences techniques such as interviews, questionnaires, focus groups and workshops, which can be combined with more specific techniques such as usability tests. Various methodologies have been put forward, which have in common an interest in engaging with potential users and understanding their needs. The 'participatory and reflective design' methodology, for example, involves users' participation and evolving stages of evaluation. Here different types of users, the project team and specialists come together to evaluate each new stage of development, from the identification of users' needs, activities' analysis, concept model, through to prototyping and implementation, until the software is ready for use, again becoming subject to the constant evaluation and feedback from users (Pereira 2001). 'Scenario-based design' is another technique, which may be used to promote work orientation according to Carroll (1995, 2000), facilitating engagement with future users. This acts out scenes of current or future envisioned work activities as mutual education of work practices, identification of technology constraints and problems, but also new possibilities and solutions (Bødker 2000; Kensing and Madsen 1991).

Grudin and Pruitt (2002) from the Microsoft Corporation argue, however, that user participation is more complex in the case of mass-market, commercial software design. They advocate the use of a new interaction design technique commonly referred to as 'personas',[13] which involves the design of fictional users. They say that, when targeting millions of users, participation becomes a challenge, although highly desirable. They argue that, although software designers have tried to incorporate the Scandinavian user-centred approach, when having to deal with a larger number of consumers they lost the real engagement with participants as well as the attention to the socio-political quality of life issues, having difficulties to define representative participants. Drawing upon the power of using scenarios in the design of software, they propose the use of personas to break the dullness of traditionally used scenarios, following up on Bødker's call to use caricatures and unrealistic extremes which are more engaging.[14] Cooper (1999) and others (Hackos and Redish 1998; Mikkelson and Lee 2000; Tahir 1997) have advocated the use of abstract representations of users to guide design, and Grudin and Pruitt (2002) built upon their experiences.

House mass customisation

Architects have traditionally had a prejudice against the prefabrication of houses and its components (at least in practice if not in concept), which – according to Colin Davies (2005) – is due to several issues, but among them was the erroneous view that fabrication implies standardisation and mass production, with no space for individual choice.[15] Davies reports a history of house prefabrication with not very successful incursions from famous architects, such as Gropius, Frank Lloyd Wright and Le Corbusier.[16] The most successful and extensive examples in practice are not developed by architects and are therefore often not considered to be 'real architecture'. Within this category a number of light-weight construction methods evolving from the traditional balloon frame technology have been used in the US in particular, such as the platform frame. In this type of frame, the floors and walls are constructed as distinct structural units or platforms, and the walls are framed as storey-height panels. Being more manageable and flexible than the balloon frame, they allow for different building methods and can be transported to the site also as 'panel built' (walls and floors framed up in the factory) or 'box built' (room-size modules). According to Davies, the more that can be done in the factory regarding assembly and addition of other necessary items (such as insulation, lining, heating, wiring and plumbing), the better, as it increases the chance of achieving a better-quality product.

Universal composite components using new material such as structured insulated panels (SIPs) have also been increasingly used on the construction of houses in the US and now also in the UK. Panels are usually about 150 mm thick, with a rigid insulating foam core sandwiched between two continuously bonded sheets of plywood or, more commonly, oriented strand board (OSB), working on the stressed-skin principle, and these are able to support roofs and floors. They are lightweight, have high thermal insulation levels, and are easily prefabricated and customised. In Britain, ironically, one of the few specialists in using SIPs in house prefabrication, the Border Oak firm in Herefordshire, specialises in traditional English timber-framed houses, using post-and-beam structures of green oak infilled with 'the modern equivalent of wattle and daub' (Davies 2005: 151). Suppliers of such prefabricated options, which can be easily customised, generally provide suggested drawings of houses via publications and on the Internet, but the houses are actually designed and built according to their clients' wishes. Within the Swedish experience, the traditional balloon or platform timber-frame technology has been used as standard for low-rise housing since the early twentieth century, when it substituted the log-building vernacular. Most of the production is done in factories, with the final buildings also often assuming a vernacular style.

More recent changes in modern industry, however, are responsible for bringing new light into the issue of mass customisation of houses. Taichii Ohno of Toyota, for example, has proved that factory products can be customised to answer clients' demands via the use of 'lean production'. Moreover, advances in 'computer-aided design/manufacturing' (CAD/CAM) allow for speedy but not necessarily repetitive production. Lean production, also known as the Toyota Production System, is an assembly-line manufacturing methodology developed originally for Toyota and the manufacture of automobiles. Focusing on reducing system response time, this production system was capable of immediately changing and adapting to market demands, with their automobiles being made to order. The house industry in Japan has also adopted this methodology, with suppliers bringing materials to the factory when they are needed and production being assembled and delivered in time to be put together on the construction site within a flexible and responsive manufacturing process. CAD/CAM technology has also had a decisive effect on this process, as it has made it possible for a computer-controlled machine to 'make a hundred different components in almost the same time that it takes to make a hundred identical ones' (Davies 2005: 144). A CAD programme can automatically work out the best economical arrangement of the shapes on the sheet in the case of a thermal-cutting machine, for example, which makes the process cost-effective. CAM technologies thus bring a new kind of freedom of form and dimensions that, combined with the flexibility of lean production, allows the prefabrication of non-standard buildings in factories at economically competitive rates – as the Japanese housing industry demonstrates.

In addition, new processes and techniques available in the industrial production of houses can also be effective in facilitating the integration and promotion of energy-efficient features. An example of how is cited by Masa Noguchi from the Mackintosh School of Architecture in Glasgow, who was invited to mass customise a PV (photovoltaic) solar house which had been designed by the Canadian Solar Decathlon Team, composed mainly of engineering students from Concordia University, for the 2005 Solar Decathlon competition.[17] Noguchi developed an interactive mass custom design (MCD) communication tool: the solar housing model is used as the display home and potential home buyers are allowed to examine the product quality, while using the MCD tool to assist in selecting standard design components which can then be customised. Noguchi believes that PV mass custom housing can be considered as a prototype of sustainable homes which will appeal to the UK market, 'where the pressure to adapt affordable, customisable, and sustainable measures to housing is being intensified' (Noguchi 2007: 9).

The Japanese housing industry is already successful in commercialising their mass-customised houses, which are often equipped with a PV system, air-source heat pump and a combined heat and power generation system as standard features. Following the failure phase of house mass production during the 1960s and 1970s, when identical houses were produced which were rejected by the public, Japanese housing manufacturers decided to invest in improving quality and customer satisfaction. Now they have acquired a good reputation in producing mass-customised houses of quality, reasonably priced and zero-energy, with the number of PV installations in Japan growing from 539 to 52,863 houses between 1994 and 2003 (Noguchi 2008).

Although varied, the above two examples of experiences from the product design field are not only highly relevant to that of user participation in the architectural design process, but also overlap and interact with it. The future of mass customisation can strongly shape the future of architecture, for example, through providing interactive tools for participation in design, follow-ing wider social engagement using open-ended software, and through mass customisation of housing to a wider set of models and styles. as desired by a client (i.e. following other forms of mass product design). To what extent these technologies will transform more traditional ways of social participation is unclear and the transfer of such experience as that of Japan is not automatic to other societies and cultures, or productive systems.

Conclusion

This chapter has highlighted a variety of key issues which arise across the range of selected disciplines including some new issues which are becoming relevant to wider social participation in architecture. Within the former, there is obvious relevance to architecture in the extensive experience of participation in planning – especially for wider social participation – and this is the main area of overlap with widening governance agendas. User participation is also a key, and increasingly statutorily required element of the management of social housing – but less so in current new housing design. Participation by users is also of relevance in facilities management and post-occupancy evaluation, as well as in environmental psychology. Areas of increased potential overlap between these and architecture have been highlighted in this chapter, including the importance of the creation of generic knowledge which can assist indirect participation in architectural design. The one area with which architecture has limited engagement as yet seems to be in software and mass customisation of product design – although this is growing, especially in housing design, and potentially could have a wider role in architectural practice (see Jenkins and McLachlan forthcoming 2009).

Perhaps the most important issue raised in the various sections of this chapter is that architects should be encouraged to see value in forms of knowledge which lie outside their core professional competences as currently prescribed – and that this should be highlighted more clearly in architectural education, without necessarily diluting these competences but instead reinforc-ing them.

Notes

1 The book includes a wider bibliography for reference in this respect (i.e. separate from the specific bibliographic references of the book per se) – see Appendices.
2 The idea is explained in two main books. Space syntax is best known through *The Social Logic of Space* (1984) by Professor Bill Hillier and Julienne Hanson, and *Space is the Machine* (1996) by Professor Bill Hillier.

3   For more details on research and theory relating to children and participation, see the special issue of the *Journal of Environmental Psychology*, Issue 22.

4   Published in 2008 by Scottish Government Social Research, this work was developed by Alexandra Albert and Eleanor Passmore from The Work Foundation.

5   Set up in 1999, CABE is funded by two government departments: Department for Culture, Media and Sports; and Department for Communities and Local Government.

6   In fact the post-1980 Conservative government initially supported housing associations and related activity as it undermined local authorities, but later directed such participatory activity to urban regeneration and cut off funding sources.

7   The non-regulatory functions of the former Communities Scotland were transferred to the Scottish government's Housing and Regeneration directorate; while the work of Communities Scotland's Regulation and Inspection division has been transferred to the new Scottish Housing Regulator. See www.communitiesscotland.gov.uk (previous site maintained as archive); www.scotland.gov.uk (information about housing and regeneration); and www.scottishhousingregulator.gov.uk (Scottish Housing Regulator website).

8   Researched by the Tenants Information Service and the Department of Urban Studies, University of Glasgow.

9   For example, Chambers and Conway 1992.

10 Sometimes described as plan, publish and protect.

11 www.communityplanning.net.

12 See the Ponoko website (www.ponoko.com).

13 Personas are fictional people with names, clothes, occupations, families, friends, pets, possessions, age, gender, ethnicity, educational achievement and socio-economic status, with photos attached to them. Their creation is based on user research field studies, focus groups, interviews and further market research which work with the highest priority segments.

14 Bødker uses a cheery utopian visual and a nightmarish, dystopian vision to foment discussion in how to avoid undesirable outcomes and focus on positive ones (see Bødker 2000).

15 Colin Davies cites the successful history of the mobile home in the US, which has been producing 'customised homes for years without knowing anything about lean production or CAD/CAM' (Davies 2005: 205).

16 Or limited application of successful experiences, such as Walter Segal's work in London.

17 Working in teams during the Solar Decathlon, college and university students compete to design, build and operate the most attractive, effective and energy-efficient solar-powered house.

Part II

Illustrative case studies

Chapter 5

Case studies of social participation in different building types

Leslie Forsyth, Marcia Pereira,
Leanne Townsend and Martin Edge

Introduction

The aim of this chapter is to illustrate the type and form of contemporary buildings that can result from a design process which is participatory. Although only
a limited selection, the examples are illustrative of and support the view that a
participatory design process can produce architecture which is recognised as
having quality and thus participatory design processes do not exclude the production of buildings which are seen as having merit by the architectural
community.

      The case studies were selected following a review of literature and
additional information obtained during interviews with key individuals involved
in participation in architecture. They are drawn from different geographical locations – Aberdeenshire, London and Liverpool – and represent three different
building types – a residential development, a school and a community centre –
each of which was subject to different forms and styles of participation processes. Two of the selected buildings have received awards for their design,
while the third was developed by an organisation with a long commitment to
user participation in the design process.

Canmore Place housing development

General information

Canmore Place is a private social housing development in Kincardine O'Neil, Aberdeenshire, designed by architect Gokay Deveci for client Andrew Bradford. It caters to a variety of users – single, disabled, old and young couples, and families with two, three or more children. There are two house types, both of which are square in plan and have a flexible layout.

One type was built as single storey with the option of developing further accommodation in the roof space and therefore has between two and four bedrooms. The ground floors can accommodate two or three bedrooms, with a large living room, kitchen, dining room (which can be converted into a third bedroom), and a large bathroom equipped for disabled users. The top floor may be used as storage or for two bedrooms and an extra bathroom.

The other type was developed as an experimental design specifically to accommodate post-occupancy participation and redesign by users. These houses – two in number – were square units with a central services 'pod' and a series of sliding partition walls designed so that occupants could potentially change the spatial layout and size of rooms in a number of ways. These two houses with pyramidal roofs were sited at the entrance to the development as a reference to gatehouses.

Each house has a small backyard garden with a shed. In addition, there are two large common green areas with benches and porches which

5.1
Canmore Place.
Architect: Gokay
Deveci Architects.
View from the
road

seem to be very popular during the summer. The houses use different cladding materials from the traditional stone houses in the area, but maintain fairly traditional proportions and roof pitches. The external finishing of the walls is wood while the roofs are shingle.

Reasons for this case study

This housing project was identified as a design which had either received or been shortlisted for awards: RICS (Royal Institution of Chartered Surveyors) Award 1999; 2000 Homes Innovation Award by DETR Construction Best Practice Programme; Aberdeenshire Design Awards 2000 – Housing; The RICS Award 2000 (shortlisted); Saltire 2001 Housing Award (shortlisted). In addition, the design process is illustrative of a variety of types of participation with a long period of generic research prior to participation beginning.

The participation process

The participation process which led to this development falls into three distinct and very different phases:

1   A large and wide-ranging research project over a number of years which, among many other activities, developed the house designs in consultation with a wide range of potential users.
2   A limited participation exercise with the local community prior to the project going on site.
3   Aspects of the design were specifically geared towards experimentation by, and participation with, users in the post-occupancy phase.

Indirect social participation in the research project

Scottish Homes and Gordon District Council funded a research project at Robert Gordon University (RGU) with the aim of designing more affordable houses by going back to first principles and challenging the nature of the house and all our assumptions about traditional rural and suburban housing. Two earlier sites were selected but were changed before Canmore Place in Kincardine O'Neil was ultimately used for the development.

The project began with no preconceptions as to the form and nature of affordable rural housing. Although concerned with building cost, the primary starting point for the project was the generic investigation of the needs and desires of potential users.

As with all social housing it is difficult to identify the group of actual occupants for a development early in the design stage. In most cases occupancy will change many times over the life of the building anyway, so it is

5.2
Canmore Place.
Architect: Gokay
Deveci Architects.
View of the rear
gardens

important to be able to accommodate the needs of a wide range of potential users. Therefore the large amount of data collected and analysed by reference to potential user groups, which was then used in an iterative research-design process, was essentially part of a design participation exercise.

Among many other activities in this project, environmental psychologists and other social scientists carried out what amounted to a series of early-stage briefing processes, with potential users as clients. They explored the users' desire for and use of space in the home at a very fundamental level. This and other data was then developed into a series of hypotheses for designers to work with in reaching possible solutions. These potential solutions were subsequently tested by reference to the potential user group and the designs were then exposed to a 'Steering Group' of institutional stakeholders, with members from the Scottish government, local authority, insurance, construction industry and housing association sectors. These designs were developed and refined over a long period by a number of designers, who had access through the project to many more resources to test social responses to their designs (as well as cost and technical aspects) than would normally be the case in a small housing project. By the end of the project a series of well-developed and tested designs were presented as part of the reporting to the client.

Once the Canmore Place site was identified, the RGU Team developed further variants of the design, specifically a terraced version with an upper half-storey which could either be fully fitted out or left as a part-build roof space for future development by occupants.

The direct community participation exercise

A number of factors delayed the realisation of the development, including the University's inability to act as architect for the project and the change of client from the District Council to a private landowner. Therefore, the designs created in the research phase were taken forward to the development phase by one of the researchers as architect for the project.

The new client welcomed user participation, expressing a long-term interest in generating affordable houses, improving community conditions and working closely with community members. As a lot of indirect participation work had been carried out prior to the exposure of the designs to the actual community in Kincardine O'Neil, in contrast to the research activity, direct participation in the detail design and development phase was more like a planning participation exercise, involving representatives of the local community, not potential occupants, in activities focusing on the external appearance of the houses.[1] At this stage the designs were substantially complete and only a few details remained which could be changed. The project was introduced to local residents in an exercise during which second-year architecture students at RGU presented possible designs to members of the community in Kincardine O'Neil. In the detailed design phase, participation focused on the internal layout of rooms, since flexibility of this was a feature of the design's external layout of buildings in relation to each other and the building materials used. The main reason for wider public participation during this phase was the need for acceptance in a small rural community: Kincardine O' Neil is the oldest village in Royal Deeside and residents are very proud of their heritage and the old buildings.[2] The architect was aware that acceptance of the unconventional housing design by the residents was important in gaining planning permission.

The community consultation process occurred over three days in the local village hall, during which time the architect was always present. This was based on a three-day exhibition with discussion of three alternative project ideas. These involved the design of 'envelopes' for the houses as well as three options for an overall landscape planning and housing layout. The architect first worked with schoolchildren, using this as a way of engaging with other members of the community (e.g. getting parents involved). Activities were informal, with a 'drop-in' format, and refreshments were provided. The architect spent roughly half an hour with each person. 3D card models, pictures and drawings showing plans, façades and perspectives, as well as sample materials (e.g. roof materials), which people could feel as well as see, were all used in the consultation. The 3D models were used by participants to rearrange internal layouts of buildings. Site layouts were presented through different pictures. Computer models were also used – these were simple and relatively primitive 3D visualisation tools. In parallel to this, second-year architectural students from RGU undertook more general exercises with the community, developing design ideas and models. These seem to have allowed the community to enjoy a rich architectural experience.

Post-occupancy experimentation

The research team designed the houses with the explicit initial intention of experimenting in the post-occupancy phase with users' use of space. For this reason the houses were designed with two innovative features: fully flexible, sliding internal partitions which could be moved easily by occupants on a day-to-day basis; and a network of underfloor sensors which would detect and monitor the movement of occupants around the house. The intention was that, for a period of six months following completion of the development, two of the houses would remain in control of the research team. Different occupants would be moved into the houses and an experimental programme was devised which would encourage people to change the layout of spaces in their home and permit monitoring of the subsequent use of space. However, in the event, this more radical design participation exercise proved impossible once the client had changed to a private landlord and the architect had changed from being RGU to a private practice.

Evaluation

Evaluation of the participation activities was undertaken in the research project and involved the iterative testing of designs, created by reference to user groups, on user groups. Researchers used data to create hypotheses for designers. Subsequent designs were evaluated for their physical performance, cost and so on, and also for their acceptability to potential user groups. It was always envisaged that the ultimate evaluation would be through a demonstration project taking one or more of the designs on site.

In 2005 an evaluative report of the demonstration scheme was made to Communities Scotland by the Ecological Design Group. This was a group founded in RGU in collaboration with the School of Architecture, University of Dundee. The research leading to the report was undertaken by the University of Dundee – this is accessible online (Communities Scotland 2005).

No formal evaluation of the participatory process with the local community was undertaken. The architect and the client both indicated in an interview for this case study that they consider the overall process successful. There was a good turnout for the consultation exercise (35 per cent of the population), and participation led to changes in roofing materials and some of the internal layouts. Participants also had some say in the timber finishes and the site layouts. The participatory activity was considered effective in informing people of what was going on and this was seen as essential for acquiring planning permission.

The loss of the experimental post-occupancy phase of the participation is symptomatic of the problems when balancing research and design aspirations with economic demands and those of the regulatory authorities.

The architect indicated that he does not believe in participation before a design has been drafted as he thinks it is necessary for people to have some sort of design with which to engage. In this case the client was in agreement, indicating that if too early, consultation may produce an impossible wish list – however, if this is too late, nothing can be changed. The fact that the whole design had been developed by an indirect participation exercise starting long before a single mark had been made on paper seems to have been lost in the process of moving from the idea to completed houses. Perhaps this demonstrates the success of the process in producing well-liked designs which are not overtly generic or obviously the product of research. However, other members of the research team are clear in the view that the long, slow process of starting design from very basic first principles and injecting information from participation exercises at an early stage was instrumental in producing radical, thought-provoking designs (Edge and Pearson 2001).

In relation to the analytical framework for participation in architecture introduced in Chapter 1, Table 5.1 below summarises the 3D aspects of this.

Kingsdale School regeneration project

General information

Located in East Dulwich (South London), Kingsdale is a secondary (lower and upper) and tertiary school. It is the highest achieving community school in Southwark in the National GCSE League Tables, being recognised for its very good management. However, Kingsdale was considered a 'sink' school some years ago and officials were pressing for its closure. Everything started to change when a congruence of factors took place: new management was installed in 1998; a new curriculum was designed and implemented; and the regeneration of the school was designed using a participatory process executed via different stages.

Table 5.1 Canmore Place house development participation phases and levels

Stakeholder	Design	Construction	Post-completion
Client	Decision-making	Decision-making	Decision-making
Users	–	–	–
Public	Information and consultation	Information	–

The project comprised a new-build construction within the occupied school, including creating a new roof over the main courtyard together with the construction of walkways and a bridge at the first-floor level, an auditorium, a library, a new dining area and assembly hall. Initially, the main school was altered, including extensions to classrooms and refurbishment to the whole building. In the most recent phases, a new-build mass timber music school and sports hall were constructed on the east of the site. Several articles mentioning the innovative design approach were published and are easily accessed via the Web.[3]

Reasons for the case study

The project used participatory exercises involving students, staff and the whole extended school community in an ongoing process, where the old and the proposed buildings were discussed. Considered to be 'radical' and 'academic

5.3
Kingsdale School auditorium. Architect: dRMM – suspended air duct and lighting rig, designed by artist Joep van Lieshout

inspiring' architecture, Kingsdale School has received several awards: In 2008 the project was highly commended in the 'Learning' category of the World Architecture Festival; the 2005 Building of the Year Award – Inspiration through Architecture (Royal Fine Art Commission); and the 2005 Excellence in Design Award (American Institute of Architects (AIA)); 2002 M4I Movement for Innovation Demonstration Award (School consultation process). In addition, the Pod or wooden geodesic dome which is used as an auditorium was winner of the structural category of the 2004 Wood Awards. The school project is undoubtedly innovative in its design and in the materials and techniques used.

The participation process

In 1998, the then newly appointed headmaster saw the change in the school physical environment as an opportunity to bring about a change in behaviour.[4] He thus applied to take part in the Architecture Foundation 'School Works' project (1998–2001), aiming to explore the relationship between educational achievement and the built environment. An architectural competition was organised via the 'School Works' project. The final 20 architects went through a selection process, which involved the participation of pupils and school staff, and dRMM were appointed as architects. The headmaster was also successful in acquiring support from the then Secretary of State for Education Estelle Morris, and received £12 million for the regeneration project. Estelle Morris was equally enthusiastic that the approach taken to the regeneration of the school was to be participatory. This extraordinary funding was instrumental in the success of the project as a whole, both in permitting more experimentation and allowing more time for participation.

As part of the Architecture Foundation ethos,[5] a participatory design process was started. An initial consultation phase took place, where the Architecture Foundation sub-contracted DEMOS to carry out the participatory exercises. However, the school management was not very happy with this initial work, as it felt patronised, and decided it should take over the process. Having said that, the participatory exercises which subsequently took place with dRMM architects were considered to be very fruitful. This later participation was initiated with dRMM one year before starting the design process and involved students, staff and the whole extended school community. Participation then took place all the way through the design, construction and post-completion phases. Most of the participatory activities took place within the school, as it continued to function during the whole regeneration process, but visits to other schools were organised.

Both the school senior management and the architects seem to have had a strong influence on the 'language' used during the design process as well as on the definition of the activities which took place. However, it

5.4
Kingsdale School.
Architect: dRMM.
Courtyard roof
comprised of
transparent
air-filled ETFE
pillows that
inflate and deflate
to regulate
sunlight and heat

appears that the architects guided the discussion of materials and technical solutions, bringing their design ideas into discussion, albeit in a very democratic and accessible way. According to them, there is always a learning curve and participants have to learn some of the technical jargon. If this is carried out properly, the learning process leads to participants having a greater dialogue with the design later in the process. They believe that in this case, the participants' design sensibilities became more sophisticated over time.

The local community was also involved from the beginning of the process, with meetings taking place every Friday evening. Several people from the relatively wealthy local community were against the school being there, as it was considered to be a 'dangerous' place. However, through their involvement in the discussions and the different stages of regeneration, their opinions changed considerably. According to the architects this was because their concerns were listened to, they became involved, and they took part in organised visits to the site. In addition, the architects believe that it did not take long for community members to see a change in the students' behaviour.

Members of staff took part in participatory activities with students. Staff members also changed their opinions regarding the school over time. Some were quite sceptical at the beginning and thought students would vandalise the new auditorium, for example, but it did not happen. Other members of the teaching staff were quite enthusiastic from the beginning, but the majority became more interested later when they started to see improvements.

The collaborative participation with students and staff took different forms, such as interviews, presentations, workshops, seminars, student

5.5
Kingsdale School.
Architect: dRMM.
Exterior – music
and sports/dance
buildings

projects, questionnaires and meetings. Examples of the 'pre-design' participatory activities used include: mock-up TV shows with students; collages; disposable cameras given to children to make pictures of what they considered to be good or bad in the school; architects presenting pictures of different school solutions or different learning experiences and students' favourites were chosen and used in presentations. It was felt that the children were empowered and able to make choices at many different stages.

During the design process, more tangible design proposals were made. More physical models were used and real-size mock-up environments were created. In order to choose a solution for covering the internal patio, different options were hung over the space for children to opt for the ones they preferred. The same process was used to choose the floor materials and colours. In some cases students' choices were not taken literally, as, for example, with the particular choice of the colour green – a palette of different greens being used instead. Students' wish for a swimming pool was not realised either, as the school management opted for using the same amount of money for the provision of three IT suites.

Evaluation

Although the regeneration project and its participatory process of this building has been the theme of different articles, exhibitions and presentations, no formal evaluation of the participatory process itself has taken place. However, good communication between architects, the school management (headmaster and deputy headmaster) and contractors (Galliford Try) is considered to have been essential in achieving the quality of outcomes. All stakeholders involved seem to agree that the mix of people with vision and good ability to communicate ideas had a great impact on the project's success. The architects recognise that a good client is essential to achieve a good architectural product. They particularly considered the headmaster to be 'inspirational' and 'demanding in a good way'. The 'clients' – the school management – regard the architects' ability to communicate well and listen to be invaluable, as well as the flexibility shown by both architects and contractors. The architects were considered to be 'fantastic', very patient, and ready to discuss different ideas, techniques and many aspects of the project.

5.6
Kingsdale School.
Architect: dRMM.
Entrance to the
music, sports and
dance buildings

The time available for the initial participatory activities (one year) allowed for a thorough investigation of issues as well as for the exploration of different techniques and ideas. However, the architects are aware that, within the everyday context of normal projects, this time was a 'luxury'. Ideally, the minimum time for the initial participation would be around six months but new procurement processes generally do not afford such time for this activity.

The quality of the final design is undisputable. It seems to have tackled the necessary issues via appropriate and ingenious solutions such as passive supervision, pleasant and efficient spaces and connections, multi-use spaces, accessibility to all floors, and sheltered and attractive social space in the courtyard, which became the heart of the school. Its architectural success may be seen by the number of awards and citations the project has received in the recent past.

5.7
Kingsdale School.
Architect: dRMM.
Courtyard lift and
entrance hall

According to the architects, the challenge to achieve a good result using participation is to identify 'design champions' (e.g. the headmaster of Kingsdale School), who share the vision and are good communicators, with a strong sense of leadership. When a good chemistry with the client exists, it is possible to set up an efficient participatory process and define a vision, setting clear ambitions, via a clear understanding of the past and the identification of the correct issues which need to be tackled in the future.

The division of the regeneration into phases was also beneficial, as it allowed the development of a certain awareness of the impact of changes, generating a positive 'snowball effect'. Seeing change take place increased stakeholders' motivation and helped attract more funds. However, the school management was always clear about the need to avoid the 'forever' factor of never-ending discussions and changes.

The overall impression is that students as well as staff felt empowered, as they were given choices and saw that their opinions were being considered in the different phases of the regeneration project. As a consequence they seem to have developed a sense of ownership of the buildings. There is a feeling of pride which can be clearly distinguished when visiting; vandalism and staff turnover have considerably reduced; and students' achievements have been continuously improving, with the school being recognised as one of the leading transformational institutions in South London (Department for Education and Skills 2004).

In relation to the analytical framework for participation in architecture introduced in Chapter 1, Table 5.2 below summarises the 3D aspects of this.

Lee Valley Millennium Centre[6]

General information

The new Lee Valley Millennium Centre designed by Comtechsa is located in Netherley, Liverpool. The centre aims to be the social focus of the six estates

Table 5.2 Kingsdale School participation phases and levels

Stakeholder/phase	Design	Construction	Post-completion
Client (senior management)	Decision-making	Decision-making	Decision-making
User (staff and students)	Decision-making	Consultation	Consultation
Public	Consultation	Information	Information and consultation

that comprise Netherley and Lee Valley areas, on the eastern fringe of Liverpool. It is the biggest Millennium Commission project in Liverpool, having also received funds from the Single Regeneration Budget, European Regional Development Fund, Liverpool City Council and fire insurance monies from the community centre that previously stood on the site.

With a floor area of 1600 m^2, the building comprises an Internet café, laundrette, sports and community hall with online film capability, community college, public library, training rooms including IT training, office space and bar. There is also a proposed 'breakfast club' for children from deprived families to be able to eat before school. Comtechsa was approached by the Lee Valley community to assist with the design of the building, as one member of the community had already used Comtechsa's architectural services.

The initiative began in 1995 and funding became available in 1998. Representatives of the local community group created a smaller group which became a limited company and a registered charity in order to be able to apply for the funding. The present manager of the community centre was part of this small group, and also took part in the participatory process.

Reason for the case study

This case study was selected to examine the participation process as carried out by an organisation which has been active in this field for some considerable time, since 1979. Furthermore, it afforded the opportunity of examining whether there was a difference in the process of participation carried out by architects working for members in a user-controlled organisation from that carried out by other architects.

5.8
Lee Valley
Millennium
Centre. Architect:
Comtechsa.
Reception area

The participation process

A key issue in participatory processes is who initiates them. In this instance it was the client, originally Belle Vale Community Centre before becoming Lee Valley Millennium Centre. The 'language' used in participatory processes is also of great importance, especially when technical and other expertise is involved. According to the participant interviewed, communication with the architect was good, and there were no difficulties either in understanding proposed ideas or in putting forward their own thoughts.

The architect had a range of discussions with various stakeholder groups at different times throughout the project. To design the public library, for example, several meetings with library staff and council architects took place, as it is Liverpool City Council who runs the library. Representatives from the Millennium Commission, which partially funded the project, were also involved in the participatory process as they were keen to see that the money was being spent in an appropriate manner. Representatives from the Lee Valley Partnership were included at suitable stages. All parties in the participatory process were keen to have a significant input where appropriate and did so throughout. However, the main discussions were attended by a smaller group of representatives who then reported back to the community group.

The community group were already quite sure of what they wanted, and as such the participatory activities were a natural progression towards their objectives. The architect spent some time with participants trying to find out what the spirit or ideal for the project was. This built on two surveys which had been carried out with local people at the beginning of the process, before

5.9
Lee Valley
Millennium
Centre. Architect:
Comtechsa.
Management
Committee chair
in the hall and
café

Comtechsa had even been contacted. These surveys sought to determine what local people felt was needed in a community centre and carrying out this exercise helped to generate the feasibility study. Once the architect was involved, participation largely took place with a small group of five or six people who were felt to be representative of the local community. The contacts between the architect and the community client generally took place in an office situated at the nearby Belle Vale Shopping Centre. These meetings occurred at regular intervals and at every stage of the project.

One of the techniques used was a three-dimensional cardboard model of the building set in its wider context, along with a model of the interior of the building. The model of the building in the wider context was useful, as this showed how the community centre would fit into the surrounding park. Participants were encouraged to discuss these models, but according to the centre manager they were not encouraged to 'play' with the models. The models were largely used to make sure that people were happy with the final design. A 3D computer model was also used, but not all participants found this to be very useful.

In practice, members of the representative group tended to delegate the decision-making to the manager of the centre and another member of the design group, who dealt more closely with the architect. The centre manager felt that her opinions were listened to and she was able to make decisions. In retrospect, she believes that some things could have been designed differently. She feels that there is not enough office space, while too much space is wasted in terms of the large community hall where there is a

5.10
Lee Valley
Millennium
Centre. Architect:
Comtechsa

large screen, which is only really used when a big football match is on. On the other hand, the architect felt that too many changes were made during the construction phase, when these could not be appropriately adapted to the design. For example, the building was not designed with automatic doors but these were added at a later stage to improve disabled access and, as a result, these do not work as effectively as they should and tend not to be used.

Evaluation

Post-completion evaluation of the project has not formally taken place. However, during the interviews with the centre manager and the architect, it became apparent that some concerns over the building may be resolvable with further effort. As the architect pointed out, this should act as a lesson that post-occupancy evaluation should ideally take place and that it could be clearer to clients that Comtechsa is always open to communication with clients and users once a project is complete. There has also been no specific evaluation of the participatory process. However, during interviews with both the architect and the user/client, both considered that issues such as the delegation of the decision-making responsibility to one or two representatives, despite being fairly typical in such processes, reduces the level of wider participation as well as placing a great deal of responsibility on the selected representatives.

From the information available and the interviews which were carried out with individuals involved in the project, there is no evidence to suggest that participation in the design process was different because Comtechsa is a user-controlled organisation. The techniques and methods used to involve the client, user and wider public were similar to those used in other projects. However, it is worth noting that the Lee Valley Millennium Centre is a member of Comtechsa and as such has direct access to the committee

Table 5.3 Lee Valley Millennium Centre participation phases and levels

Stakeholder	Design	Construction	Post-completion
Client*	Decision-making	Decision-making	Decision-making
Users*	Decision-making	Decision-making	Information and/or decision-making
Public	Consultation and information	Information	Information

Note
*In this example, the client was the community group which applied for funding for the building. Some of this group were potential users of the community centre. However, only a very small group participated in the main discussions. When viewing the above table it is worth bearing in mind that the wider public are also the potential users of the building.

responsible for the employment and performance of the technical staff who organised the design and participation processes used in their project.

In relation to the analytical framework for participation in architecture introduced in Chapter 1, Table 5.3 above summarises the 3D aspects of this.

Conclusions

The above case studies show that what is perceived as successful user participation in the design process can be both complex and varied. It can take different forms and can happen at different stages involving very different kinds of stakeholders. Also apparent is the range of issues that can affect participation: governmental demands, funding requirements and the organisation of communities and clients comprise a small selection of the variables that are illustrated in the experiences of Canmore, Kingsdale and Lee Valley. However, there are a number of crucial relationships which are also illustrated in the case studies and of these the relationship between the architect and client seems to be fundamental. If this relationship is respectful and inspiring, the chances of having a better design process, with more satisfying results, seem undoubtedly greater. The time available for participation during the whole design process is another important factor which can contribute to a successful process and product. A good participation exercise needs time for preparation, to motivate participants, to build up trust and demonstrate results. However, the way to incorporate this time into the design process is less clear. These and other related issues are discussed further in Chapter 10. The limited number of examples described in this chapter cannot prove that participatory processes necessarily produce better design, or better user satisfaction with the resulting buildings. However, they show that user and wider social participation in the architectural process can result in quality buildings which satisfy clients and users and are also capable of recognition among the architectural and built environment communities.

Notes

1 It is important to note that although participants were not necessarily future users of the buildings but just interested community members, one or two may have gone on to live in the housing.

2 Another initiative that was underway in Kincardine in parallel to these projects was a £50,000 funded project at RGU looking at the overall sustainability of the village.

3 Examples include *Frieze Magazine* (Issue 87, November/December 2004: www.frieze.com/issue/another_brick_in_the_wall) or *Architecture Week*, an article on 'Recovering Kingsdale' by Don Barker (November 2004: www.architectureweek.com/2004/1103/building_1–1.html).

4 In fact since 1999, when the project began, the school has gone through a complete change. Morale and student behaviour has improved as well as their achievements. Staff turnover and vandalism have considerably reduced.

5 The Architecture Foundation aims to be 'a catalyst for architecture, creating many kinds of projects', and one of its aims is to 'foster a social culture, of collaboration, participation and debate' (www.architecturefoundation.org.uk).

6 The authors gratefully acknowledge the inputs from key members of Comtechsa in preparing this case study.

Chapter 6

Case studies of organisations with community-based practices

Leslie Forsyth, Marcia Pereira and Leanne Townsend

Introduction

The two organisations chosen for the case studies in this chapter have a long, successful history of involvement with participation in the architectural design process. Both were established in the 1970s and at that time there were many organisations carrying out similar work, but only a very small number survived the decline in participation that was seen in the mid- to late 1980s.

ASSIST is a community architecture organisation with participation at the centre of its philosophy from its beginnings. It has successfully managed to survive changes through time and political regimes without abandoning its community ethos and responsiveness to users' needs. Equally, Comtechsa has been involved in participatory activities in community technical aid for almost 30 years and remains the only user-controlled technical aid centre in the UK.

This chapter presents the history and organisational structure, financing and approach to participation, of ASSIST and Comtechsa. By considering these characteristics we aim to highlight the similarities and differences between them and in their respective ways of involving clients, users and the wider public in the participation process. But more importantly we seek to examine also what might be the qualities both organisations have displayed which have enabled them to survive over the last quarter of a century and that is integral to their continuing survival.

ASSIST Architects

General information

ASSIST Architects is a community-based architectural practice that offers services relating to housing, local employment and community facilities. It has a wide experience in master planning and neighbourhood studies, having been closely involved with community-led clients and the housing association movement since its inception.[1] ASSIST has offices in Glasgow and Edinburgh.[2]

Historical development[3]

ASSIST was set up in 1972 by the Department of Architecture at the University of Strathclyde in Glasgow. It developed from a degree thesis by Raymond Young in 1970. Young developed his graduate work focusing on a small area of Govan by offering a free technical aid service for the rehabilitation of tenement flats called TIP (Tenement Improvement Project). TIP developed both innovative technical and participatory solutions with its services going considerably beyond the traditional architectural professional remit to include accessing government finance, negotiating with lawyers and assisting with building management.

To implement this on a larger scale, ASSIST was set up in a shop in Govan Road by Raymond Young and Jim Johnson, his university supervisor, with initial funding from the Wates Foundation and the Scottish Development Department. ASSIST developed the concept of community-based housing associations to act as project managers and clients to overcome the complex problems of mixed ownership of the flats being renovated. In 1973 the first housing association, Central Govan Housing Association, was set up and began the work of rehabilitating the 212 flats in the Taransay Street Treatment Area. ASSIST was then partially funded by Glasgow City Council through fees for home improvement grants.

In the mid-1970s Young was appointed as the first Director of the Housing Corporation's Scottish Office, set up by Lord Goodman after his visit to ASSIST's work in Govan. This triggered interest in other tenement areas of Glasgow. ASSIST staff helped in setting up several more community-based housing associations – in Govanhill (where ASSIST started its second office), in Linthouse, and later in Dennistoun (where after the completion of its work in Govan, ASSIST started an office for Reidvale Housing Association in 1976).

In the late 1970s ASSIST diversified from housing into other building types, working for Govan Workspace Ltd converting a redundant school and a bakery into low-cost workshop units to stimulate local employment. ASSIST also helped to set up a building preservation trust to save the listed Victorian Glasgow Fish Market building from demolition, and convert it into a speciality shopping centre and food market. By this time ASSIST employed upward of 20 staff and it became increasingly impractical to run it as a Strathclyde University 'action research' project. As a result ASSIST bought itself out of the University and in 1984 the project was re-formed as ASSIST Architects Ltd, the first architectural cooperative in Scotland. Subsequently other architectural firms engaged with housing associations in participatory design work, and a Technical Services Agency (TSA) was set up in Glasgow in 1984 with Urban Aid funding, mostly offering tenants training and technical advice to either help them campaign for improved housing conditions and/or set up their own co-ops. The TSA's work was focused mainly on Glasgow's huge stock of council houses.

ASSIST continued to grow as an architectural practice working closely with clients and users, strengthening the foundation of its ethos of community-based architecture. Through the late 1980s and 1990s, housing associations (HAs) turned their attention to developing housing on derelict brownfield sites to create more dense urban developments. This city centre regeneration was followed by a new breed of fully mutual housing cooperatives located in the housing schemes developed in the 1950s. ASSIST has worked with a range of these associations on refurbishment and new-build projects, including housing and community building activities to meet local needs. In the mid-1990s ASSIST established its Edinburgh office and developed a new client base in the East of Scotland.

Now more than 35 years old, ASSIST Architects has developed into a successful architectural practice with a diversified set of services, working not only with building rehabilitation and regeneration, but also new-build, conversions, streetscaping/landscaping services, innovative projects, partnering procurement processes, sustainability, wider action and inclusive and barrier-free design. However, it still maintains strong links with its housing association and community regeneration roots. In addition, some architects in ASSIST spun off at various times to set up their own practices, mostly initially continuing with the same kind of community- based rehabilitation work contributing to a strong heritage of socially oriented architecture in Scotland.

Organisation

The initial organisational structure of ASSIST was as a research and development unit of Strathclyde University with Jim Johnson as the (academic) unit director. All those working for ASSIST had research posts and were contracted by the university on one-year appointments. ASSIST had a turn-over of some £250,000 per year, which funded the staff. When ASSIST bought itself out in 1984 it set up as a cooperative architectural practice with a very flat organisational structure. At first this was based on small jobs run by individuals until the larger fish market project was taken on and a re-structuring was considered necessary.

The organisational structure has changed over time, as well as the number of staff. When it left Strathclyde University there were around 20 members of staff. During the mid-1990s there were around ten. Now the number of staff is again just above 20.

The current structure of ASSIST consists of a Board of Directors with six members, mostly architects: four directors of the Glasgow office and two in the Edinburgh office. The Glasgow office has a design team with eight members and an administration team with four members, while the Edinburgh office has a design team with two members and one administrative assistant. The design teams have architects and architectural students, as well as architectural technologists, technicians and assistants. The work teams consist mostly of architects or architectural students, with four to five administration workers. They had a social worker at the beginning, but not any longer.

The practice does not have difficulties attracting staff, but indicated that students coming out of architecture school are often shocked by the participatory approach, generally not expecting to be challenged concerning their expertise in dealing with people.

Funds to pay for all expenses come in from project fees; however, community projects do not always cover all their costs and it is usually necessary to do some cross-funding. When the practice makes profits these are shared by the workers.

Participation

All of ASSIST architectural projects involve an agreed structure of participation with the client, community group, housing association or cooperative. The practice is particularly concerned with having 'good communication' and good use of appropriate techniques. It makes it clear that the communication of ideas and information is very important to ensure that people understand the choices and therefore are able to participate in the decision-making process. They use a variety of communication and presentation techniques to facilitate the process, such as model-making, 3D computer simulation and image manipulation.

ASSIST Architects is normally the initiator of the participatory process, but it has also been the case that it is asked to work in a specific project due to its experience with participation. During the participatory process the architects act as 'listeners' and 'guides' and organise events, where users can take part. The participation activities usually take place 'on the users' territory', in people's houses, in a school, or somewhere else in the local community. The architects say there are situations where housing association venues are not advisable, due to political issues. Every so often participatory events have to be run twice, at different times, to allow those who work to participate. Crèches are also organised. In an initial phase they collect information and users' views; in a second phase they go back to the community with three to four options for a feedback workshop; and in a third phase, having chosen a preferred solution, they develop it and go back for another feedback workshop or present it via a newsletter.

Open days are also held as an integral part of urban regeneration processes in which ASSIST is involved, where there is wider public engagement and communities are given opportunities to influence design proposals for their areas. Tools and techniques used to encourage participation in these situations include: digital 3D basic models, 3D cardboard models, sketches, drawings, photographs of similar solutions, similar projects, wall panels with titles for adding users' contributions and votes.

Concerning participation, the firm often finds that most people tend to know what they do not want to have, and only some know what they do. The architects try to bring new ideas and expand people's understanding of neighbourhood (e.g. the importance of maintaining local shops, post offices and local schools). They guide the process in a respectful way, as they are aware of the danger of manipulating participation in an attempt to turn the results towards a specific design solution.

Evaluation

ASSIST does not carry out formal processes of evaluation of the participatory exercises; however, its buildings go through an audit process 12 to 18 months after completion. The relationship with users is sometimes so close that they still receive phone calls from ASSIST after ten years and the success of its architects could be taken as proof of the usefulness of the participatory

Table 6.1 Usual participation phases and levels in ASSIST's projects

Stakeholder/phase	Design	Construction	Post-completion
Client	Decision-making	Decision-making	Decision-making (audit one or one and a half years after completion)
User	Decision-making	Information	Information (visits)
Public	Decision-making	Information	–

methodologies they apply. ASSIST has been able to develop a wealth of experience in different aspects of community regeneration, as well as work in new-
build, with the public and commercial sectors, being recognised by its ability to
successfully bring in participation and sustainability aspects. As mentioned on
its website, ASSIST is able to offer a 'collective expertise that reflects its successful working relationships with many clients in developing solutions to local
housing needs and responding effectively to the requirements of individual end
users'.[4]

Survival as an organisation

The organisation has survived political changes when many other community-
led practices disappeared. This seems to have happened because ASSIST was
able to adapt over time, from a research-based unit into a cooperative; having
first been a very flat organisation, but then changing when bigger projects
came in. From the original work with housing regeneration, it also diversified,
working not only with building rehabilitation, but also with a wide range of architectural and related activities. These adaptations have been in response to its
ability to read what is right for the time. The initial work in the late 1960s and
early 1970s on the rehabilitation of tenement buildings came when Glasgow
was waking up to the value of its architecture and becoming more conscious of
the unsuitability of a planning strategy generated during the post-war era. Later
on, in the mid-1970s, the whole idea of community regeneration took off when
the Housing Corporation came to Glasgow. As the political changes of the mid-
1980s took place, ASSIST Architects had not only built up a reliable reputation
but was also able to diversify its work into more entrepreneurial areas.

Comtechsa[5]

General information

Comtechsa, a community technical aid centre, is based at 60 Duke Street,
Liverpool. It is a non-profit-making cooperative society working in Merseyside
and surrounding areas, aiming to help community groups and voluntary organisations make the best use of their land, buildings and environment; and to
provide high-quality, fully accessible accommodation for community groups and
voluntary organisations. It carries out architectural and building services, largely
in community-based contexts. Services are offered on an 'at-risk' basis, enabling groups without funding to establish the viability of their ideas and construct effective fundraising applications. Comtechsa typically works closely with
clients and users and describes its approach as 'user-led'. Historically these
users have been community, faith and voluntary groups.[6]

Historical development

Liverpool has always had a very active voluntary sector. However, community organisation members had little understanding of the architectural and building processes concerned with obtaining leases for buildings, planning permissions or funding for a project; consequently projects would often fail. Moreover, people did not think about the long-term sustainability or maintenance of a building. The late 1970s was a time when many people were moving out of the city and there was an initiative towards trying to reuse some of the vacant industrial premises in the inner city by a concerned group called the 'Vacant Land and Building Steering Committee', which was formed of representatives from the local authority, voluntary and private sector.

Buildings becoming vacant gave opportunities for the creation of community facilities and this led to a need for technical support. In 1978, Nigel Mellor (present Comtechsa Management Committee Chair), who was Community Development Officer of Liverpool City Council at that time, had the opportunity to organise a bid to set up a community technical aid centre. Through this bid £30,000 was obtained in November 1979 from Liverpool City Council's Inner City Partnership Programme to set up and fund Comtechsa's work for a five-year period.

In 1983, the Labour Party took overall control of Liverpool City Council, with a strong left-wing orientation and policies which included municipalising the voluntary sector. According to reports, the council view at the time was that if services funded through the Urban Programme and provided by the voluntary sector were bad they should be ended, if good they should be municipalised. Discussions regarding the municipalisation of Comtechsa went on until 1987, but no real intervention took place and the core funding was not completely cut.

In 2001 Liverpool City Council finally withdrew its participation from the Management Committee, but continued to provide the core funding for Comtechsa, although in constantly decreasing amounts. From 2000 the Council funding of the voluntary/non-statutory sector moved towards a more contract-oriented approach.

Organisation

Structure

Founded in November 1979 with a grant from Liverpool City Council's Inner City Partnership programme, Comtechsa was initially constituted as an Industrial and Provident Society to provide services to member organisations: community or voluntary sector organisation in Liverpool, Merseyside and the surrounding areas. The membership fee was, and still is, a symbolic one-off payment of £1. Since its foundation, it has attracted over 700 member groups.

Comtechsa is now a Charitable Society for the Benefit of the Community, and can therefore provide services to a wider range of organisations.

Comtechsa members can nominate a representative of their group for election to the Committee of Management. The Committee is responsible for managing the overall service provision and has policy, financial, legal and staffing responsibility for the organisation. There are currently 11 members of the Management Committee and Nigel Mellor, who represents the Oaktree Education Trust, has been its Chair since 2002. The Committee meets about ten times a year, with meetings having very detailed agendas. Its members are volunteers who do this work in addition to their normal jobs. The Committee can have a maximum of 20 people, but having about 12 participants is considered to be more efficient in a meeting. Eighty per cent of committee members have to be from community organisations. There is an election every year to elect one-third of the committee. There is capacity also to involve other individuals committed to the work of Comtechsa.

Having a Management Committee elected by the community organisations which are members of, and served by, Comtechsa represents a great advantage. This means that the committee can draw upon the experience of its members, who are or have been users or clients of Comtechsa, to contribute to the overall management of the services. This makes Comtechsa a 'user-controlled technical aid centre'. In the original organisational structure, users had to be community, voluntary or faith organisations, with some flexibility within this to allow the participation of schools and housing associations. The City Council was also a member, as the main provider of funds. However, more recently the structure of the organisation has been changed to allow individuals to become members, although their participation within the Management Committee is restricted to 20 per cent.

Originally, Comtechsa had six members of staff: project leader (architect/planner), deputy project leader (architect/planner), two project workers (landscape architect and architectural technician), an administrator and a clerical worker. Since then it has expanded and now has 12 members of staff. There is a director who reports directly to the Management Committee, and three team leaders responsible for the technical team, administration team and property team. The technical team has one project worker specialised in landscape, three project workers specialised in building/design and one trainee (architectural student). The administration team has one administrator and two administration workers, with one of them being also responsible for the building reception. In the property team there is one property services manager and one cleaning operative. Comtechsa also offers training opportunities to help people determine whether a career in the built environment is suitable for them as well as providing an opportunity for disadvantaged individuals to move towards employment.

There has been a low turnover of staff at Comtechsa. When jobs are advertised, typically only a few people apply. According to the Management Committee Chair, one needs to be a special type of person to work in this participatory way – to have a social interest and be committed to work with the community. People tend to be attracted to such jobs because of their social values. In terms of staffing, he believes there is a potential to promote better links with universities for the organisation of students' placements.

About five years ago a decision was made to change the legal structure of Comtechsa, turning it from a cooperative (Industrial and Provident Society) into an exempt charity (a Society for the Benefit of the Community). This was done principally for funding reasons, so that the range of funding for which the organisation was eligible would be broadened. Moreover, Comtechsa can now work for anyone, not only member organisations.

Funding

Comtechsa obtained £30,000 per annum from Liverpool City Council's Inner City Partnership Programme for its initial five years of existence. Core funding continues to come from Liverpool City Council, allowing the realisation of feasibility studies and other similar services on an 'at-risk' basis. Currently, funding of this kind is accessed in competition with other applicants, and in recent years the amount has been decreasing: £215,000 (2003), £200,000 (2004), £175,000 (2005), and £150,000 (2006–2007–2008). A recent bid for £200,000 was submitted for the period 2008 to 2011 but only £100,000 was approved.

Increased competition and reductions in funding from the City Council have resulted in a need to look at new streams of funding, and a more commercial approach may be necessary; for example, there may have to be more private commissions. This is becoming a pressing issue. Despite the need for changes, Comtechsa is still keen to retain its original aims and objectives and uphold its philosophy to empower members of community and voluntary organisations through its involvement in the design and building development process. However, it is now working more in partnership with other types of organisations (e.g. Groundwork Trust) and also trying to work more with housing associations.

When Comtechsa began it had to return all fees generated to the then Department of the Environment (DoE), but after successful negotiations with Liverpool City Council (LCC) and the DoE, it was able to retain fees generated in return for no further increase in the core grant. Comtechsa currently depends on some £80,000 to £100,000 a year from fee income.

In the late 1980s Comtechsa acquired a building and undertook the complete refurbishment scheme to provide attractive, accessible, high-quality office accommodation for small community and voluntary organisations that could benefit from some shared services. The development has been very successful and Comtechsa secures rental income from the building which, along with fee income, contributes towards salaries and running costs. The building is now fully owned by the organisation and Comtechsa rents the other offices, which realise £30,000 to £40,000 annually. There is also a commercial coffee shop on the ground floor which generates £10,000 a year. This rental income has been crucial in the organisation's survival.

Participation

It is Comtechsa's philosophy to encourage and enable members of community groups to be fully involved in their building development projects. Through this involvement Comtechsa aims to promote education and understanding within the community of how change in the built environment is managed and achieved.

The nature of Comtechsa means that often the idea of participation is what attracts people to the organisation. Generally it is community and voluntary groups that use Comtechsa which are keen to be involved in the architectural process from the start. In most cases, therefore, the initiators of the participatory process are the users. However, it has always been part of the Comtechsa approach to involve users as much as possible even where this was not necessarily expected.

Participation generally takes place all the way through a project and Comtechsa encourages groups to participate as much as they want to. In most cases the participating group is the client group, but at some stages participation may be opened up to a wider public. Such wider engagement occurs where buildings are to be used by the public.

Comtechsa is aware of the need to explain technical jargon and to make the architectural process accessible to all, which then becomes a 'process of informal adult education' that builds confidence and empowers people. This approach has been a core value within the organisation from the very beginning. A wide range of techniques are used during meetings, workshops and open days, such as 'Planning for Real' exercises.

Table 6.2 Usual participation phases and levels in Comtechsa's projects

Stakeholder/Phase	Design	Construction	Post-completion
Client*	Decision-making	Decision-making	Decision-making
User*	Decision-making	Decision-making	Informed and/or decision-making*
Public	Consultation and information	Information	–

Note
*Usually Comtechsa's clients are community groups and, therefore, also users.

The need to be able to maintain relationships with organisations in the post-completion phase is also something that Comtechsa is conscious of. Ongoing support entails an open invitation to get in touch if any defects are identified. In addition, if Comtechsa sees potential enthusiasm from clients, they are encouraged to come along and stand for election to the committee. If elected, these individuals bring their experience of having been a past client and, therefore, are able to relate better to the experience and concerns of groups and individuals with whom Comtechsa works.

Evaluation

No formal evaluation of the participatory process takes place after a project is completed, which is perhaps surprising for an organisation which stresses its commitment to participatory approaches. However, informal feedback and post-completion contact is routine. Any issues that arise are taken into consideration as early as possible and the community members normally keep in touch with the organisation. Members of the Committee of Management and staff recognise that mistakes can happen, but over the period of the organisation's existence they maintain that there have been a minimal number of instances when poor advice has been given.

Comtechsa has been involved in a social accounting exercise which was quite productive although very time consuming, and the Committee would like to be able to integrate this approach into the normal running of the organisation to avoid the otherwise high additional cost in time.

Survival as an organisation

It appears that a number of factors have been instrumental in the survival of Comtechsa for the past 29 years. First, it has always been very responsive to change. There have been one or two occasions when decisions by Liverpool City Council have caused serious problems for Comtechsa, but on each occasion these have been overcome.

One of the factors which seem to have been fundamental to the success is the long-standing involvement of its current Committee Chair, guiding the organisation through different times and political changes. Also important is the continuous involvement of professionals who believe in the organisational community-focused ethos. Bringing the right people together seems to have generated an environment where the commitment to involving users in the process of designing and building has remained consistent.

Comtechsa has always been very aware of the economic responsibilities of the organisation. Perhaps instrumental in the success is the early vision for the organisation to own its own building and rent space to other organisations. Certainly this income stream has proved to be very important over the years. The fact that Comtechsa was prepared to change its legal structure in order to increase the potential funding sources was another development which could be helpful in taking its work forward, along with a decision that Comtechsa may need to diversify into more commercial work in the future, while at the same time maintaining the overarching ethos of the organisation. Comtechsa has also developed strong skills in fundraising as sources of finance became more competitive. Finally, there is a belief that, because similar organisations are now so rare, this may give Comtechsa an opportunity to expand its work in the future.

Conclusion

The preceding descriptions and evaluations illustrate that there are significant differences between ASSIST and Comtechsa. The former has developed through a series of stages from a research-based community architecture organisation which was part of Strathclyde University to a private practice constituted as a company and managed by a board of directors. The latter has retained more of its original organisational structure in that it remains a user-controlled technical aid centre, but it has had to change to broaden its potential to gain funding and work. Comtechsa has evolved from an Industrial and Provident Society (IPS) through a hybrid of IPS with a charitable arm to its current state as a charitable Society for the Benefit of the Community. However, importantly, ASSIST and Comtechsa both have in common the retention of their original ethos of operating for the benefit of users.

The main distinction in the respective attitudes to participation lies in who is expected to initiate the process. ASSIST is usually the driver, introducing clients to the benefits that this method of working can bring, although it is often approached by clients who have heard of this approach and wish to follow that process. Comtechsa, on the other hand, expects the client to instigate the participation process. As a user-controlled organisation which works for members this is an understandable position.

With regard to survival and continuing operation, the two organisations appear to have much in common. In both instances it seems to have resulted from the presence of key people and flexibility. People with strong ideals, conscious of the social importance of architecture, were present at the foundation and throughout the history of these organisations. These individuals were able to attract like-minded people who have been able to maintain the social ethos. Both organisations have been very practical and flexible, being able to reorganise themselves financially and structurally, to cope with different demands and policies. They are both good examples of learning organisations:

learning from and changing with the circumstances, while maintaining the ethos which drives the work.

Notes

1 www.assistarchitects.co.uk.
2 Glasgow office: 100 Kerr Street, Bridgeton, Glasgow G40 2QP (glasgow@assistarchitects. co.uk). Edinburgh office: Sanderson House, 35 Water Street, Edinburgh EH6 6SU (edin-burgh@assistarchitects.co.uk).
3 The authors gratefully acknowledge the inputs from key members of ASSIST in preparing this case study.
4 www.assistarchitects.co.uk.
5 The authors gratefully acknowledge the inputs from key members of Comtechsa in preparing this case study.
6 For more information see their website (www.comtechsa.org).

Chapter 7

Case studies of architectural educational institutions

Marcia Pereira and Leanne Townsend

Introduction

Architectural education has been mentioned previously in this book as one of the reasons for architects' lack of skills and interest in promoting participation in the design process. Within the UK, two institutions have been identified which include user participation in their architecture curricula and have developed innovative ways of involving their students and staff in participatory design. The case studies presented in this chapter look at the experience of these institutions – the Department of Architecture and Spatial Design at the London Metropolitan University and the School of Architecture at the University of Sheffield – to examine how they approach the subject and how successful they have been.

Department of Architecture and Spatial Design, London Metropolitan University[1]

General information

Located in North London, the Department of Architecture and Spatial Design at London Metropolitan University (LMU) has a good reputation for the quality and innovation of its courses. Students have had success in numerous competitions, including the RIBA President's Medals, and their accomplishment, as well as that of their tutors, was highly praised by the former RIBA president George Ferguson. The willingness to combine experimentation with practical experience is said to be a characteristic of the staff. There are around 300 undergraduate and 250 postgraduate students (LMU Department of Architecture and Spatial Design n.d.).

Reason for the case study

The Architecture Course at LMU is one of the very few in the UK which has participation embedded into the curriculum as well as having a dedicated module on participation. The participatory approach is used in several design studios and students have the opportunity to work on real design projects, with clients, resulting in buildings being built. There is also an in-house architectural office, which facilitates the involvement of students and staff in real projects.

Motivation to include participation within the curriculum

The inclusion of participation in the curriculum was inspired by Professor Robert Mull, Head of Architecture, who has a history of working with participatory design. Torange Khonsari, who is leader of the module on participation, was one of Robert Mull's students and also has a particular interest in user participation.

Approach

Module

There is a special module on participation entitled 'Design: From Participation to Realisation'. This is a 30-credit module, with the following description:

> Working with a range of projects/tasks the module introduces a variety of techniques in the practice of participatory design. The module develops students' skills in working as a team, in researching, planning and implementing a project. It enables exploration of a broad and innovative range of presentation techniques to communicate with a range of clients and users. Working towards the resolution of a project within a workshop this module develops students' understanding of the design process as a record of the development, realisation and response to a built project. One part of the module will particularly investigate issues of construction and materials and of the design of components and processes of assembly.[2]

Students on this module attend taught sessions which consist of a series of five seminars, eight lectures on participation and realisation (four each) and four lectures on drawing techniques. Process, resolution and attendance are assessed. Students are instructed to document the development of the work as well as to record and reflect upon their own participation in the process. This module is offered to second-year architecture students and it runs in parallel to the design studio. The projects are of a small scale, as the aim is to allow students to experience the whole process, from briefing and design to construction/realisation.

One example of this is the project 'Living Units', in which students investigate the affordability of student halls of residence and how the halls become an important part of their experience. The project is to develop a prototype for student accommodation for a developer and goes through three phases: 'Events in the Hut' (participation), 'Spatialising the Narratives' (transformation of participation findings into design solutions), and 'Realisation' (prototype construction). In the third phase, prototypes are built and tested on a real site.

Design studios

Teaching in the design studios within the department takes place in groups of between 15 and 25 students, and participation is embedded into several of these studios. Students have the opportunity to engage with live projects locally as well as internationally, in places such as Kosovo, India, West Belfast and the former Soviet Union. These experiences provide students with a chance to interact with local users and communities as well as to learn from different cultures. An example of this is described later by one of the students involved in an international project.

Several architectural offices that work with a strong focus on user participation run studios within the department, such as 'erect architecture', 'Fluid', 'East' and 'Public Works'. Live projects are an essential part of different design studios, where students become involved with real clients and users. An example is a project developed by students in Marrakesh, Morocco. As part of their studio work, students organised an event in the main square of Marrakesh using colourful umbrellas, which elicited a positive reaction from the wider public and helped them to interact with the local population. Another example was the commissioning of students to investigate a 'dead area' around Hampstead Theatre and this led to the involvement of local people in interesting participatory exercises.

ASD Projects

ASD Projects is the live projects office embedded within the Department of Architecture and Spatial Design. It was set up with higher education (HE) funding, as HE institutions are now encouraged to generate income. According to the ASD director, the aim is to provide a supportive professional environment for students and staff. The office allows them to undertake consultancy commissions, research projects and also provides project management to live projects carried out by students as part of their course work. They are committed to 'socially engaged design, where students, academics, and practising architects come together to enhance the built environment for the benefit of others' (Mull and Markey 2005).

The office has been in existence since 2004 and is supported by the Department and the University. It employs year-out students as well as diploma students. All the office projects follow a 'participatory ethos'. They particularly give support to the module 'Design: From Participation to Realisation', where students develop small-scale projects, going from the initial contact with clients and users until construction of at least a prototype. The ASD Projects office supports the module regarding financial, legal and practical issues and clients have to follow the semester/academic time restriction. The existence of the office allows for flexibility and acts as an enabler. It does not want to compete with commercial practices and encourages teaching staff to bring in projects that incorporate research and participation. Other examples of work carried out and/or supported by the office are: the organisation of the London Architecture Biennale as well as the continuation of design projects initiated within the design studios, including the design of an architectural school in Cuba, the design of the Oral History Centre in Iran, and designs for sanitation projects in India.[3]

Student experience

A fifth-year architecture student was interviewed concerning her experience of participation in architecture within the school. In her third-year studio she undertook a design project with tutors from the architecture firm 'Public Works'. The tutors emphasised the importance of working with 'live projects', entering real competitions and 'speaking to real people'. During that year, there was a competition taking place in Iran and students were encouraged to participate. The aim of the competition was to design something that would help to regenerate a local community. The tutors' approach was that students should not try to define a priori what the design would be.

The student contacted an Iranian community in London and found out about an Iranian women's group, which met regularly in a school. She went to their meetings, spoke to them and asked them to fill in a questionnaire about their daily lives. She visited them in their houses and listened to their stories. Many times the women used objects to tell their stories. In this way, the student identified a number of common objects, such as bread, headscarf, tea-making objects and flowers.

She used the objects collected from stories from Iranian people in Britain to generate stories in Iran. She then created 'The Cabinet of Narratives', with objects and stories. She took the cabinet to an Iranian school and asked Iranian students to read stories. She also introduced the cabinet to a school in Britain. More stories were collected and, hopefully, also a better understanding of the two different cultures was achieved. As a result, her proposal for the design competition was an 'Oral History Archive'. She used the idea of drawers in a cabinet to generate the design proposal.

In a second phase of the project, the student spent one week in Iran where, with the support of a translator, she used the identified objects to speak to people. This resulted in a community archive centre being set up which was filled with objects and stories resulting from her research. The idea was to create a forum for socialisation in a culture where this can be interpreted as being discouraged.

In the two phases of the project, the student's aim was to allow people to communicate and share stories within a culture where this is not easily done. She found the whole process was a very rich experience, but seemed less happy with the translation of the narrative into the design proposal itself.

During her year out the student worked in the ASD Projects office. She was commissioned to design an extension of a classroom for Kingsmead Primary School in Hackney. However, during her interactions with users and staff, she ended up identifying other needs: a parents' waiting area, an outdoor learning area and a storage area. She interacted with users in their daily activities, joining the children in what they were doing, observing, speaking to teachers and to the caretaker as well as to parents and taking part in parents' evenings.

This student has noted different approaches within the department, between units that use participation and others that do not. She believes that some tutors are more interested in 'form' and 'technique', whereas others are more concerned with the social relevance of architecture. She would welcome a real academic and transparent debate about participation. At the time of interview, her present unit had a more formal approach, where participation has less weight. The student indicated that she is using this as an experience which she will reflect upon and later make up her own mind on how it might inform her professional career. In her opinion both formal architecture and participatory architecture can have good or bad results.

Political and social issues

According to the Academic Leader of the Undergraduate Course and Year 1 Coordinator, there is a general view within the department of architecture as being a 'social event'. There is no 'demand' as such to embed participation into teaching, but there is a realisation of its importance. She sees the concept of participation in a broader sense. When students camp on the site, bring models and make interventions to generate reactions, in her opinion these can elicit participation.

A concern of the Year 1 Coordinator regarding participation in architecture schools is the definition of 'where participation stops and design starts in a studio'. She cites the Architectural Association architectural school as an example, which went through a phase where first- and second-year students were getting so involved in participation that they ended up not designing a building. Close to this issue, she stresses the importance of the 'conversion' stage, when ideas generated via participation are transformed into 'real buildings'.

Although there are different opinions, in general there seems to be a view among the staff in the Department that participation is important. The participatory projects carried out in different design studios show that there is a lively interest in such an approach. However, it would be worthwhile investigating how the different degrees of acceptance of participation as an approach to the architectural design process co-exist with each other. There seems to be a concern that participation takes too much time and students need that time to 'learn how to design'. Some students and staff doubt that participation can effectively inform design and generate good architecture. A healthy, transparent academic debate could be beneficial. However, it appears that despite these concerns participation is an important component of the school's ethos.

School of Architecture, University of Sheffield[4]

General information

The School of Architecture at the University of Sheffield is one of two institutions offering architecture in the city. It is a well-established school with an excellent reputation offering programmes at undergraduate BA (Hons.) and postgraduate level MArch, as well as research degrees. There are over 400 registered students. The University of Sheffield scored highly in architecture and the built environment in both architecture and landscape architecture in the 2008 Research Assessment Exercise and received an 'Excellent' in teaching according to the latest government ratings.

Reason for the case study

The Sheffield School of Architecture is one of very few in the UK which has participation embedded into its curriculum. The concern with development of social skills, with students learning how to communicate well with clients and users, as well as the promotion of participation, is well represented within the school. Moreover, 'live projects' embed students into the whole process of participation, design and production.

Motivation to include participation within the curriculum

The interest in the development of students' social skills and participation started with a project developed by Professor Bryan Lawson and Simon Pilling: 'Clients and Users in Design Education' (CUDE) which was a Higher Education Funding Council for England (HEFCE)-funded teaching and learning project. Developed in the late 1990s, the project proposed a series of methods and tools to help tutors in the process of encouraging students to develop their communication skills. In 1999, Jeremy Till joined the school and 'picked up' on the findings of the CUDE project, developing it further within a critical educational approach.[5] Prue Chiles' contribution has also been fundamental, as she set up the Live Projects programme in 1999, building upon her own experience in practice.

Approach

Although there is an overall critical educational approach that permeates the whole course, there is a stronger focus on participation during the diploma years or MArch (ARB/RIBA accreditation at Part 2). In Sheffield, the former diploma course has been restructured and replaced by a two-year MArch, which aims to prepare students for the diversity of architectural practice through 'a combination of transferable analytic skills in research and synthesising design skills' (University of Sheffield School of Architecture n.d.a).

Live Projects programme in the design studio

In the first year of architecture education students develop a project for a live client and some of the third-year projects also involve live clients. However, it is only at the diploma stage that real participation takes place within the studios. Students at this stage are considered to be mature enough for this kind of work. Initiated in 1999, the Live Projects programme[6] allows students to interact with a range of clients including local community groups, charities, health organisations and regional authorities. In some cases the projects involve actual building; in others, the design of urban master plans or consultation exercises. In every case the project is real, happening in real time with real people, and always with a defined end result. Importantly, Live Projects must pass an ethical test generating social and sustainable benefits – therefore clients are typically charities, community-based projects, schools and hospitals.

Having Live Projects at its core, the MArch is based around a number of design studios, six at the time of this study. These studios promote in-depth investigation of themes developed out of the studio leaders' own research interests. The Live Projects run during the first six-week period of each autumn semester for fifth and sixth years, with students from both years working together in teams of four to 12 people. This allows for an interesting 'mix' and is seen to provide a very productive collaborative learning process.

Clients and students benefit from Live Projects: clients have access to an architectural input which draws on the research base and innovation of the school; while students have 'the opportunity to bring their developed skills into the real world, often with immediate social benefit, developing their communication and group working skills, essential for practice' (University of Sheffield School of Architecture n.d.b).

Live Projects constitutes a 15-credit design module from a total 120 credits/year. The learning objectives emphasise the process rather than only the final product. Importance is placed on design quality, but also on consultation practice.

The Live Projects programme is now responsible for over 50 completed projects and more details about it may be found on the website.[7] The following are some examples of completed projects.

The 'Entrance Space/Courtyard Space' projects were developed in 1999/2000 as two Live Projects over consecutive years. This work was undertaken at Paces School for Conductive Education, an organisation concerned with providing a positive learning experience for children with motor disorders. The first project involved reconfiguring a previous building exit into the main entrance space for the school, while the second aimed to enliven an existing courtyard by providing new decking and bench structures. Work on the school's new entrance space required the students to design and build a new waiting area, reception desk, lit display shelves and coloured light diffusers. To do that, existing walls had to be removed and old science furniture reused. Hung coloured kite fabrics were added to a long roof-light, providing a soft rainbow of banners below and bringing the reconfiguration to life. The second group used coloured shapes formed from standard timber sections to create a series of multi-level platforms that could act as tables, benches, walkways and decks to lie out on.

The Ballifield Primary School 'Primary Ideas' project was also developed in 2002. The initial brief was to design and build a number of small-scale interventions in order to improve the built environment of the school. The financial backing came from the school itself. Students consulted on a number of occasions with school staff and led activity classes with school pupils. Three ideas resulted from these participatory exercises: refurbishment of the ceiling within a classroom, creation of a sheltered external area, and refurbishment of some of the children's toilets. The toilets and the sheltered external area were actually rebuilt by students within time and budget, and the school greatly appreciated the improvements that were made.

Teaching courses

Two types of teaching give support to the Live Projects. During the projects, teaching on communications and creative techniques in participation are delivered. This takes places via communication and brief building workshops, as well as via seminars on consultation and participatory techniques. Emphasis is given to learning the role of the architect, how to assign tasks within the group, leadership roles, group hierarchy and the complexity of dealing with a multi-headed client organisation, often examined through stakeholder mapping at the beginning of each project.

'Management and Practice 1' is a ten-credit module offered to fifth-year students. This 'introduces students to aspects of briefing and team-working within an architectural project, together with an overview of factors related to the running of an architectural practice' (University of Sheffield School of Architecture 2007). Very importantly, it also encourages students to reflect on the nature of architectural practice based on a critical self-appraisal of their own experience in their year out and in the Live Projects developed in the studio. Students work on group assignments, putting into practice the issues they learned and working in a collaborative way. In individual assignments, students write an essay about their individual input in the group work. The module assignment is based around the 'Live Project' which the students have undertaken in the first semester, thereby contextualising potentially abstract ideas.

The Bureau of Design Research

The Bureau of Design Research (BDR), set up in 2002, is a design-led research and consultancy unit based in the School of Architecture. It resulted from a symbiosis between Prue Chiles' private practice and the work developed within the department. The key driver is 'sustainability through design' as well as creating environments which are socially sustainable, resulting from good design and close relationships of communities with the public and private sectors. At the time of interview, the BDR was staffed by one director, two associated directors and eight internal consultants.

Seeing themselves as design-led researchers, the BDR staff's aim is to bring ideas and research methodologies together and apply them successfully in the real world, allowing connections between people and projects to be made, and combining innovative ideas with rigorous research methodologies. Positioned as an autonomous research unit within the university, the BDR can have the dynamism of a small organisation (changeable, responsive and flexible) while benefiting from close links with external consultants and internal specialists at the university. It develops collaboration with industry and community groups as well as staff and students of the university.

BDR work has focused on three main areas: learning environments, strategic and community-led regeneration, and 'new futures': predicting new scenarios to address questions posed by post-industrial developments. The BDR also plays a key role in the development of the Live Projects programme, running studios and providing support for the continuation of projects when necessary. Its projects are presented on its website along with information on published work, some commissioned by organisations such as CABE (Commission for Architecture and the Built Environment) and DfES (Department for Children, Schools and Families).[8]

Student experience

Working with participatory methodologies, BDR personnel seek to enable people to think spatially and to help groups to create shared visions, using art and design practices as well as encouraging community involvement, and arming stakeholders with the relevant skills to be fully empowered in the process. Of particular interest are the participation exercises where BDR works with users and communities to collect narratives. A good example of this is the work on the regeneration of North Sheffield, where 'multilayered narratives ranging from an image of the whole city right down to personal stories of residents in the communities underpinned the whole process'. In her contribution to Blundell-Jones et al. (2005), Prue Chiles discusses the pros and cons of 'narratives' and emphasises their importance in 'breaking through professional codes, appealing to the majority – to lay people uninitiated in the private world of conventional architectural or regeneration "language"', facilitating 'bottom-up – insurgent or radical – broader processes'.

For this study, ten students from fifth and sixth years took part in a focus group, discussing their experiences with Live Projects. All students indicated that the opportunity to work on a live project was very interesting and attractive, with no feeling of being exploited. On the contrary they felt empowered by the opportunity to work on such projects. These students see the clients as fundamental for the success of Live Projects. All students indicated that they had quite different experiences. According to them, there are different types of clients – while there are some who see participation as a public relations exercise or 'ticking the box', there are others who are really open-minded with good and interesting ideas, who happily take part in the whole participation process. As a good example they mentioned a school headmaster who wanted to have a zero-carbon school and was able to really engage staff and students in the project. One student, however, expressed the wish to have a very commercial company as a client, to see how challenging the work would be in that situation. Some students pointed out that working on live projects makes the whole experience more complex, because they are faced with real-world constraints, and have to resolve issues such as the inflexibility of clients or confusion over who the real client is in a process. Some clients were said to have low expectations at the beginning because the designers are students but ended up really surprised with the quality of results; whereas others are much more ready to listen to the students' ideas from the start.

For the students, Live Projects are useful not just in the ways described above, but also in their understanding of other areas of their work; for example in the writing up of management essays. In general, the students feel that Live Projects are very effective in increasing their confidence as well as in improving communication skills. Students were keen to point out that although all Live Projects involved communication with stakeholders, the level of participation varied from project to project.

Students see participation as a powerful way to amass design ideas that are responsive to users' needs, and several cited with enthusiasm the different participatory approaches they used. An interesting example is that of a group which was initially asked to design a youth shelter in a park. A series of different events, which could attract different types of people, was organised, such as 'Jazz in the Park' (music performed on a stage within the park), 'Arts and Crafts in the Park', 'Football in the Park', as well as simple interventions such as running along with joggers and distributing oranges. After these actions, where different kinds of reactions were generated, students were able to identify a series of other community needs regarding the use of the park. This resulted in their identifying the construction of a football pitch, for instance, as a much more effective way to answer young people's needs.

Students are critical of large architectural companies and developers, seeing these as having a highly patronising view of users, and seeing participation as a problem instead of a source of ideas. However, they are also aware of the danger of using participation to manipulate participants and authorities, as well as the issue that many have a preconceived idea of participation. Their opinion is that true participation involves people both in the process and the product, and is not merely carried out for its own sake. They add that laypeople do not tend to understand architecture fully, so participatory processes must be designed to be easily understood. One student in particular held a very strong belief that participation should not result in a mediocre product but in ideal circumstances should actually lead to design which excels.

He added that it is important to him to maintain aspiration and ambition and to see himself as a specialist – the divide is not always a bad thing. He also thought that the word 'participation' could be interchanged with the idea of 'conversation'. Finally, he argued that students could also benefit from an evaluative stage in Live Projects.

Students concluded that working on Live Projects led them to adopt a more critical approach to individual situations. The approach taken by the architecture staff in terms of participation is not about brainwashing the students – they believe they are still able to arrive at their own ideas and take away with them a more socially aware approach. They acknowledge that there is a large gulf between university-based architectural experience and the real world. Students see Live Projects as a subject which should be made available in other schools, within a participatory ethos.

Political and social issues

The political views behind the setting up of the Live Projects programme are driven by a desire to educate future architects as well as a reaction to a more traditional approach to architecture in which a remote set of values is argued to define the way in which architecture is carried out. It is contended that this perpetuates a myth of the architect as someone who creates the built environment in the absence of any connection to those he or she is designing for – the sole author or imposer of architectural appearances. In contrast, Live Projects aims to foster a social awareness and responsibility in future architects.

According to Jeremy Till, the participatory approach puts the Vitruvian triad into a social context, going against the view of architecture as a service industry, where having a 'sexy' building is a commodity value, while participation is not seen as good commodity value. He thinks the typical view of the architectural profession is that the 'delight' part of the Vitruvian triad is imperative and will always be dominant. However, he sees some change taking place, as architectural offices start to look for 'participation' in students' CVs. He cites Fluid, a London-based architectural office, as a good example of a practice which has been successfully working in a participatory manner.[9]

Despite considering participation to be highly important, another lecturer in the school responsible for the management module thinks that the participatory approach should not be imposed by all architectural schools: 'people should believe in it', and each school should develop its own approach. As every school has a duty to make its ethos understandable, students should be relatively well informed when they make their choices about whether this is an area of interest for them.

Students' assessment during Live Projects was said to be an issue. As part of the philosophy the projects are student-led, with the tutors assuming a more advisory role. Consequently, the projects are assessed according to the success with which participants have worked together to manage this process. Intended to help students to work collaboratively rather than in competition, assessment is made of the group as a whole rather than of individual contributions. Presentations are made to the other Live Projects groups at the end of the process and judged according to the success with which a group has worked together to develop and manage the brief and deliver the final result. Students are also encouraged to mark their own work. This is very new for students, who sometimes have difficulties when valuing their own work and specifically the learning experience that took place during the whole process. There is no formal evaluation of the participatory approach as such, but students do reflect upon the process during the assessment, as well as via the management module.

Members of staff are constantly producing research and presenting and publishing their experiences, and therefore creating opportunities for individual and collaborative reflection on their practices. Transparency seems to be a positive feature in the way participation is implemented within the school. Documentation on all projects and guiding materials for students and clients are available and easily accessible via websites. Aims, expectations, methodologies, forms of assessment, as well as the underlying ethos, are clearly stated.

Conclusion

The participatory engagement programmes within the two architectural schools investigated share similarities in the way they approach participation. In both cases, participation was introduced to the curriculum through 'live projects' and also as a course module. Live projects allow students to become involved in the execution of real design projects and the course module gives them the theoretical preparation they need to accomplish the participation exercises. Both institutions have an architectural office as a common feature, which allows flexibility between the demands of the academic timetable and the execution of real projects.

However, they differ in the emphasis on engaging with participation at different stages of their programmes. London Metropolitan focuses more on participation during the second year, while in Sheffield this happens at postgraduate level during the final two years. Both approaches have advantages. Introducing students to participation and live projects at an early stage in their architectural education is likely to ensure that they become aware of the social dimensions of architecture and are able to carry that awareness into the later stages of their education. On the other hand, allowing more mature students to take part in participatory processes with live clients means that students are able to bring the sum of their architectural education to bear on the issues, which can lead to a more thoughtful and reflective approach to the processes.

In addition, a significant number of staff in both institutions seem to have a social ethos which makes their work on participation possible, providing good examples for how this might be done elsewhere.

Notes

1 The authors gratefully acknowledge the inputs from key members of London Metropolitan University Architecture staff and students in preparing this case study.
2 Internal document made available to the authors.
3 For more details about ASD Projects please contact Anne Markey (a.markey@londonmet.ac.uk).
4 The authors gratefully acknowledge the inputs from key members of Sheffield University Architecture staff and students in preparing this case study.
5 Professor Till left Sheffield in 2008 to become Dean of Architecture and Built Environment at the University of Westminster, London.
6 See the Live Projects programme website (www.liveprojects.org).
7 www.liveprojects.org/.
8 For more info see BDR website (www.bdr.group.shef.ac.uk).
9 Thanks to Professor Till for this and other inputs into the case study.

Chapter 8

Case studies on the use of participatory computer-based techniques[1]

Marcia Pereira and Leanne Townsend

Introduction

New technologies, in particular digital visualisation techniques, present a new set of possibilities for communicating design ideas and creating the possibility for interactive development among alternative propositions. The purpose of this chapter is to explore how these techniques have been used in the participation process, and whether or not they provide advantages over more traditional techniques, through two case studies. The first case study examines the use of the Glasgow Model, a digital model of the city of Glasgow developed by the Glasgow School of Art, Digital Design Studio, while the second looks at a variety of participatory tools that were used in the development of the Cornton Housing Development in Stirling, where designers used more traditional methods as well as computer visualisation.

The Glasgow Model

General information

The Glasgow Model is a computer model of a large portion of Glasgow City Centre, commissioned by Glasgow City Council at an overall cost of £450,000.

It was developed by the Digital Design Studio within the Glasgow School of Art. The commission comprised an online model, a massing model and a high-detail photo-realistic model, plus training in its use. Accurate up to 20 cm, the model has won an award from BAFTA and, according to its developer, is likely to be the most accurate city model.

At the time of fieldwork (February 2007) the model had been used twice, once for presentation purposes at the Six Cities festival (2007) and once for the presentation of competition entries made by architects for the redesign of George House in George Square, Glasgow. This case study is concerned with the use of the Glasgow Model in the presentation of entries to the competition run by Glasgow City Council.

A large number of practices were invited to submit proposed designs for the redevelopment of George House on George Square. George House is currently a tired 1970s building and the plan is for the competition winner to realise the winning design. Competition entrants were shortlisted and those on the list were required to present their ideas using the Glasgow Model. It is this presentation process that is considered as the participation in this case study, as the Glasgow Model was still in its infancy and had not yet been used for any wider public participatory events. In this case, the 'users' are those members of the Council who watched the presentations in order to select a winner. Glasgow City Council is the client, as it commissioned both the competition and the Glasgow Model itself, and a number of Council employees were involved in an evaluation of the model, one being interviewed for this study. One of the practices presenting an entry for the competition was also interviewed, as was the creator of the model.

The participatory process

The Glasgow Model was commissioned by the Council for a number of purposes. First, there is a move to open up the planning process, making it more accessible to those who cannot physically access the public library or the planning office within the Council buildings, both being locations where plans are held for public viewing. This accessibility will be improved by making the model available to people online. A number of other organisations and groups will also benefit from the model, including the police, land services, fire and rescue, the Urban Design Panel and Historic Scotland.

The George House competition

As part of the entry requirements to the competition, the architects were asked to submit an accurate 3D model of their entry as well as to use the Glasgow Model to present their designs. The Council believed that this would be a good way of testing the Glasgow Model's effectiveness. The architects interviewed were using computer modelling before their experience of the Glasgow Model; however, typically they would use such technology for the rough, early stages of design. They had tended to use a model called Abacus, which they describe as being much more primitive than the Glasgow Model, and therefore only useful in the early stages. They claim that the use of a more sophisticated model allows for more focus on details.

The architects believe that the use of the model in participatory processes would be beneficial, but that the benefits may depend upon the audience. They contend that some people have expectations that computer imagery will be used, but that there are a number of issues which may need to be addressed before the exclusive use of computer imagery will be acceptable in participation processes. They believe that more traditional approaches are still important and that it is sometimes better to present ideas in a 2D drawing if they are early design ideas, as the computer format can demand a degree of detail not yet available. However, they are aware of a number of projects using computer models for presentations to users; for example, the proposal of an extension of the Buchanan Galleries in Glasgow, which will lead to an extension of the Glasgow Model, in order to inform the local population.

According to the Council, from the perspective of the user, the model was very useful in judging the competition. It was possible to switch between the six shortlisted designs at the touch of a button when in discussions, effectively viewing the six different designs in the same context. Apparently some of the models were less sophisticated than others, and this was disappointing in that the degree of sophistication of the Glasgow Model had not been fully utilised in the process. In terms of seeing and understanding the designs, the interviewee felt that the 3D images embedded into the Glasgow Model were far more useful than looking at drawings. She believes that computer images are more helpful in participation because one can view a design from different angles and the ability to navigate encourages more interaction. However, she found that there was a difficulty in getting a feel for some materials, although this problem was dealt with by some of the entrants better than by others. In addition, she felt that the use of the model had been the best approach, as it makes design projects more understandable to non-design professionals. In a computer model there is a very close approximation to reality, thereby giving a good impression of how something will look, should it be built.

According to the Council interviewee, the Glasgow Model will be used more and more with the public as was the original intention, since she feels that it is much easier for laypeople to understand 3D images than drawings. The model may also help to improve communication among professionals within the Council and between the Council and third parties. If this is the case, then probably the massing model and the high-quality photo-realistic model will be used among professionals, whereas the online model will be used mainly by the public.

Evaluation

According to the developer of the Glasgow Model interviewed for this case study, although modern techniques in presenting to the public have a number of benefits, there is a danger in rejecting older methodologies. Contemporary computer visualisation can be very efficient but sometimes lacks quality when produced at low cost. The model developer does believe, however, that people understand 3D images far more easily than 2D images; therefore the use of computer models can bring people into the design process much more easily. He points out the danger inherent in participatory processes when using computer models, since it is relatively simple to be dishonest (e.g. by always having sunny weather and well-lit buildings). Sometimes this may be unintentional, but nevertheless, the temptation to use the tools at hand to make something look its best is always there. This problem also exists in 2D modelling but can appear more 'real' in 3D models. This is one important way in which the use of 3D computer models can affect the language of the participatory process. In addition, he suggests that all new means of representation in design have an effect on the ways of illustrating and communicating design and ultimately on fashions in architecture.

The architects interviewed, however, believe that sometimes a 3D model can seem cold and attract a negative emotional response. There is also a greater cost and longer timescale involved in the use of this technology than with more traditional methods. They believe that hand-drawn images may be more attractive to people because they are softer. They also point to the problem of people expecting computer models to be 100 per cent accurate when this is not always the case. They argue that a computer model tends to be much more accurate and real towards the end of a project which is often too late for any real user empowerment to occur. However, they also say that real empowerment may be more likely through the viewer's own navigation of computer models, because designs cannot then hide behind 'best views'. Overall, the architects believe that a model itself cannot improve a participatory process, as this depends more on the framework which is in place.

Cornton Housing Project, Stirling

General information

This case study examines the Cornton Housing Development in Stirling, Central Scotland, designed by FBN Architects for Castle Rock Housing Association. The project was built on the site of 1950s' housing which was deemed uninhabitable and demolished. Stirling Council owns the land and housing, Castle Rock Housing Association was the developer and it chose FBN Architects to carry out the design work. FBN tends to work on community-based projects in which participation is a key requirement.

The participatory process

Cultenhove, a neighbouring estate to Cornton, was the subject of a housing regeneration process which took place at the same time, also led by FBN Architects. The initial consultations for both projects started in May 2005 and design groups were established with members of both communities working together in the initial stages. These voluntary design groups included local tenants and house owners: house owners were often in the majority at Cultenhove meetings. Open days were carried out in the community centre at each estate. The initiator of the participatory process was Stirling Council, as it is now compulsory for participation to occur in Council-led urban regeneration projects. According to reports, there tend to be two motives for this: either to smooth the project process and reduce objections or to arrive at the best possible design, although it could be argued that the reality of participation tends to lie somewhere between these two. The main aims of the participatory exercises in this case were to gather information from local people as well as to find out their preferences and priorities.

At Cornton, the design group comprised local people (house owners and tenants) contacted through a local community group known as CAPP (Cornton Action Planning Partnership), together with Council representatives, housing association members, the architects, and later the building contractor. At the beginning of the process, the architect involved took the design group participants to Glasgow to visit recently completed housing projects. They found this to be a very good experience, as it allowed them to see how similar houses could be designed in different ways. Meetings were chaired by the housing association as well as members of the Council's Community Department. The architects would give a presentation, with projected images, to inform and update participants on the progress of the project. In design terms, they led the participatory process and encouraged residents' involvement by inviting them to discuss and voice their opinions about house layouts and the general form and style of the design.

The consulted participants reported no problems in communicating with the architects and were very happy with the level of participation they had. According to them, the architects used a 'normal language' to explain the project and they did not feel inhibited in any way. They felt the architects were always open to answer all questions, even the most 'stupid' ones.

The architects mentioned a clear difference in the results of participation between Cultenhove and Cornton communities. At Cultenhove many of the participants were neighbouring owner-occupiers who would not occupy the houses being designed, while in Cornton the participants were mostly tenants who could expect to be rehoused in the new development. Even when shown the same images to illustrate design solutions, the choices made by the participants of the two communities were very different. The architects noted more engagement from Cultenhove participants, who expressed a strong wish for a more contemporary look to their houses and for a more environmentally friendly approach.

Participation was carried out before and throughout the design phase, as well as during the construction stage, but in the latter stages it revolved mostly around issues arising from construction and people's experiences of living very close to a building site.

Tools and techniques used

A number of two-dimensional images were used, such as the layout of the entire community, site plans and house plans with internal layouts, elevations and landscaping. In addition, photographs of comparable landscaping features were presented.

Visits were arranged to recent housing developments in Glasgow, by the architects along with the housing association client, and participants were encouraged to go on the visit. They then discussed what they did and did not like at a subsequent meeting. In addition, a number of traditional participatory techniques were used, including questionnaires to identify general issues and obtain feedback from the wider public during open days. Images were grouped at 'stalls' under subject billboards such as 'streets/parking', 'elevations', 'security', where people could speak to the professionals manning the stalls. According to the architects, incentives to attend were offered aimed both at children and adults, including balloons and a range of competitions and prizes. Conventional focus groups were also organised, but were not considered to be very effectively chaired by the Council, with some participants being much more vocal than others.

Different three-dimensional techniques were applied in the participatory process. First, 3D card and polystyrene models which showed the layout

Table 8.1 Cornton housing development participation phases and levels

Stakeholder/phase	Design	Construction	Post-completion
Client (Castle Rock developers)	Decision-making	Decision-making	Decision-making
Users (local residents)	Consultation	Information	–
Public	Consultation and information	Information	–

of rooms as well as street layouts were presented to participants. Computer visualisation – 3D exterior and interior images – were projected, to display possible layouts and assess preferences. Three-dimensional walkthroughs were not used, however, as there was no time in the fast-moving process to produce these, although the architects emphasise that this is now easier to do with more recent software. The software packages used were: VectorWorks for 2D-images, Sketch-up and VectorWorks 3D to generate 3D images, and Atlantis for rendering.

Images generated by computers were printed out during the participation exercises and presented on paper or posters as well as shown via PowerPoint presentations. The use of the technology was not made in an intrusive manner. It even went unnoticed by some of the consulted participants who, when asked, said that computers or computer-generated images were not used at all during the meetings. This combination of old and new techniques seems to have worked well, according to the participants' feeling of ease in communicating and understanding the ideas. The architects pointed out that verbal communication is still the most important method in participation and that this relies on the skills of the individual as a communicator, who should avoid the use of jargon, be clear, and transmit enthusiasm.

The use of 3D images is hugely beneficial according to the architects, if they are 'honest' and if they are used for a specific purpose; for example, to show what a front garden would look like when partly occupied by a car. 3D computer models can often be better, as they can be more realistic than a 2D plan or even a traditional 3D cardboard model. The architects were of the opinion that the use of 3D imagery was a very effective means of stimulating communication between the various parties in the participation process. However, during discussions around the computer models it was often necessary to refer to the 2D maps in order to fully appreciate the context. 3D visualisation proved particularly useful in showing potential interiors. In future the architects also plan to use 3D flyovers of entire estates in participatory exercises in order to illustrate a neighbourhood context. They believe that a combined approach, which includes an interactive technique (such as movable models), is the most effective method in participatory exercises.

Evaluation of the participatory process

The user participants who were interviewed indicated they were happy with the process and believed that the architects had been very informative. As noted above, the use of computers seemed to have gone unnoticed by some participants. People also found the trip to similar housing projects in Glasgow very useful. Overall, the future residents felt the participatory process had been helpful, and that those leading the process were very approachable, particularly the architects.

According to the architects, the format used for the participatory exercises was not ideal, as they would have preferred to work with smaller groups of maximum six people in consultation meetings, combined with larger open days designed to investigate wider opinion. In Cornton, there were often 20 people in meetings. Another problem in any participatory exercise is that some participants are too shy to speak, while others are very vocal and even aggressive. A stronger chairperson would have been desirable.

Regarding the groups' composition, although participation was open, at Cultenhove house owners often outnumbered tenants. A power discrepancy between owners and tenants was observed, with house owners clearly feeling themselves entitled to have more of a voice because they had made a financial investment in living in the area. The Council and the housing association never dominated the process, though it was felt that at times they might have tried to harmonise the participation.

On the whole, the architects felt that the participants were responded to through the design process, but were not fully integrated into it – they made choices between options rather than really contributing novel ideas. In the architects' view, earlier (especially 1970 to 1980) participatory processes were more effective, perhaps because there was more political activism then. People nowadays seem less knowledgeable about the wider issues, and less assertive about expressing their opinions. Overall, however, the architects believe the process was useful for gaining an understanding of important local matters – for example, where trouble may be expected from gatherings of disaffected young people – and in collecting residents' opinions on different proposed solutions. They believe that participation works best when both architects and the client are thoroughly committed to it. The client must want the building design to succeed, and be interested in not just the financial soundness of the venture, but also in the quality of the building and the satisfaction of residents.

Conclusion

The case studies demonstrate that there is value in both new and in more traditional media and communication techniques during the participation process. As demonstrated by the Glasgow Model, there is a significant advantage to be gained if a three-dimensional, detailed city context model is available to test alternative proposals. By facilitating visualisation in this way users, or councillors in the case of Glasgow, are able to have a better understanding of how suitable design options might be. However, it is important that the use of the model is ethically appropriate and not manipulative. On the other hand, some participants appreciate the value of more traditional two-dimensional methods at the early stages of a design, whether they are guiding the design and involvement or otherwise taking part.

Regardless of the tools which are used to communicate and facilitate the design, there seems to be agreement among the architects and users in the Corton Housing Project that social and verbal communication skills are vital ingredients in generating a successful participation process. An ability to discuss and explain the project using no jargon and plain English is important. Making the other participants feel that their opinions are being valued and facilitating constructive contributions to the discussion appears to be a key component in the development of a successful participation process. Therefore, overall, social skills seem to remain more relevant than sophisticated techniques for the success of participatory activities.

Note

1 Members of staff at Glasgow School of Art, Glasgow City Council staff, the architects who pioneered the Glasgow Model and those involved in the Cornton Housing Project in Stirling (architects and local community members) are thanked for their important inputs to the authors of these case studies through interviews.

Part III

Findings and recommendations

Chapter 9

Analysis of findings

Paul Jenkins

Objectives and methods of the research

This book is based on a research project, the main objectives of which were: to map out the scope of existing knowledge of relevance to wider social participation in the architectural design process; explore existing methods of fostering forms of such participation; point to gaps in both knowledge and methods, and in so doing propose an agenda for further research of national and international relevance. As such, the work had an inductive focus, identifying key research issues and gaps in knowledge for further investigation, as opposed to providing any fully definitive responses. In addition, achieving a balance between conceptual analysis and review of professional practice (and related policy) has been an essential aspect of both the research objectives and the methods implemented in the study. Reporting on the study, this book thus aims to assist both in *theory-building* as well as encouraging *reflective practice* and sites itself within a transformative knowledge tradition. In this context, before discussing the findings, some contextual background is required to clarify these transformative aims.[1]

The initial conception of the study in 2005 was seen as responding to perceptions, especially within government and related policy organisations, of the need for more socially inclusive practice in architecture. An initial analysis of public policy in this respect indicated that this has taken two main lines: the promotion of participation by users in building design, which is mainly focused on public buildings such as health and education, but also residential design; and the promotion of wider understanding of, and engagement with, architecture in society. In parallel with these, essentially 'supply-side' approaches, the editors, as originators of the study, were well aware that there continues to be an interest in user participation in architectural practice, with some perception that this is increasing – albeit not reaching the levels of engagement experienced from the mid-1960s to mid-1980s.

Again, the study was created with an awareness that, while participation in the related discipline of planning has been statutory since the mid-1960s – and this has led to the evolution of debates and substantial literature on the objective, nature and mechanisms of such participation – the architectural literature of relevance is relatively sparse and fragmented. A limited number of key texts on participation in architecture exist, many of these rather dated, but there is no core text that examines the range of key issues concerning wider social participation in the architectural process, and that recommends a range of appropriate responses to these issues in contemporary social, economic, political and cultural contexts.

In addition to the limited debate and literature within architecture on participation, and weak engagement with other relevant debates within related disciplines and literatures, the background to the study also identified limited communication on this between researchers and practitioners. This was seen as partly due to the way knowledge is perceived within professional practice and academia, but also relates to the way value is attributed to architecture.[2] Embedded within this are issues concerning the relationship between the generic and specific in terms of user needs and architectural approaches, with architects tending to approach knowledge on a project-specific basis and not invest in, or use, more generic knowledge generation and application techniques, as has been noted in previous chapters. In the light of the above initial contextual analysis the research project was structured as follows, mapping to a great extent on to the structure of this book.

An initial literature review was considered a key activity for two main reasons. First, to review the existing architecture literature of relevance, examining the historical development of social participation in architecture since the 1960s, as well as key concepts and practice – with an emphasis on the UK experience but reference to wider international experience. Second, a wider scoping review of related literatures in associated disciplinary areas was proposed, to investigate other experiences of participation which could be of relevance to architecture. Allied to these two objectives was a third of using these review activities to produce a database resource of wider literature of relevance for broader use.

This desktop study was followed up, as in much social research, with fieldwork activity, in this case through identifying institutions and good practice of relevance and, within these, identifying appropriate themes and sites for case studies.[3] It is important to stress that the case studies were seen as primarily illustrative, since this was a scoping study, and were structured through initial reviews of relevant background material: site visits with 'transect walks' and participant observation, backed up by some key informant and focus group interviews.

These two main methods were used to collect information as the basis for this analysis, but importantly for a study which examines social participation, and sites itself in a transformative epistemological tradition, the research was structured to engage with a range of 'stakeholders' or 'peers' to provide key information, oversee the emerging analysis and validate the research findings as they developed, permitting a flexibility in praxis that made the most efficient use of the study resources and helped to tighten the focus of the research. To achieve this the study set up four discussion mechanisms: engaging researchers with significant relevant experience in group discussion; creating a forum[4] where key informants within relevant institutional settings and disciplinary areas could provide input, including through semi-structured interviews; as findings emerged, these were disseminated and discussed through focus group discussions with relevant invited institutions engaged in various ways in participation in architecture; and finally widening the public dissemination and discussion of findings and conclusions through a web-based wiki and participatory workshops.

Not only has this participatory research method been essential in widening the scope of the short speculative project but the study also thus became a form of action research (or more accurately perhaps research action) in that the *research* activity has led to investigation and stimulation of possible follow-up *action* – which is the focus of Chapter 10. It is, however, stressed that this is primarily a scoping study and thus, while the discussion aspects of the project have highlighted forms of action that may well build on the study – e.g. other forms of resource provision such as through websites, focused debates through conferences and within professional organisations, policy changes for practice – these have not been per se the main objective of the project as a speculative research project funded by the Arts and Humanities Research Council. That said, however, this chapter summarises findings from various sources in the study and highlights issues emerging in response to some key questions that the study investigated.

Another important element of the study is that the nature of the definition of the core research area as the architectural process has inevitably focused on the role of architects in practice and education, as well as the role of supporting professional and government policy-making bodies. This should not limit the impact of the study to these groups, however, as architecture activities are part of wider social activity. As such the final dissemination events of the project were deliberately seen as an initial way to present the findings of this specific focus to a wider audience which inevitably has a wider social basis. The study clearly identifies the need for interdisciplinary, interinstitutional and interactive follow-up within a multi-layered and multi-actor approach to the role of architecture within society and the book is aimed at stimulating this.

Research questions

A number of research questions were seeded into the investigation from its inception, and summarised responses to these, drawing on the information reported in previous chapters, are presented first. This is followed by a reflection on conceptual and analytical issues and then on action-oriented issues which the research raises. Chapter 10 then presents recommendations of relevance for key actors: academia, the profession/practices and policy-making institutions, as well as for future research – part of the original focus for the project.

Responses to the research questions drawing on the evidence presented in the previous chapters are tabled below. Responding to these questions raises a number of issues, some of which are dealt with in more depth in the subsequent sections of this chapter, but many need further investigation beyond this initial scoping exercise.

Who gets involved in wider social participation in the architecture process and how does this affect other roles and relationships?

Wider social participation activities in specific architecture design processes are usually led by architects, due to their role in the process (albeit sometimes with community facilitators, social workers and/or engineers).[5] While few other professionals are directly involved in wider social participation in the architectural design processes, others may be indirectly involved in analysing generic needs/demand, such as environmental psychologists and sociologists. A conspicuous gap here is engagement with facilities managers, who – while perceiving added value in ongoing building costs through user participation – have no tradition of engaging with wider social groups or closely in the architectural design process (see also below on post-completion feedback). This needs further investigation.

The role and attitudes of clients to wider social participation are of great importance, whether permitting/encouraging this, or accepting the results of the participatory process. In the end clients are responsible for *inter alia* the economic impacts of design and, while they may value inputs on social aspects of design through consultation, they may not necessarily take these on board in final decision-making – see discussion below on power. Participation by users may lead to some higher capital costs, but generally these may be seen to be offset by either higher user satisfaction (and possibly higher productivity) or lower ongoing costs (e.g. running costs and maintenance).

Clients can also be social organisations and, in these circumstances, are more likely to initiate and drive the participatory process (e.g. community-based Housing Associations, or community and voluntary organisations);

however, who represents the wider client/users (and how) in these situations is an issue that needs further investigation.

The direct engagement with building users needs a proactive approach by both architects and clients, and this takes time and resources to develop. While it has been possible for this to be embedded within normal architectural practice (and does not necessarily require special resources), the current tendency in publicly driven architecture/building procurement processes (whether because of increasing scale of delivery or new public–private partnership approaches) seems to make direct participatory activities in the architectural process less likely. Again, while the research project has initially engaged with this issue, this needs further investigation.

The architecture process overlaps with the planning process in various ways, and this is where engagement with the wider public is more likely to take place. Indeed, permitting wider participation in the architectural design can make a planning application process more difficult, although some local authorities seem prepared to allow greater flexibility through, for example, a multi-staged planning process – this can also be investigated further.

Stimulating demand for participation within society, and/or specific social groups, needs to be based on a wider public understanding of architectural design issues, and here government, policy-making bodies and the professional organisations need to play key roles.

What activities in the architecture process are participated in, and to what extent does the architect see this role as guiding the client/user/wider public as opposed to investigating their existing interests/awareness?

Generally, wider social participation in architecture focuses on aspects of the design stage, although this may continue into construction with changes to design. Rarely do users get involved in construction per se in the UK, exceptions being in 'self-build' activities. Although growing in incidence this still represents a small proportion of buildings designed in the UK. This is very different in other contexts (e.g. the US and the global South) where residential and other social architecture often has user input in design and construction.

While self-building is a small part of architecture in the UK, much private sector housing design does not necessarily involve architects and the trend to private sector leadership in other public building procurement is also tending to reduce the role of the architect and architectural design. As noted above, this tends to also reduce opportunity for specific direct participation by users or other social groups, while it may not increase engagement in generic forms of user needs/demands. This has been the subject of recent research undertaken for the Scottish government which begins to identify this lacuna (Scottish Executive 2006).

An increasingly important aspect of this issue is the nature of wider social participation that can take place in the early brief development stage of design – as with larger-scale building projects and programmes this is the more likely opportunity than in the specific design process. That said, in large-scale urban regeneration projects, architects (as well as planners) can have significant resources and requirements for wider participation in the design process.

While architects may tend to initiate and lead direct participatory building design processes, these can be more effective when they are prepared to relinquish some of their customary role – e.g. working with people on the creative aspects of design and not only on the social aspects. However, this tends to be against the dominant ethos of the role of the architect as creative director, which is reinforced in education albeit often constrained in practice.

Also of significant importance here is that there is very little evidence of any systematic post-completion feedback, whether architect/project-specific or more generic. This is seen as an ever more important issue given the changes in procurement processes for public buildings and the need for better generic information informing brief development.

Linked to this is the increasing need for clearer understanding of ongoing running costs in the design of buildings (e.g. energy costs) and the role of users in managing this, and hence forms of post-completion measurement to assist in refining such activity (in management as well as in prior design).

How can social and technical tools for participation be used to communicate more openly in the process, and how can this affect the use of resources?

While there is a variety of new technical tools for visualisation which are becoming less resource-intensive and thus more utilised in practices, and some new IT-based social networking possibilities (e.g. interactive websites such as wikis), the key issues in participation are still the process issues such as:

- What is the objective of the participation?
- Who gets involved and who drives the process?
- How does participation take place (what is the dominant 'language', what level of engagement is seen as possible/acceptable: information, consultation or decision-making)?
- Where does the participation happen (e.g. what sort of venue and how can this affect the process)?
- Which resources can be made available (financial, time and skills/level of understanding)?

As well as new IT-based visualisation software, there are also more public resources available concerning participatory tools and techniques (e.g. books, manuals and websites), and architects need to be more acquainted with these and how to use them in practice.

A few architecture, built environment and planning schools now provide training which includes exposure to more specific participatory tools and techniques, but there is room for more initiatives in this regards – including possible curriculum guidance (ARB/RIBA) on social/user engagement.

There seems to be a need for more institutional support for participation in architecture/built environment – e.g. some form of common resource base(s) and some form of highlighting the importance of this within the discipline/profession.[6]

Which types of buildings might be more or less suited to participation of users and the general public in the design process?

'Social' architecture such as housing, health, education and recreational/community buildings/spaces are probably seen as more typically appropriate for participatory processes; although, other buildings involving multiple uses are also potential candidates (e.g. workspaces, public buildings).

However, in fact it is in corporate building design that significant active use of indirect/generic and direct/specific participation in design takes place – including at brief development stage (which may be a separately funded activity). Potentially more can be learnt about this in other forms of building procurement. The same is true for post-completion feedback, where larger architectural (and other professional) firms tend to realise the need for investment of time and resources to avoid 're-inventing wheels'.[7]

There is generally a weak tradition in the UK of involving wider social participation in the architectural design of specific public buildings (e.g. through publicly voted competitions) compared to other countries (e.g. in Germany and the Netherlands). This could be further promoted.

While architects do have relatively high wider social status, their products often do not, and thus modern architecture is often seen as alienating by wider social groups (Scottish Executive 2006). The recent trend in popularising self-designed architecture in the mass media may continue to contribute to maintaining the social status of architecture, but may not provide any mechanisms for wider social engagement.

Why is there limited communication between research into, and practice of, wider social participation in the design process?

Research into wider social participation in architecture has become to some extent caught up in issues of the 'silo' approach to knowledge with different disciplines and professions developing separately with limited joint activities.

Planning and social housing management are examples of disciplines/ professions with a long evolution of activity and discussion around forms of social participation, yet this has limited impact on architecture. Similarly, investigation of other values in the built environment through environmental psychology and sociology have had limited impact. This is reflected in architecture education where social science has less significance than visual arts, humanities and natural science-based technology.[8]

While architecture is essentially interdisciplinary in practice, the role of research in practice – as systematic knowledge development and transfer – is weak across the profession. While many architects would consider themselves as reflective practitioners to some extent, any systematic form of reflection drawing on post-completion feedback is limited (Jenkins *et al.* 2005). This impacts on development of the wider knowledge base within the profession, which may then need to rely on other disciplines/professionals.[9]

While architecture plays a wide social role, the direct or indirect engagement of wider social groups, including users, will inevitably be evidenced in different ways today compared with the previous traditions of the 1960s and 1970s in the UK (or in other countries), as this depends on political and economic contexts as well as wider social and cultural values. For instance, a major driving force for wider social participation in architecture in the late 1960s and 1970s was political, drawing on social protest roots; however, current political impetus for such participation is more oriented to economic concerns to reduce delays in achieving outcomes and engage wider social actors (individuals and the private sector) in implementing public policy due to lower state capacity to invest.

In addition to globally related economic challenges currently facing the state, increasing cultural diversity in the UK drives a need for both government and professional organisations, as well as civil society organisations, to promote wider social participation more explicitly in the architecture design process in practice, and hence also in architectural education and research activities.

Conceptual and analytical issues

In addition to providing a basis to begin to answer the above research questions, the study has thrown up a series of more conceptual/analytical issues which Chapter 1 initially outlined in defining the scope of the investigation. Other than the definition of the, albeit fuzzy, conceptual limits of what is considered the relevant scope for investigating wider social participation in the architectural design process (arguably inevitably 'architect-centric' in this approach), the three main conceptual and analytical issues which the study raises are those of knowledge, value and power.

Concerning knowledge, the research has attempted to widen the search for knowledge of relevance across different disciplinary areas, across any (perceived) theory/practice 'divide' and across professional and public policy borders – all of which define useful and relevant knowledge in different ways, as well as conferring different values on knowledge and evaluating 'valid' knowledge differentially. For example, in academic knowledge, systematic rigour and attempted neutrality are key bases for evaluating the nature of knowledge across many disciplines, although how these concepts are applied differs considerably between – for instance – the natural and social sciences, the arts and humanities.[10] In contrast, the instrumental nature of knowledge (i.e. how useful this can be) tends to dominate practice and hence professional interests, and also to a significant extent government interests. However, while government and other related bodies may play a strong role in promoting forms of practice aligned with public policy, such bodies also play a key role in determining professional boundaries and quality of practice (on behalf of society), as well as the content of professional education (now channelled through academia). In approaching this study the core research team have drawn on their practice experience, policy awareness and academic understanding to seek as wide a range of relevant knowledge as possible. This has been through more traditional academic methods such as literature reviews, interviews with key informants and case study investigation, but also – as noted above – through less 'academic' methods to access a wider range of experience through wider discussion, which also serves as a mechanism to socially validate findings.

It is not only the wider scope of relevant knowledge of the defined research subject that is of interest, but also the role of knowledge in the architectural design process. As professionals, architects undergo a long and somewhat rigorous education, overseen by a government-appointed regulatory body as well as professional and academic quality control institutions. They are – largely as a result – given a relatively high-status position in society as professionals, albeit now with limited protection (i.e. only that of title) vis-à-vis other actors in the design and building process. In this, architects inevitably consider themselves to hold a privileged position in relation to the design of buildings, and this is heavily reinforced by the trend over a long period of time to defend the profession from other knowledge-based professionals as well as other actors in the building process.

More recently the pressures within academia concerning teaching quality control as well as growing research activity, allied to growing stipulation of educational content by the regulatory bodies, seems to have led to increasingly protective views of the uniqueness of architectural knowledge in education and hence also in practice. This has its counterpart in an increasing alienation of society in relation to architecture, compounding the vicious circle of limited social participation and appreciation of architecture throughout society. While this is perhaps true for many contexts, the relative isolation of architects from society and society from architecture seems particularly marked in the United Kingdom, especially compared to other European countries.

This context leads to a situation where architects create a value system for architecture which is not necessarily that widely accepted socially – this closed value system being used in many situations as a defence mechanism. In this situation architects then prioritise their own peer-group evaluation system in relation to other, wider, social values, and this is reflected in the educational, research and practice processes which architects undertake. Architects thus generally consider their own peer-group knowledge as of higher value than those of other participants in the architecture process – more specifically concerning design of the visual, cultural and spatial aspects, with less emphasis on exclusivity of knowledge for technological and perhaps managerial knowledge. These represent key elements of the three main forms of knowledge and value in architecture (*firmitas, utilitas, venustas* – i.e. strong/durable, useful, beautiful), although the social and economic (or political) aspects of architecture are less fully engaged with in education and research. This perhaps also represents a reaction to the trend in the immediate post-World War II period when state-led architecture was highly influenced by social, economic and political values and the disciplines which support these (e.g. sociology, economics and political science) – seen by many in retrospect as a negative period for architecture in wider social and aesthetic terms.

Essentially, widening social participation in the architectural process comes down to how value is created and who creates this value, and how it is affected by power relations and played out in terms of knowledge. The architect is obliged to understand and work with the values of the client in the architectural process, but if he/she does not value the values and knowledge of the other major non-professional stakeholders in this process (e.g. the user and wider society), inevitably there is little opportunity for widening participation, even if this is required in some way. Again, while some architects may value the social knowledge of users – as this will affect how the building is used – they may not value the aesthetic knowledge of users. This does not mean architects need to ignore their own specialised knowledge on a wide variety of issues of relevance, but it does focus on to what extent architects may want, or find the necessary resources (e.g. time), to share this knowledge with that of others in the design process.[11] Such sharing, however, becomes more difficult the further apart these knowledge sets are – for example, specialised architectural knowledge has become less accessible by users and wider society, who will, however, have their own forms of knowledge and values concerning any building or architecture, probably based mainly on their own experiences, the wider values of the social and cultural milieu they live and work within, and important influences such as mass media and education.

While perhaps not valued as important by architects, these social values are all the same real and can exert their own form of power.

Apart from social (nature of knowledge and value) and economic (resource) barriers to wider social participation in the architectural process, other barriers can have political significance and reflect the wider nature of decision-making within society on either generic or specific issues. The driving force for social participation in the architectural design process in the 1960s and 1970s was to a great extent political as a reaction to the social, economic and political exclusion from decision-making in the welfare state. Then higher value knowledge was expected to be best channelled through experts, such as architects, planners, sociologists – as 'scientists' – mediated by government.[12] The more recent government exhortations, inducements and requirements for wider social participation in architecture (e.g. in urban regeneration) have both an instrumental objective (impacting on post-completion social problems) as well as fit within a more general government agenda to widen political participation through 'governance'. This has come about to some extent as a reflection of the reduced resources, but wider role, of government in society within a globally competitive economic system. This represents a very different political economy from the 1960s to 1980s and one with much more emphasis on activity beyond government – whether private sector or within civil society and the wider public, and hence the trend to engage with different forms of partnerships – although private-sector partnerships tend to dominate these arrangements.

While politics is inevitably linked to issues of power, in fact power is embedded in all social relations and as such participation is neither as simplistic as a 'zero-sum game' (where power is seen as finite and one group always needs to wrest power from another) or as 'empowerment' through providing the resources and getting the tools and techniques right (and where power is seen as infinite and can potentially expand to deal with any situation). Power affects all relations and is constantly negotiated and renegotiated between related power holders, some dominant and some subordinate in any specific situation. In this understanding of power, subordination alternates between being an accepted state and a challenged one with different forms of equilibrium reached at different times/locations in negotiation processes. Such negotiations continue over relatively long periods of time in most socio-political relationships and are both negotiated in the specific situation as well as drawing on other forms of formal and informal social power and capital. Hence the relationship between an architect and a client or user will depend on both their direct negotiation and the indirect social values which determine among other things social status and attitudes (i.e. socially created values) such as the expected role of the architect.

With this concept of power, participation is not always about decision-making, although this may be seen as the most powerful form of negotiation on any issue, such as an architectural design, but is also about pro-viding and sharing information, whether generic or specific. The power relation-ships in a process such as architectural design are complex as there are typically various (actual and/or potential) participants and these may have differ-ent formal power (e.g. the client has a contractual relationship with the archi-tect and the architect is legally bound by a professional code), as well as informal power (e.g. the architect may have a high status and thus expect to dominate the client). There are different ways of sharing information, some one-way and some two-way, the essential difference being encapsulated as between information-giving and consultation. Consultation, in turn, differs from joint decision-making as there is no obligation for the dominant decision-makers to take account of the results of consultation. In practice these power relation-ships are usually not very explicit, either because they are assumed to be clear (e.g. the client–architect relationship) or are not clearly thought through and made explicit (e.g. when clients agree to user participation without considering wider consequences such as costs).

Thus an analytical approach which clarifies the nature of appropriate knowledge, values and power in any activity where there can be participation, such as the architectural design process, can assist understanding of what is possible and appropriate in terms of objectives for participation, the tools and techniques which can be used and the resources these are likely to take, and the eventual role in decision-making.[13] Many years of experience in participa-tion in planning, however, demonstrate that even where participation is pro-moted or required, the nature of this is seldom clearly defined and the result can be even more alienation of users and wider society from engagement and/or negotiation in the process.

The above discussion refers more to direct engagement in a specific architectural design process, but issues of knowledge, value and power affect more indirect forms of 'participation', such as the production of generic know-ledge (e.g. from systematic post-completion feedback on buildings, specific research into users/building/processes and/or research of relevance undertaken in related disciplinary areas) which are often seen as of limited relevance to architects, whether in practice or academia. However, the political process may require architects to engage with such findings, (e.g. regulations), and increas-ingly through policy guidance and other indirect and partly formal expressions of power relationships, which draw on such forms of generic research and knowledge.

To conclude this rather brief examination of the conceptual and ana-lytical issues in wider social participation in the architectural design process, some self-reflection is needed by architects on the values, power relations and forms of knowledge this requires, and which actors or stakeholders can have different positions within the process. As posited in Chapter 1, inherent within this are two differing fundamental positions that can drive such interest: first, that which sees such analysis as the basis for encouraging an inalienable right by social groups to engage specifically and generically with architecture as a social activity which affects them, and second, that which accepts that such an analysis can make the architectural design process more effective in some instrumental way. Of paramount importance in both approaches is an ability to read power relations, differentiate values and identify relevant forms of knowledge, but also importantly to assess interest and demand for wider social participation and whether this may need stimulation given the wider (historically influenced) context. Forcing participation on users, or even wider society, generally leads to adverse reactions and also opens up to different forms of oppression.

Action-oriented issues

The structure of the architectural process

Bearing in mind the need for clearer understanding of the conceptual basis for wider social participation in the architectural process as discussed above, a range of action-oriented issues have also been raised in the study. These can perhaps be best approached using the analytical framework that was set up in the early concept paper and applied to the case studies, as this embeds – albeit to some extent in a simplified manner – the conceptual and analytical issues discussed above.

The analytical framework identified three main types of (potential) participants (clients, users and the wider public), three phases of the architectural process when participation could take place (design, construction and post-completion), and three forms of participation (inform, consult and decide). The three types, phases and forms provide potentially 27 (3 × 3 × 3) options for participation. However, there is limited user participation and even less likelihood of public participation in the construction process in the UK – although for a wider global analysis these categories have significance and are thus a valid part of the analytical framework. This latter can thus be set aside in a simplified analysis of the UK context. In addition, clients are usually involved in the construction process as changes to approved designs are needed; however, as this usually includes all three forms of participation – information, consultation and decision-making – this can also be set aside in relation to this simplified analysis. Given this, there are some six major 'opportunities' for wider social participation in the architectural process, and in each of these opportunities different forms of participation can be envisaged, as shown in Table 9.1.[14]

The 'normal architectural process' is one where the client is informed, consulted and takes part in decision-making on a wide range of

Table 9.1 Six major 'opportunities' for wider social participation in the architectural process

	Client	User	Public
Design			
Post-completion			

Table 9.2 Participation in the 'normal' architectural process

	Client	User	Public
Design	Decision-making		
Post-completion	Information		

aspects of the architectural design, and this may involve prior research into the nature of the appropriate brief as well as the design process per se (e.g. for large corporate clients). Typically, however, as noted above, there is no systematic and/or in-depth engagement with the client in the post-completion stage and hence no generic knowledge developed either by the client or the architect – whether for their own use or wider dissemination. This again is less so for large corporate clients, although the role of facilities managers in this regard may not include any significant engagement with the architects.

This 'normal process' also usually does not involve participation of users who are not considered the client in some form (e.g. not a social client organisation), and this is also true of the wider public, except inasmuch as wider public opinion may be expressed through, for instance, public media on the completed building. This, however, generally has no direct effect on generic knowledge used by architects, although it may come to affect public clients such as the government in terms of future activities in architectural design and associated guidance. Considered more valuable, for architects at least, is the professional peer group's assessment and the way a building is evaluated formally through awards or informally through publication in the architectural press, and this has significant influence in future architectural design as well as the education of future professionals. This 'normal architectural process' may be shown diagrammatically (see Table 9.2).

A second 'partial participatory architectural process' may be identified where clients and/or architects engage with users in at least part of the process, with varying degrees of engagement which will certainly include information provision, probably some form of consultation but less likely any significant form of negotiated decision-making. Here again it seems that clients are often not engaged in any systematic post-completion feedback per se although they may take on board their post-completion experience in future

Table 9.3 Partial participatory architectural process

	Client	*User*	*Public*
Design	Decision-making	Consultation	Information
Post-completion	Consultation		

Table 9.4 Wider participatory architectural process

	Client	*User*	*Public*
Design	Decision-making	Consultation	Consultation
Post-completion	Decision-making	Consultation	Information

commissions, and as such consult with architects more adequately in future. Users are also not necessarily involved in formal or informal post-completion feedback of this type, except when this is seen as important for future building programmes by large corporate or government clients. The public also generally does not participate in such processes, although in large-scale architecture programmes where no fixed user group exists, the wider public may be the source of generic information of user needs. This 'partial participatory architectural process' may be shown diagrammatically (see Table 9.3).

There is a third possible 'wider participatory architectural process' which takes account of possible direct and indirect user engagement in the design and post-completion feedback processes, with the latter systematised in some form for the benefit of the participants and wider society and profession, with this being used as a way to engage wider society more effectively with architecture as well as architects with other social knowledge and values. This could also include direct wider public participation at times in the design process through public competition, as well as indirect generic information production through, for example, social research affecting brief development. This 'wider participatory architectural process' may be shown diagrammatically (see Table 9.4).

While it is suggested that this analytical framework can be useful in stimulating discussion on who gets involved in what stages of the architectural process, in the form used above it is overly simplified and hence needs to be translated in practice. One way that this could be considered is in adaptation of the existing professional Plan of Work,[15] recognising especially the possibility of a separate, or extended, brief development stage. However, it does specifically help to highlight the weakness of any post-completion knowledge production stage in the Plan of Work.

Equally, the simplified framework does not differentiate adequately between various forms of engagement within the inevitably complex design process, nor does it permit analysis of the way participation takes place within these (i.e. power relationships issues such as language, venues, procedures, as well as more socially embedded ones such as gender, age and ethnicity). It also omits the dimension of user involvement in the management and running of technical aid services, where client organisations of a (user-controlled) design service may be members of the organisation which delivers the service, and they have the opportunity to elect members to the Committee of Management and so bring their knowledge of the service into its decision-making arena, as in the example of Comtechsa (see Chapter 5). That said, the above typification of praxis using the analytical framework does permit the study to highlight key issues concerning the practice of participation in the architecture process, namely resources, skills and attitudes.

Key issues oriented to action

In relation to the act of participation in architecture, resources are predominantly taken to refer to both time and financial resources, as social resources are covered under skills below. The evidence from the scoping study is that participation in the architectural design process – and also in any post-completion feedback process – requires time, which translates into finance for architects and probably the client, as well as possibly that of users (less so for the general public, as their participation is voluntary and less accounted for financially). Users may be prepared to put in time, but this may also be at a cost to the client, depending on the user–client relationship. As clients can be expected to put in time since this is in their interest (although to what extent varies enormously), the crucial issue here is time for the architects to engage in participation.

As may be seen from the historical review, case studies and other forms of evidence presented in previous chapters, this is increasingly critical as architects compete for work through fees and have to cope with cyclical swings in workloads. It is also affected by the structure of the profession, with many small firms with limited scope for any flexibility in working practice. Thus, if any form of wider participation is not prioritised by the client and factored into the fee structure in some way, the time allocated may be minimal. The same applies to post-completion feedback, and this stage has been effectively ignored in the professional Plan of Work due to no clear fee status, the extra costs involved and the fact that this does not have a direct impact on the building which is funding the fee income.

As a result, although initially most architecture firms were unwilling to engage in 'participatory processes', such as described above in the 1970s, this changed as the possibility – indeed need – for such fee income grew at a time of low workloads due to general economic downswing. When a new government came to power which encouraged private sector competition as opposed to civil society engagement, fee-based resources continued to be made available through government funding as an alternative to direct government engagement and many architecture firms engaged with community clients. However, in the subsequent rapidly growing competitive professional environment in the mid-1980s eventually the UK (and also US) government funding cut-backs led to this form of participation in the architecture process largely disappearing.[16]

The case studies of two of the organisations which survived this regime change demonstrate how accessing other forms of economic resources has been key to their general survival and targeting specific project-related funding essential to their continued participatory engagement with users. This situation, as noted above and in previous chapters, has changed again with a different government orientation, supporting wider governance and significant public funds for, for example, urban renewal, including stimulating user participation. However, in other areas of public funding the increasing reliance on private finance through public–private partnerships – and an associated scaling up of delivery (e.g. in health, education and residential development) – has led to enormous challenges to the direct participation model.

One of the possible responses to this, significantly advocated by government and related policy organisations, is more reliance on generic information as an indirect means for engaging with wider social need and demands. Although this has been mooted for some time, many of the initial attempts to influence private sector actors, through such policy and practice guidance, have had limited effect to date – although this may be changing. This approach also, however, requires investment of resources (financial and temporal) in forms of knowledge development such as research, and there has been limited availability of this in the field of architecture (e.g. to investigate differentiated housing demand within the private house-building sector, or to ensure that adequate resources and time are set aside to permit and encourage wider participation in the earlier stages of the design brief development process (often the most crucial in larger-scale contracted public programmes). This approach to encouraging indirect participation, as noted previously in the literature review on widening governance, also includes stimulating demand through wider information provision and consultation on architecture more generally in society, with architecture centres as examples of where this takes place. These, however – while having successes – have had a limited impact across the whole of the UK, as there need to be significantly higher levels of funding to reach out more effectively to broader social groups through wider localised coverage, such as is the case in the Netherlands.

Two issues which arise here are therefore the need to have adequate resources built into the architectural process, especially at design brief development and post-completion stages, for direct forms of participation, and the need for greater levels of investment in indirect knowledge development (e.g. research) and dissemination (including knowledge transfer) in terms of wider professional and public engagement in architecture in more generic/ general ways. The provision of such resources, however, will not emerge spontaneously from private sector actors – although these may well engage when initial resources are made available, bringing their own financial and/or time resources to bear[17] – and hence the onus is on the profession and public sector to act.

Linked to resources is the issue of skills. Even where public resources and regulation and/or guidance require and/or encourage wider social participation this still needs skills in participation within the process – for the architect and other professionals, clients and users who might be open to wider participation, and the wider public in raising interest and ability to engage. The skills required do involve imparting information on aspects of the complex architectural process and know-how to focus on these, as well as which participatory tools and techniques to choose given the circumstances. As the study has determined, new IT tools and techniques permit different forms of information delivery, but do not reduce the importance of social aspects of participation.

As far as architects' training is concerned there is, as noted previously, a weak engagement with social issues in education, and only a few architecture schools/departments aspire to any skills training for participatory engagement – and the long-term effect of this is deeply embedded within the profession. This can potentially be changed through re-emphasising the social aspects of architecture in education, including (but not limited to) stimulating more participatory engagement, and widening this education through continuing professional development for existing professionals. This requires action by the professional organisations and the relevant government regulatory body. Such training can prepare architects to share knowledge and develop more participatory tools and techniques in practice with clients and users, if these have access to necessary resources as noted above. Given stated policy objectives, government could also provide more counterpart resources through the wider public participation mechanisms, such as competitions and architecture centres, to encourage relevant architectural and participatory skills development within wider society as a part of this approach. However, although government has a key role to play, there is also an important role here for other organisations in civil society which promote wider social participation in public activities, to engage more specifically with architecture and the built environment and move beyond general governance issues or highly specific activities (e.g. conservation lobbies).

The role of wider organisations in civil society, as well as government, professional, educational (in addition to lobbying organisations representing wider private sector interests) is not only in assisting the development of the skills base for engaging with either direct or indirect participatory activities in architecture, and finding ways to fund these, but also in changing attitudes. As has been argued above, public attitudes to architecture are possibly at a low point (although possibly not as low as the late 1970s) and the realisation of this has driven government and related organisations to invest in wider social information activities. Professional and educational organisations need also to engage with changing attitudes through direct and indirect mechanisms for participation in practice as outlined above, and could play an important role in supporting other private sector and civil society organisations in changing attitudes to wider programmes of architecture/building delivery (such as in private housebuilding, as this is the dominant form of production of the built environment).

However, it is not only the attitudes of the public and professionals that need to change, but also that within government, which needs to be prepared to invest in less tangible, longer-term change and to coordinate its efforts better between stimulating more participation on one hand but reducing the options for this on the other.[18] There is no 'quick fix' for the public sector to encouraging wider and deeper social participation in any form of process, especially where this has been rather instrumentally implemented in the past. While policy-oriented guidance and regulation are key public sector proactive mechanisms, government and related bodies need also to provide reactive mechanisms which permit spontaneous and/or organised participation on issues to emerge and find its own 'space'. In the end, arguably the most difficult issues for widening social participation in architecture are attitudinal, as even if more resources and better skills are available, assisting 'supply', the nature of participation needs to be developed through increasing demand.

Notes

1   Those more interested in the analysis per se can skip this research-focused section.
2   Concerning attitudes to knowledge and research within architecture see, Jenkins 2008. On values within architecture, see Key Concepts chapter.
3   After some deliberation these case studies were focused on four themes which are the basis for the previous chapters: the institutional basis for community architectural practice/technical aid over time; the relationship between user participation and perceived quality in architectural design; the inclusion of participation issues with architectural education; and the balance between social and technical mechanisms for participation in architectural design (especially new forms of visualisation).
4   This was through the project steering group, with participants from practice, academia and professional/policy bodies.
5   There also seems to be an increasing participation of 'design facilitators' and artists, especially in urban regeneration projects.
6   One possibility here is perhaps a conference to encourage less 're-inventing of the wheel' in practice, permitting tools, techniques and practice experience to be more widely disseminated and better understood.

7   For more discussion, see Jenkins *et al.* 2005; ScotMARK/gm+ad 2007.

8   In 86 different criteria established by the Architects' Registration Board for inclusion in accredited educational courses there is no mention of client/user/public engagement.

9   While this might entail some specialist knowledge with commercial value which practices would be unwilling to share, the RIAS research has shown that in most cases the result is partly in the public domain. This is thus not a major hindrance for wider sharing of experiential knowledge if the mechanisms for this are easy to engage with and seen as useful by initial practices which developed the knowledge, as well as others who can utilise it.

10 A useful reflection on this may be found in Groat and Wang (2002).

11 This is reminiscent of the debates on the various participatory planning positions as described in Chapter 4.

12 This 'rational' approach to the exercise of professional activity over time in planning changed to one focusing, first, on technical systematisation and then widening social participation, in line with changing attitudes to governance – the so-called 'three paradigms' of planning.

13 I.e. the objective of the participation; who gets involved and what is their level of engagement and who drives the process; where the participation takes place (venue, dominant 'language'); and which resources can be available (financial, time and skills/level of understanding), as discussed previously.

14 This does not include the potential for participation in the more general management process of architecture practice or community technical assistance within which the architectural process sits.

15 See note 7, Chapter 1.

16 As was noted in the case studies, left-wing governments do not necessarily support such direct participation, assuming they provide representative systems for state–society relations, whereas right-wing governments may use civil society and non-governmental organisations as a way to reduce government activities; see Carley *et al.* (2001) for examples referring to wider state–civil society relationships in the built environment in different countries.

17 As noted previously the corporate private sector has considerable experience in this field and more could be expected for corporate bodies in terms of social responsibility in this regard – especially large employer organisations.

18 Parallels exist here again in the recent changes in the planning system where local-level planning is required to have more evidence of public participation but this is restricted concerning strategic issues.

Chapter 10

Current challenges and recommendations for the UK

Paul Jenkins and Leslie Forsyth

Introduction

A key aspect of this research has been to go beyond academic boundaries and seek inputs concerning the study and its implications from architectural practices, professional and policy organisations, as well as the interested wider public.[1] The main issues discussed in these events were: identification of any further contributions to the project findings; discussion on the current relevance of these findings; and comments on possible future follow-up activities. As such it was hoped that the study would generate some discussion and possible action in these organisations which would take forward findings and recommendations. This chapter reports on the results of the participatory workshops/ dissemination events which discussed and prioritised these, and sets out a succinct set of recommendations and areas for further research, which is part of its remit as a scoping study. It then concludes by reasserting the relationships between architecture and society, and the role of participation in this, as a key part of the architect's normal activity. This needs to be interpreted in different ways within different political, economic, social and cultural contexts, and the study includes an Appendix with initial thoughts on the relevance of this for contemporary policy and practice in the Scottish context, which emerged in discussions with policy-makers, profession/practices and academics in the process of research.

Participatory workshops

These events were held at The Lighthouse, Glasgow (Scotland's Centre for Architecture and Design) on 21 April 2008 and at the Commission for Architecture and the Built Environment (CABE), London, on 16 May 2008. The events were facilitated by the Education Projects Officer at The Lighthouse, and consisted of a brief project presentation by the Research Team, followed by group work activities. This included focusing on how participation in the architectural design process ideally should operate, indicating skills, opportunities, barriers and threats regarding participation in the architectural design process and identifying practical activities linking these to achievement of the ideals, as well as identifying which actors could implement them. In the last stage of the process participants received a limited number of votes to prioritise the most important activities.

The above events produced the following priorities:

1   Architecture centres, policy-support organisations (e.g. CABE and A+DS) and architecture schools should contribute to raising public awareness of the benefits from and need for wider social participation in the architecture process, creating higher demand for this in the architecture process and underpinning the added value created through time in such participatory processes.

2   Interested architecture practices should lobby their professional organisations and regulatory body to further develop the role of consultation within practice documentation, raising the profile of wider social participation in practice and advocating the inclusion of social aspects of architecture in professional curricula. Continuing professional development may also be used in developing skills for other participants in the architecture process – i.e. clients, users and wider social groups.

3   Architecture centres, professional and policy-implementing institutions, and civil servants involved in delivery systems such as Partnership for Schools should influence policy-makers to generate supportive policy as well as funding – for appropriate user/social participation. One possibility suggested here was the creation of a Minister for the Built Environment. It was also recommended that funding should be made accessible by interested users/ social groups and other non-governmental funding organisations.

4   Architecture practices, professional organisations and academic institutions should engage in benchmarking/assessment and dissemination of the practice of participation in actual projects. This will require funding and/ or fees to be built into building costs or other research streams. On this basis practices should be encouraged to develop their internal research and development and knowledge transfer activities.

5   Academic institutions, architecture centres and relevant policy-making/ implementing organisations need to look at the impact of current policy and how this is being implemented, advocating a coherent 'joined-up' approach across government departments.

Project recommendations

The recommendations are structured around target groups for possible action – academia, the profession and policy-making institutions – which were engaged with during the research. They focus on follow-up action to the study and include initial ideas for follow-up research as seeded into the original Arts and Humanities Research Council Speculative Research proposal. Within each of the target groups the recommendations are considered under the categories of attitudes, skills and resources.

Academia

Attitudes have been identified in the preceding analysis as perhaps the most difficult, but most important, barrier to wider social participation in the architectural design process. One key issue here is the attitude of architects to why this might be of value – as many architects would see their personal and professional skills and values as more important than those of users or the wider public (even than clients). While this research has not attempted to prove that any specific architectural design will be improved by wider social participation, it has addressed the claim that such participation reduces the likelihood of good architecture. The key issue discussed here is the nature of value and who defines good architecture. This will undoubtedly remain a matter of considerable debate, but the dominant tendency in the profession to uphold the exclusivity of peer group values seems unlikely to change significantly. However, the research has challenged this in two ways. First, the study has investigated how architecture that is valued by the architecture peer group can be produced through participatory processes, without claiming the converse, and second, by highlighting that wider knowledge of relevance to architecture, such as through post-completion feedback mechanisms or more generic research, is not generally systematically developed or used. The reasons for this are various, but it does lead to replication of knowledge production (or 're-inventing the wheel').

While it is considered that professional organisations play a critical role in attitudinal change, this is probably most important within academia, where attitudes and related value systems are largely created. Again, there is no assumption that all architectural education in academia needs to promote specific participatory approaches, but it is recommended that the social role of architecture be more clearly identified in academic and professional training syllabi, creating the possibility for those in architectural education who have an interest in wider social participation to strengthen the engagement with this in academic education and research. This would entail engagement with associated and relevant sets of knowledge and literatures than those currently engaged with, as highlighted in the wider literature review. The statutory Architects' Registration Board (ARB) could facilitate this by including a criterion or competency to this effect in the requirements for prescribing academic awards in architecture.[2]

Such a broader, syllabus-based approach would permit a range of different aspects of the relationship between architecture and society to be developed, including specific skills for social participation, as is now becoming more common in planning schools. To do this, as noted in the relevant academic case studies, entails some real engagement between students and clients/users/wider public and this can present some difficulties due to the nature of academic calendars. The way this has been resolved in the UK case studies, and as noted in the US through the wider literature review, has been through having architecture practices closely associated with the schools/departments. In some cases these have a specific social orientation, but in fact this may not be necessary and most schools of architecture will have at least sessional members of staff engaged in studio activities which might provide a vehicle for such work. Care is needed to ensure that these initiatives do not undermine existing practices through unpaid student work, although this may provide missing resources for participatory engagement.

Profession

Obviously, professional organisations play a role in changing attitudes across the profession in practice. This may be through supporting the changes in education recommended above, as well as through promoting an extension of the skills training aspect in existing practices by making this available through continuing professional development (CPD). As the profession engages with public bodies and policy-making institutions, it can also adopt a role in promoting attitudinal change within these bodies concerning the role of the architect. This is especially relevant given the impact of public–private initiatives in the procurement and management of buildings and the need to promote indirect participation, as well as to ensure the continuing (and even increased) possibility for direct user/social participation in the architectural process.

Recommendations for the profession are:

1   To stress the importance of user and social participation in the brief development and design stages of the professional Plan of Work.

2   To consider the viability of reasserting the importance of a post-completion feedback stage within the Plan of Work (including engaging more with facilities management issues).

3   To promote the role of social engagement with architecture in education and continuing professional development – including participatory skills training.

4   To consider other mechanisms which encourage architects to engage with (participate in, develop and/or use) other generic forms of knowledge that represent indirect participation. This latter aspect would include promoting the systematic 'capture' of experiential knowledge/research within architecture practice and the wider dissemination of it.

5   Action on some of these recommendations entails recognition that the commercial imperatives which drive private practice can mitigate against investing time in post-completion analysis and sharing experiential knowledge.

While not having the key to unlock adequate resources for permitting and encouraging direct and/or indirect wider social participation in architectural design, the profession plays an extremely important role in lobbying for such resources to be made available. This might be through fees, promoting a separate brief development aspect of the Plan of Work at least for complex and large-scale architectural buildings/programmes, reinforcing the need for post-completion feedback in the fee structure, providing guidance on pro bono activity and finding resources to stimulate practice-based and other forms of knowledge development, transfer and research, especially from major client bodies. Concerning practices, it may well be that only a minority aspire to widening social participation in the architectural design process. This may only change over time through a change in attitudes, a growth in demand for such participation, and structural changes in work availability, practice size and so on. However, this study recommends that architects who have this aspiration should be encouraged and not discouraged from such practice. Receiving support from the profession in this respect, especially in structuring the needed resources, is particularly relevant in complex public–private and large-scale procurement processes.

The study also proposes that the government and profession encourage architecture practices to invest in knowledge development and transfer through research in practice, using post-completion feedback as a source of knowledge not only for the specific client and practice but for the wider profession and public policy. Practices should be encouraged also to engage with publicly funded research and policy-making as ways of developing indirect participation. Both direct and indirect participation processes in architectural design require skills and, although some of these are embedded within education and practice such as the use of visualisation techniques, practices should be encouraged to invest in human resource development in social participation through CPD.

Policy-making institutions

As may be seen from the previous sections in this chapter there are a number of recommendations within which government, regulatory and other relevant public policy-making bodies can act to promote both direct and indirect wider social participation in the architectural design process. These institutions play important roles in: (1) promoting skills development; (2) providing direct and indirect resources to support activities; and (3) inducing attitudinal change across the wider public, private sector and profession.

Skills can be developed through regulation of professional training in academic schools/departments and inclusion of wider social aspects of architecture in curricula; assisting funding CPD activities, especially where these are directly relevant to large-scale public investment projects; and funding support for this through architecture centre(s) in promoting wider social engagement in architecture and related areas.

Resource provision should include research funding (or specific practice-oriented and generic research as well as support for civil society organisations in both specific and generic participatory activities – i.e. a reactive programme as noted in the conclusions above).[3]

Inducing attitudinal change across the wider public, private sector and profession needs to be through supporting regulation of public and public–private procurement processes to ensure adequate social engagement; and also promoting wider social information/consultation processes such as through architecture centres and public involvement in architectural competitions.

Future research ideas

The following are initial suggestions for future research arising from this study. There is a need for research that examines the nature of direct participation in current architecture projects, including community-based client bodies and urban regeneration projects, to understand the level and form of participation of users and wider social groups. This research should investigate good practice beyond the range of that investigated in case studies in the scoping project. Another necessary area of research is one that focuses on mechanisms for architecture practices to engage more actively in accessing generic information of relevance to practice, post-completion feedback on practice and the development of other forms of relevant design inputs from practice as well as mechanisms for transfer of such knowledge (i.e. the indirect forms of wider user-oriented participation).

The study has also highlighted the necessity of continued research into the nature of public participation in wider public engagement with architecture such as architecture centres and architecture competitions – including experience in other parts of Europe – as a means to encourage wider public participation in architecture in the UK. Of specific importance in the light of recent major public investment programmes, there is also a need for research that focuses on the changing processes for procurement of new buildings (including the planning process) and the impact this has on user and wider society participation. Potentially related to this will be research into how corporate clients engage with their own building users in brief development.

Finally, there should be continued research to support wider understanding of social participation in architecture through associated literatures identified as relevant in the scoping study and investigating the wider international experience. This would contribute to the possible new architectural training syllabus focus on architecture and society, recommended above.

Concluding remarks

The key message of this research for the contemporary policy environment, current practice context and also actual educational practice is how the historical, geographical, wider disciplinary and practical (case study) experiences presented, analysed and channelled into recommendations in the study can be brought together more effectively. On the one hand, the evolving policy environment reflects both political and economic structural change and has inherent contradictions in relation to direct and indirect user participation as well as wider social participation in architecture. On the other hand, there is a continuing strand of participatory agency in architectural practice which seems to be reviving with a strong social and cultural emphasis. In parallel, there is limited emphasis in the education process on these issues, let alone the engagement with academic resources in related disciplines.

At the risk of over-simplifying, the key is perhaps in how we see the role of the architect vis-à-vis the client, user and wider society. If architects see themselves as avant-garde specialists, they will resist policy influence unless forced to act differently (through, for instance, economics) – and in this they potentially lose ground in relation to other built environment professionals. If also, in this self-perception, architects decry the values of clients, users and wider society, they will resist wider, and earlier, communication of ideas and options as well as negotiation on decisions and limit direct participation in the architectural process. In addition, the essentially competitive and exclusionary nature of such an avant-garde position will lead architects to avoid collaboration with each other in – for instance – creating common knowledge bases or drawing on generic knowledge sources. In this (continued) scenario, some architects who have a particular interest in social issues will continue to engage in participatory activities, and government will continue to set the scene for and against these activities with little coherent input from the profession – and as such this form of 'community architecture' or 'community technical aid' will retain a niche role in policy, practice and education.

On the other hand, if architects perceive their role as providing an important and specialised service to society, which entails an understanding of social values and interests both in the particular and general, as well as the role of government in addressing social issues, the social nature of architecture can become embedded as a normal and not a niche role – without in any way detracting from the value of the continuing specialised knowledge that architects are trained in and should practice. In this scenario good architectural practice would naturally encompass user and wider social participation (as well as that of the client) and architects would be aware of, and engage with, the processes associated with participatory design and production of buildings. This would of course be expressed in a wide range of ways as architects, buildings, clients and societies are complex and interact in complicated ways. Having a firm grounding in the relationship between architecture and society in education would be essential to this approach. As such, rather than architects as self-defined avant-garde specialists encountering an increasingly restricted role in the wider built environment, wider social participation in architecture would become an everyday issue and more fully represent a broader and deeper role for architects in society.

Notes

1 The main mechanisms for this were through the Steering Group, with representatives from architectural practices and policy and professional organisations as well as academics, and the Focus Group Discussion Events, with representatives from a wider set of policy and professional organisations, social and private sector actors and voluntary organisations (in Scotland and the UK generally). These were followed by two participatory workshop dissemination events, when interested parties were encouraged to participate with a view to identifying priorities for action and key actors in relation to these priorities. The workshops were open to the wider public and advertised through the two hosting organisations.

2 The range of such knowledge could also be reinforced through some form of social networking, for example, a dedicated conference or other more constant resource (such as a specific research/teaching/training/information and/or web-based resource), perhaps shared across architecture centres. This could bring in practice experience, thus helping to cross academia and practice approaches.

3 Such state–society programmes exist in various countries, the US social architecture experience being such a case – albeit where significant resources are also made available from private charitable organisations.

Appendix I

Relevance of the study to the contemporary policy and practice context in Scotland

Paul Jenkins, Marcia Pereira and Tim Sharpe

Introduction

As noted in the Introduction to this book, part of the initial impetus for proposing this scoping study was the policy environment where government and related policy organisations are encouraging the promotion of participation by users in building design (mainly focused on public buildings such as health and education, but also residential design) and wider understanding of, and engagement with, architecture in society (through – for instance – architecture centres).

In addition, there continues to be an interest in user participation in architectural practices, with new forms of activities as well as focus, in a very different general context from the 1970s and 1980s 'heyday' of community architecture and community technical aid. While these initiatives are very important, their impact is still relatively limited and in fact there seem to be some major challenges to their wider social and practice impact. This research – as well as future work on the subject – is seen as highly relevant in helping these new practices to situate their experiences not only within a historical context but also within a broader contemporary picture. As such, the final section of the book briefly reviews some new initiatives within which the study may have an impact as an example in Scotland.

Contemporary policy environment

Examples of policy initiatives include the Scottish government's Architecture Policy Unit activities through The Lighthouse (Scotland's Centre for Architecture, Design and the City). These have – for instance – focused on engaging wider social groups in school design, through the Future Learning and Teaching (FLaT) programme.[1] There have been a variety of activities in this area targeted at the large-scale new investment in educational buildings, much of which is through public–private partnerships (PPPs). These have included publications such as design guidance and web-based resources. In addition, The Lighthouse hosted an exhibition 'Senses of Place: Building Excellence' (February to April 2008) which highlighted the outcomes of a series of workshops, under the government's 'Curriculum for Excellence', in which teachers, pupils and other school users from five local authorities across Scotland worked with leading Scottish architects and designers to influence the design of learning spaces for the future.[2]

These initiatives are highlighted in the Scottish government's new statement on architecture policy of 2007, *Building Our Legacy*, based on a review of the previous policy document (Scottish Government 2001). This new architecture policy statement highlights the need to provide a supportive climate for debate on architecture and an appreciation of the role architecture plays in society as well as to encourage community involvement in architecture.

> In order to create a climate in which good design in the built environment is the rule rather than the exception, we need to continue to raise public awareness of the value of good design, and to encourage greater interest, debate and involvement in built environment issues.
>
> (Scottish Government 2007: 37)

The main vehicle for this in Scotland has been The Lighthouse, through exhibitions, workshops, seminars/talks, a website (www.scottisharchitecture.com) and downstream funding of projects. This includes a new ACCESS to architecture campaign, following on from previous activities, focusing on two main activities: (1) promotion of the best new architecture, young talent, emerging trends and topics for debate by means of exhibitions, publications, digital resources and other events; and (2) a programme of outreach and community engagement aimed at bringing the debate about architecture into the heart of local communities throughout Scotland.

While there has thus been considerable success in engaging with users and wider society in the architectural design process for some schools in Scotland, the key issues highlighted in the current policy environment are the need to encourage more local authorities to undertake such participatory design processes and provide resources for these, as well as the building of capacity to widen such programmes (i.e. requiring resources and skills in various organisations). A similar initiative potentially needs to be developed with regard to residential design, and here again the Architecture Policy Unit has initiated activity, through commissioning research into the perception of, attitudes to and practice in design within the private sector housing developers across Scotland. This research identifies key issues for changing the focus on private housing development to place 'design at the heart of house building'.[3] The research potentially opens up a debate concerning how residential design can be better developed, including the role of direct user participation and indirect generic housing demand research.

Concerning wider social participation in architecture across the UK, while there is as yet only one architecture centre in Scotland, there are 22 in the rest of the UK.[4] As such, this is still a relatively limited resource and widening the social impact requires more initiative being taken at local level. Due to state budgetary limitations, such initiatives do not have to be – and probably cannot be – of the nature and scale of nationally funded resources such as The Lighthouse or CABE, but can be based on voluntary, private sector and local authority, as well as on central government, initiative. Apart from resource centres sponsored, or supported, by government, other initiatives may include design champions and design panels which can create interfaces between local government, private sector, professional and wider public interests. Key to the success of design champions is their clear role within the decision-making processes – i.e. not just a role concerning information and consultation.

Another example of UK-wide governmental initiative in widening social participation, which has been extensively debated, is the Building Schools for the Future (BSF) Programme, aiming to rebuild or renew nearly every secondary school in England. According to the government, 'every child will be educated in a 21st Century environment within 15 years' (Office of the Prime Minister 2004). Considered to be an ambitious programme due to its aims, costs – worth £2.2 billion in its first year, 2005 to 2006 (Teachernet 2007) – and timescale, this has significant support from politicians. However, it also faces criticism, for example, on their procurement methods (also PPP), among other issues (Abrams 2007). But more relevant to this work are the complaints from practitioners, who argue that there is not enough time within the process that can be allocated for a proper engagement with users, risking a tokenistic approach to participation.

Contemporary practice context[5]

Concerning continuing interests in architecture practices to engage directly with users in design, there is evidence of a growth of this practice in relation to workplace design (e.g. the increasing engagement with architects to develop briefs and building programmes prior to the commissioning of design[6]), and the government sponsors such community participation in urban regeneration projects. However, there seem to be growing challenges to the direct participation of users in other forms of social housing. The trend to increasing volume and speed of delivery through consolidation of housing associations is such a situation, for example, in Glasgow, where the creation of the Glasgow Housing Association in 2003 is leading to implementation of processes which reduce the funding and time for architecture practices engaging with tenant communities, as has been the tradition for some three decades.

'Firm Foundations' is a draft paper from the new Scottish government on the future of housing from a central perspective, proposing major changes in the way in which social housing/area regeneration is developed and procured. While there are strong and positive aims within this strategy (e.g. higher quality and increased delivery), the push towards lower cost, larger-scale provision and centralised development may well detract from these aims. Focusing on the unit cost of housing as the main criterion could lead to shorter-life-less desirable housing provided through a mass-procurement process with little local input or contact, leading to local people playing almost no part in a major element of area regeneration – housing. In addition, the current policy focus on the need to design and deliver successful places could be sidelined in faster larger-scale procurement processes. Centralisation and predominant use of private developers as the main new housing delivery mechanisms – rather than decentralised social housing providers – will undermine traditions of community and governance in housing associations which have long-term commitment to housing, unlike any private sector provider. As a result the strong history of participation and community involvement in social housing provision in Scotland, with a number of architectural firms providing socially participatory design, is at risk in the new approach. On the contrary, the future validity of the community-based model for area and housing regeneration should re-emphasise the importance of process, while not detracting from delivery.

While the above focuses on contemporary practice context in Scotland, similar tensions exist across the UK. The most important issues which concern practices that consciously attempt to carry out participatory exercises which promote direct user engagement in the architectural design process are those regarding: time for and costs of participation (issues associated with the non-statutory status of participation in architecture and to the existing procurement processes); and the need for cultural change, where clients in particular become more conscious of the value of participation.

Notes

1 The 'Sustainable Schools Project'-funded FLaT Programme explored new design scenarios for school buildings through a workshop-based model centred on real schools, with collaboration between local authorities, international and local design professionals, teachers and young people themselves. See www.scotland.gov.uk/Topics/ArtsCulture/arch/schooldesign and www.flatprojects.org.uk/index.asp. One example of stakeholder consultation in school design is the Carlibar Community Campus, East Renfrewshire. Here, exemplar designs had been commissioned by the local authority to guide the PPP process, and extensive consultation with stakeholders (parents, local residents, pupils, staff and unions) was held at regular intervals from the initial design brief through to construction over a period of four years.

2 The Senses of Place Programme was commissioned by the Schools Division at the Scottish government as part of their Building Excellence Programme. The local authorities involved in the project are Argyll and Bute, North Lanarkshire, Orkney Islands, Stirling and West Lothian working alongside architects and designers 3DReid, DEGW, Gareth Hoskins Architects, JM Architects and Sam Booth, and Lisa MacKenzie.

3 This research was published in 2008, and was undertaken by a consortium of higher education institutions based in Edinburgh, led by the School of the Built Environment (Heriot-Watt University), with the Architecture School at Edinburgh College of Art/ScotMARK and Architecture at Edinburgh University. See www.scotland.gov.uk/Publications/2007/11/08110758/0.

4 See www.architecturecentre.net/directory.asp.

5 Practices on the project Steering Group and who attended the participatory workshops have contributed to this section.

6 These were highlighted in the Royal Incorporation of Architects in Scotland's Health and Happiness research project. This pilot project was initiated by an in-depth literature review which set the conceptual basis for presentations and workshops in a research seminar. The findings from the literature, together with the ideas discussed and presented in the conference, form part of the first of a series of publications based on similar projects for knowledge development that the RIAS has began to produce.

Institutional resources

*Joanne Milner, Marcia Pereira and
Leanne Townsend*

The Architecture Centre Network

The Network provides opportunities for over one million people in the UK to engage in activities related to the built environment. A number of Architecture and Built Environment Centres (ABECs) are currently active across the UK. The purpose of these centres is to increase education and involvement in design and planning of the built environment. The Architecture Centre Network is responsible for coordinating and managing the activities of these centres, having as a key agenda built environment education and the engagement of young people in issues relating to this (www.architecturecentre.net).

Example: Knowle West Media Centre (KWMC), Bristol

This is a community centre which brings the local community the resources to engage in photography, film and digital media activities. It occupies a run-down 1950s medical building. The building itself has become a barrier to the progress of the initiative, and a new building was decided upon. As the KWMC staff had little experience of design/architecture, they approached the Bristol Architecture Centre (2004). The project's main priority was the involvement of local young people in every aspect of the design of the new building. A 'core group' of young people was asked to identify their priorities (e.g. sustainable building, cutting-edge design). They were walked around the city to discuss architecture and taken to London's South Bank and the Centre for Alternative Technology (CAT) in Wales. They were even involved in the selection of the architectural firm. The new building was scheduled for completion in early 2007.

*Example: Regeneration of East Dunbartonshire's School Estate,
The Lighthouse, Glasgow*

There was a procurement of six new schools in this area. A commitment was made early on in the process to engage all school users/members in the process, particularly pupils of the schools. One of the people involved attended a three-day conference at The Lighthouse on the best practice in developing new schools. This introduced him to the architecture centre. A brief was then produced with The Lighthouse. The schools themselves identified pupils who would be interested and motivated. Younger pupils discussed the use of materials and colour, and the older pupils worked directly with architects on issues of space, form, layout and so on. The first school was due for completion in 2008 and it was hoped that pupils' involvement would remain high until completion.

The Architecture Foundation

The Architecture Foundation is the UK's first independent architecture centre and was established in 1991. Aiming at actively bridging the gap between decision-makers, design professionals and the public, it organises numerous projects, which have included over 100 public exhibitions, design initiatives, competitions and debates, attracting a large number of people. Organising debates with famous and influential practitioners, it also generates a variety of publications. It is a registered charity and has a growing membership of supporters and a Board of Trustees composed of individuals from a wide cross-section of interests and professions – design and architecture, the arts, media, education and business. The Architecture Foundation is an active member of the national Architecture Centre Network (www.architecturefoundation.org.uk).

Example: the Architecture Foundation 'School Works' project

'School Works' was a 'design initiative' project generated by the Architecture Foundation aiming to explore the relationship between educational achievement and the built environment. The school selected for the project was Kingsdale School, Southwark SE2. The project started in December 1998 and finished in January 2001. As part of the Architecture Foundation ethos, a participatory design process was started, with the participation of school pupils, staff, as well as of the extended school community. The school management, the architects (dRMM) and constructors (Galliford Try) were able to develop a rich partnership and the project, developed in stages, achieved enormous success. The school buildings received a series of design awards and, more importantly, the school improved considerably, being now the highest achieving community school in Southwark in the National GCSE League Tables. For more details, please see the Kingsdale School case study in Chapter 5.

Asian Neighbourhood Design

Asian Neighbourhood Design (AND) was founded in 1973 by Asian architecture students at Berkeley California. They started using teaching cabinetry to high school drop-outs via the Comprehensive Employment and Training Act (CETA) and also used federal grants to help with housing rehabilitations in Chinatown. With the decline in federal funding in 1981, they decided to sell their architectural design and furniture-building services. They then became the architects for most of the housing rehabilitation projects undertaken by non-profit organisations, due to their past experience with communities. Their work evolved over time to provide a wider set of community development services such as family and youth (including employment creation), community planning and development, and construction management services. They play a key role in the participatory process, even prior to the selection of the architect, and work through the whole building programme with the client/user (Blake 2003) (www.andnet.org).

ASSIST

ASSIST Architects is a cooperatively run architectural practice with over 30 years' experience in sustainable design, social housing and community regeneration. With offices in Glasgow and Edinburgh, it provides a successful participatory design service to both community-led organisations and the private sector.

Example: Clovenstone Park, Wester Hailes, Edinburgh

Completed in 2001, this work was developed in collaboration with Wester Hailes Community Housing Association, City of Edinburgh Council (CEC), Scottish Homes and Clovenstone Tenants Group. The primary purpose of the commission was to produce a detailed master plan for the area that addressed the issues facing the local community, gain the support of the key partner organisations and propose a programme for implementation. ASSIST carried out a detailed house condition survey and a disruptive survey of each house type, ensuring a full knowledge of the existing structures. The aim was to develop a plan that achieved social and physical integration within an existing community, involving comprehensive refurbishment, demolition, new-build and environmental improvements, according to the guiding principals of sustainability, community and visual integration, design quality, affordability and marketability. Public consultation was a key feature of the redevelopment process, with regular reporting to the Steering Group, open days, design workshops and planning weekends. The process was successful in achieving a common vision for the area, which was embraced by all stakeholders involved.

For more information see the ASSIST case study in Chapter 6 (www.assistarchitects.co.uk).

Association for Community Design

The Association for Community Design (ACD) was formed in 1977 in the USA and holds an annual conference as well as Internet site and forum, supporting community design centres (CDCs) in capacity-building in architecture and planning across a range of base organisations such as universities, NGOs and other 'not-for-profits'. ACD has individuals, organisations and institutions as members, all sharing in common a commitment to increase the capacity of design and planning professions to better serve communities (www.communitydesign.org).

Collective Architecture

Collective Architecture, an architectural practice based in Glasgow, was originally established in 1997 as Chris Stewart Architects. It was decided to formalise its working approach to become Collective Architecture in February 2007. The company is owned by an employee-run trust, which intends to regard and further involve staff in the development of the practice. It has been working successfully throughout the UK with private and public clients aiming to generate buildings which are environmentally and socially sustainable.

Example: Moorpark Regeneration

Having the Williamsburg Housing Association as client, this project (2006) involved the integration of a significant part of the primarily residential area of Moorpark in Renfrew. Fifty-four new-build houses and flats were constructed along with 24 tenement flats that were refurbished. Key to the design process was an involved community consultation. This effective relationship with the community was maintained and the design of the housing reflects the tenants' needs, but remains simple, cost-effective, and flexible for conversion to future needs. An emphasis was made in promoting further community involvement and efficiency via the use of local companies and materials (www.collectivearchitecture.com).

Commission for Architecture and the Built Environment (CABE)

CABE is the government's adviser on architecture, urban design and public space, aiming to improve people's quality of life through good design and via its work with their main stakeholder groups: policy-makers; planners and councillors; developers and designers; clients; and the public. CABE strives to support all these stakeholders, inspiring the public to get involved in the design process, and documenting and disseminating the experiences. Set up in 1999, CABE is funded by two government departments: Department for Culture, Media and Sports; and Department for Communities and Local Government (www.cabe.org.uk).

Examples: CABE report: Better Public Building (2006)

This report is based on a philosophy that good design should benefit everyone. It stresses that not only is user participation an important part of the design process, it is the responsibility of clients as well as architects to ensure that users are given *enough* of a say in the end-product:

> User involvement can be poorly planned: Involving end-users and stakeholders early and often in the design process is a key part of delivering a successful project and so clients need to ensure that this happens. Failure to involve them enough is likely to diminish opportunities for improving service delivery. It runs the risk of delivering buildings that do not work for the people using them.
>
> (CABE 2006: 10)

The role of the client in ensuring good-quality design is further stressed and the report states that guidelines are provided to ensure good design and assist with a participatory approach to the project:

> Ultimately, the responsibility for delivering high-quality projects rests with the client ... Thanks to CABE and the Construction Industry Council, specific help is now available in recognising good design. The design quality indicator, or DQI, is a tool that all public sector clients should use in assessing the value of design in delivering a public sector building. The DQI poses set questions to help assess the quality of a design.

Clients should use the DQI early in the consideration of a project to help structure discussion, establish shared design aspirations and feed into the brief.

(CABE 2006: 23)

Comtechsa

Specialised in working with communities and based in Manchester, Comtechsa is a non-profit-making cooperative society working in Merseyside and surrounding areas, aiming to help community groups and voluntary organisations make the best use of their land, buildings and environment; and to provide high-quality, fully accessible accommodation for community groups and voluntary organisations. Comtechsa typically has worked closely with clients and users since its foundation in 1979 on everything from nurseries to community centres, redevelopments and renovations. It is an important requisite of every project that a consensus is built among community members and design professionals.

For further information on Comtechsa and examples of their work see Comtechsa case study in Chapter 6 (www.comtechsa.org).

Community Places (previously called Belfast CTA)

Community Places, which was called Belfast CTA until 1 April 2008, is a not-for-profit voluntary organisation based in Belfast. It provides advice on planning issues to disadvantaged communities and support to community planning, consultation, research and building projects.

One of its aims is to improve participation among disadvantaged communities. Participation in this sense relates to planning and public policy-making. Involved with the new power of community planning which is to be implemented by the government, it is vocal in advising on the way in which this new power should be used to empower local communities with increased engagement in planning decisions and processes.

Community Places provides assistance to community groups and projects through:

- planning support for community groups;
- planning advice for individuals;
- community planning;
- community consultation and engagement;

- advice on community building projects;
- research and strategy development.

Example: Lisburn Road, South Belfast

There are a number of active community groups in this street – an area with a busy community life housing shops, pubs, restaurants and cafés. The areas around this street have become attractive to young people, particularly students. This has impacted, often in a negative sense, on the once stable family life of the area. One community group focused its efforts on the impact of an increasing number of multiple occupancy households (e.g. those occupied by students and young professionals). CTA was approached for help in facilitating a community exercise session to assist the community group to assess the impact of these households. Issues to arise were traffic, change in local character, noise and antisocial behaviour. A number of actions resulted, including the implementation of a code of conduct at the university. The group also succeeded in lowering the government's target for the area in terms of multiple household occupancies from 30 to 20 per cent of total households (www.communityplaces.info).

Community Self-Build Agency

Created from the success of a 1985 self-build project in Bristol, this agency provides opportunities for communities to build their own homes. People are encouraged to participate in every stage of the project and gain skills along the way. Self-builders are usually not existing home owners, and tend to be in low-income or unemployed groups.

Example: Darwin Road, Tilbury

Tilbury Self-Build Project, Darwin Road, Tilbury, enabled ten young unemployed people to build their own homes and also provided 'National Vocational Qualifications' (NVQ) training. The scheme, which was supported by New Essex Housing Association, a subsidiary of New Islington and Hackney Housing Association, was successful in helping the self-builders find paid work and realised many of the positive benefits associated with self-build (www.communityselfbuildagency.org.uk).

Department of Architecture and Spatial Design at London Metropolitan University (LMU)

The architecture course at LMU is one of the very few in the UK which has participation embedded into the curriculum and a dedicated module on participation. The participatory approach is used in several design studios, and students have the opportunity to work on real design projects, with real clients, resulting in real buildings being built. There is also an in-house architectural office, which facilitates the involvement of students and staff in real projects.

The module on participation entitled 'Design: From Participation to Realisation' is a 30-credit module which introduces a variety of techniques in the practice of participatory design and aims at getting students working with a range of relevant projects and tasks.

Several architectural offices which carry out work with a strong focus on user participation run studios within the department, such as 'erect architecture', 'Fluid', 'East' and 'Public Works'. Live Projects are an essential part of different design studios, where students become involved with real clients and users.

For more information and examples of Live Projects carried out within the LMU architecture course, please see (www.londonmet.ac.uk).

Detroit Collaborative Design Center

The Detroit Collaborative Design Center (DCDC) was established in 1994 as a non-profit subsidiary of the School of Architecture at the University of Detroit-Mercy. It focuses on education in an undergraduate neighbourhood design studio, providing internships for students. DCDC provides services to non-profit organisations at neighbourhood level. The focus is on organisational capacity-building and education collaborative design processes, bringing together the main stakeholders in architectural design (e.g. funding organisations, community organisations and residents). The design work has won a range of awards from local to national level (www.arch.udmercy.edu).

Fluid

An architectural and urban design practice established in 1996 and based in London, Fluid offers an approach to urban regeneration and architecture that builds on participation as a key to the production of sustainable communities and high-quality design. Fluid believes that a commitment to consultation and participatory processes adds value by ensuring that there is a match between community, stakeholder and client demands, and a deliverable design outcome.

Fluid is an architectural practice, which works as a think-tank and a research unit, bringing together architects, interior designers, urbanists and academics. The practice wants to help define a new approach to the generation of urban design. It sees public consultation, dialogue and participation as central to the design process and it uses a wide variety of methods of engagement. It is its view that new technologies and change in traditional methods of working provide opportunities to address social and spatial problems in innovative ways. However, Fluid also recognises the need to provide different ways to generate participation. Younger people react better to digital media, with computers playing an important role in provoking their engagement in the design process. Finally, according to Ciron, Fluid has been working with a variety of projects, where it is involved with innovative methods of consultation, aiming to give communities affected by change an opportunity to make real decisions.

Example: 2012 Olympic bid – the Lower Lee Valley

In May 2003 the government decided to bid for the 2012 Olympic Games, and settled on the Lower Lea Valley as the site for the Olympic Precinct. Fluid is a member of the EDAW consortium[1] appointed to masterplan the project and to make the necessary applications. Fluid had responsibility for all aspects of partner, stakeholder and community consultation, and for ensuring the master-plans were shaped in accordance with the consultation outcomes. Ongoing consultation targeted residential groups that would be affected were the games to come to London. The brief required the definition of a robust consultation strategy that would engage key partners, the major stakeholders and local communities whose input would be directly fed into the masterplanning team. Fluid was also required to work with several other major stakeholders to ensure broad programme alignments, and to identify and build synergies with existing regeneration projects and initiatives. As an outcome a 'Statement of Community Involvement' for one of the largest consultation exercises ever carried out in England for an area-based regeneration project was produced. Fluid has continued to work on the Residents Relocation Strategy and extensive accommodation needs surveys and reports have been completed with members of a 450-home housing co-op and residents of two traveller communities within the Lower Lea Valley (www.fluidoffice.com).

The Glass-House community-led design

The Glass-House is a registered charity based in London. It supports and encourages better working partnerships among communities and professionals who are working together to improve the quality of a neighbourhood. They offer design advice, training and project support to projects focusing on neighbourhoods, housing, public space, community buildings, play areas and facilities for young people.

They aim to:

- provide communities with the tools to lead the design process;
- give design, housing and regeneration professionals the tools to work more effectively with user groups on the design of regeneration projects that affect them;
- promote a wider understanding and practice of community-led design.

Example: Townsend, Stoke on Trent, England

Townsend is a residential area in Stoke on Trent with a lot of young families and few facilities for young people. The Townsend Residents Association was set up in July 2002. Their plans were to see two playgrounds successfully installed, to raise money for a sports pitch and teenage hang-out area, and to get a community house fully up and running. The group first attended a Spaces by Design course, one of the courses provided by The Glass-House, which subsequently provided them with information on fundraising, helping them to write an action plan and to draw up a design for the community garden, based on what the residents told them they wanted. Townsend Residents Association has also been awarded a Glass-House grant of £2600 to buy tools and materials for the community garden. Once the garden is set up, the tools will be available for hire to local people. The Association worked closely with the play workers at Stoke Council to regenerate the local park into a play area/recreation area for all ages. A fun day was organised, when the local kids were consulted about what kind of play equipment they liked best. The first two playgrounds have been designed and drawn up by the council. All the funding has been secured, including £50,000 from the Neighbourhood Renewal Fund, and funding from the Single Regeneration Budget (SRB2) and Sure Start. They are currently applying for funding for the teenagers' hang-out and kick-about area. They are working with the local secondary school, who own part of the site, so that the sports pitch may be used by both the school and the local community. Townsend community house is now open and it is very popular with the community. The community house attracts up to 40 young people a night and hosts a senior citizens' group. They are also planning to start up a mothers' and toddlers' group and a 'teen-time' youth forum. The Townsend resident community group was awarded 'Community of the Year' in 2003 (www.theglasshouse.org.uk).

The Lighthouse

Opened in July 1999 and located in Glasgow, The Lighthouse is Scotland's first national centre for architecture and design. A charitable trust, it draws its income from a combination of public and private funds. From an annual turnover of £2.5 million, around £1 million is derived from government grants to promote its Architecture Policy for Scotland.

With a strong belief in the transformational power of architecture and design to improve people's lives, The Lighthouse organises interesting exhibitions which stimulate interest and debate, attempting to engage the public and professionals. With the aim of creating a culture of learning and professionalism based on excellence and critical thinking, it organises a series of activities, also including festivals, lectures, talks, debates, events, seminars, conferences, networking events, building and city tours, awards, publications and product development.

Example: The 'Senses of Place: Building Excellence' project

This project was commissioned by the Scottish government, aiming to demonstrate the great value of involving children and young people in the school design from an early stage. This project, led by Anne Cunningham and Kate Kenyon, began with the thesis that 'if designers are skilful and the procurement method is conducive – the key to unlocking good design must be effective consultation between all of the key stakeholders'. The book (*Senses of Place: Building Excellence – The Toolkit and Outcomes*) as well as the exhibition (21 February to 13 April 2008) show the outcomes of a series of workshops, in which teachers, pupils and other school users from five local authorities across Scotland have worked with leading Scottish architects and designers to influence the design of learning spaces for the future (www.thelighthouse.co.uk).

MIND – improving mental health environments

MIND – a mental health charity in England and Wales – is working to improve the lives of those experiencing mental distress. In May 2006 MIND held focus groups across England and Wales to evaluate the state of health environments, according to users. It came to the conclusion that service users should be involved in the design of new hospitals and that guidelines as to the best way forward should be produced by the Department of Health and NHS Wales. Based on this research, MIND itself has compiled a list of key recommendations, which includes that patients should be regularly consulted in order to give them a chance to improve their own healthcare environments.

Example: SEED (Supporting Environment Encouraging Development) Group

This is an award-winning Morecambe Bay project to redevelop mental health services at a hospital in Lancaster. Service users were involved in the redevelopment process and engaged with architects, for example, to find ways of providing single bedrooms where they had originally been told that none were possible. Personalisation of space with ornaments and soft furnishings (e.g. squishy bean bags) was in evidence through the choices of the service users. Furniture appears less institutionalised and more personal and homely. This approach has challenged the traditional rigidity of the design of mental health facilities (www.mind.org.uk – See the report: 'Building Solutions: Environments for Better Mental Health. Improving Mental Healthcare Environments').[2]

Minnesota Design Team

Minnesota Design Team (MDT) is a volunteer organisation formed in 1983 which works across a range of activities vis-à-vis the built environment from regional planning to interior design, as well as economic development, tourism and so on. Volunteer teams composed of architects, urban designers, planners and other experts in design and community development engage in action research with communities (expenses being partly paid by the community) and in 'charrette'-type community design processes with a focus on implementation methods. They also provide follow-up progress monitoring (www.minnesotadesignteam.org).

Neighbourhood Initiatives

Neighbourhood Initiatives (NI) is a national charity based in Telford, Shropshire, specialising in community participation, training and development. NI works with local authorities, housing associations, voluntary agencies and community groups.

NI attempts to find simple, effective ways to involve unempowered people in decisions affecting their own neighbourhood. NI provides an external, independent approach, working with and through local groups, voluntary bodies and public bodies to effect lasting change.

Example: Sheppey Heritage Trust

The Neighbourhood Initiatives Foundation was appointed in December 2006, by Sheppey Heritage Trust, to undertake a community consultation exercise to support the development of the final stage application to the Big Lottery Living Landmarks Fund for the Flying Start project. The Flying Start project seeks to mark the Isle of Sheppey's place in aviation history by developing a facility that is of local, national and international interest. The existing buildings at the former Eastchurch Aerodrome and airfield, which was, until recently, the Prison Farm for HMP Stanford Hill Open Prison, will be transformed into a touristic attraction, a centre for courses, conferences and sport facilities, among others. There is a strong training element proposed within the project, and this makes it still more relevant to target the consultation to enable the inclusion of young people's views. Prisoners of the island open prison as well as other community members are involved in the project. The purpose of the consultation was to promote the opportunities for local people and visitors that will be available within this new facility. Local people were also able to highlight facilities and training opportunities that could be provided within the new facility and that would fill existing gaps and benefit people of all ages and abilities. The engagement of local people from an early stage in the project is seen as an opportunity to develop a 'local ownership' of the facilities and a commitment from the surrounding community to take advantage of the opportunities provided, therefore ensuring their long-term sustainability (www.nif.co.uk).

Nick Wates Associates and communityplanning.net

Nick Wates Associates is a company specialised in public engagement in planning and urban design, undertaking consultancy on a wide range of regeneration and planning issues as well as conducting research and producing good practice materials. Working with public, private and voluntary sector organisations, both in the UK and overseas, they provide the following services:

- design and facilitation of community involvement strategies for all kinds of environmental, planning and design projects;
- productions of books, reports, newsletters, feasibility studies and websites – complete service including research, writing, design and production;
- training workshops and seminars.

Nick Wates, who leads all projects, has over 25 years' experience in the field and is the author of important books and other resources on community participation (see the Bibliographic resources list, Appendix II).

Examples: Petersfield Town design statement; Bristol Re:Invigorate workshop facilitation; communityplanning.net

The work for Petersfield, Hampshire, was initiated in March 2007 and consists of training and advice on the production of a Town Design Statement for Petersfield Tomorrow. Bristol Re:Invigorate project (March 2007) consisted of the planning and facilitation of a workshop in the Filwood neighbourhood. An extensive list of projects and publications may be found on its website.

Communityplanning.net is a website owned and managed by Nick Wates Associates, which contains an extensive amount of resources and how-to-do-it best practice information of international scope and relevance in community planning and participation
(www.nickwates.co.uk and www.communityplanning.net).

Peabody Trust

The Peabody Trust aims to 'provide homes that people love, in communities residents are proud to live in'.[3] The Trust works with people of all ages on engaging community activities to develop their skills and enable them to contribute to their community.

Founded in 1862 by American philanthropist George Peabody, the Trust owns and manages nearly 18,500 properties across London, providing affordable homes for over 50,000 people. It has many award-winning buildings, such as Beaufort Court, a multi-award-winning estate on Lillie Road in Hammersmith, and Fulham and Raines Court in Hackney, which is Peabody's second scheme to employ modular off-site construction using the Yorkon system.

Example: Engine Room

At the request of the Bricklayers Arms Tenants' Association which wanted to develop an ICT centre on its estate to bring long-term benefits to the residents and surrounding community, the Engine Room UK Online centre was set up. Initiated in 2003, the project received a grant from the Housing Corporation covering a two-year period. A training programme was developed for those wishing to be assistant trainers and for the management committee, incorporating all skills needed to run a successful project, including recruiting and managing staff, managing performance, fundraising and financial management, as the eventual aim was to hand over the centre to the Resident Management Committee to run as their own social enterprise.

The first few months of the project focused on the engagement of residents and local stakeholders, with the use of a series of outreach methods to engage hard-to-reach residents, promoting the centre and raising awareness of the courses and services available. As a first step towards encouraging people from the target groups to come in, 'hook' taster ICT sessions were set up and had a very positive response. Following on from this, residents were encouraged to become involved in the management committee, and those who were willing to join were offered training. Sixteen people showed interest in the training programme and in being part of the management committee. In addition, a range of activities aimed at young people and their parents were organised. The sessions were facilitated by the Trust's youth workers, who already had a relationship with young people on the estate via a football coaching scheme. Thirteen young people aged 14 to 18 took part. As a result a number of youth forums have been set up. A positive 'can-do' attitude has been developed within the community and, through the local management committee, residents feel empowered and engaged, being enthusiastic about managing their own centre and planning and delivering local training initiatives. The enterprise also helped half of the initial trained volunteers to find jobs (www.peabody.org.uk).

The Pratt Center

The Pratt Center for Community Development in Brooklyn, New York, is one of the oldest and longest running university-affiliated community design centres (CDCs) in the US. It was founded in 1963 and engages in technical assistance, education and policy advocacy (Curry 2004). The Pratt Planning and Architectural Collaborative, a division of the Pratt Center, was established in 1975 to provide design, development and planning services based on community organisation and mainly within affordable housing. The Pratt Center is linked to the architectural graduate programme of the Pratt Institute, with its teaching staff and students working in the Center. In 2003 there were some 20 full-time staff, including five architects and a number of planners, as well as an operating budget of around US$2 million (Blake 2003) (www.prattcenter.net).

The Prince's Foundation for the Built Environment

The Prince's Foundation is an educational charity which seeks to improve the quality of people's lives by teaching and practising timeless and ecological ways of planning, designing and building. It is based in London's East End.

Example: Castletown Village Masterplan Framework, Heritage and Regeneration Action Plan

A three-day enquiry was held by Design workshop to draw up a vision for the sustainable growth of Castletown and to integrate the reuse of redundant buildings. The workshop brought together key stakeholders including Castletown Community Council, Castletown Heritage Society and the Highland Council, as well as other local groups and residents.

The first day was spent listening to technical briefings related to the site including planning, housing, community facilities, tourism, business, landscape and ecology, heritage and local identity. Attendees then analysed the characteristics of the village in terms of the hierarchy of movement, walking distances and village structure. The groups subsequently focused on aspects of an emerging masterplan, including a subregional strategy; village structure; ecology and sustainability, and development around heritage buildings.

Throughout the second and third days, the groups continued to refine, test and redraw proposals through discussion with local people and local architects. The final products of the three days included a masterplan framework for the Castletown and Castlehill area, a landscape strategy, a movement strategy, a heritage and regeneration action plan and a phasing plan, accompanied by illustrative sketches (www.princes-foundation.org).

Public works

Defining themselves as an art/architecture collective practice, 'public works' consists of architects Sandra Denicke-Polcher, Torange Khonsari, Andreas Lang and artist Kathrin Bohm, who have been collaborating since 1998. Based in London, the practice has public participation as core to its working approach, with each project being a special opportunity to obtain users' participation in the design of their spaces. They develop a unique approach to each project, attempting to identify the potentials of each specific situation and context. They have been working on a series of projects with both public and private clients, who mainly contact them due to their participatory approach.

As Sandra Denicke-Polcher and Torange Khonsari[4] emphasise, the collaboration between architects and artists is essential to their work and allows them to achieve a transformative participation in their projects. Working 'in the fluid space between Art and Architecture', they use informal and playful forms of social engagement to facilitate community-led design. According to Torange,[5] 'full or transformative participation throws architects and the architectural profession outside its comfort zone', as 'in pursuit of aesthetics and efficiency, Architecture detaches itself from the everyday desires and needs of social life'. Unlike architects, however, artists do not have to be tied down to this type of obstacle or to professional practice codes of conduct, thus being more able to 'engage in producing change in collaboration with the community', acquiring better access to their everyday reality. More importantly, in the participatory art practice, 'value is given as much to the process of transforming the community as it is to the final product'. Torange cites four types of methodology, which they have been using:

1   Participation as a method of understanding social relationships in a particular place and the physical spaces these social networks create.
2   Participation as a method to set up and expand social networks in and around places, allowing for empowerment of individuals as part of a bigger group, being able to help sustain a social project.
3   Participation as a collaborative act to challenge mainstream aesthetic values held by both design professionals and citizens.
4   Participation as a method of testing programmes and future uses for a place.

Example: The Podium project, Bunhill Row, London

A collaborative architecture commission between Public Works and Diamond Architects, the Podium project was commissioned by EC1 New Deal for Communities. The aim was to improve the existing concrete landscape shared by Braithwaite House, a 1960s tower block, and Quaker Court, a low-rise estate, via the development of an urban landscape proposal. From the beginning, a community garden was specified. Two participation methods were employed: first, participation as a collaborative act to challenge mainstream aesthetic values held by design professionals and citizens; and second, participation as a method of testing programmes and future users for a place. A residency of the artist/architects took place in the foyer of tower blocks, where they could be in constant contact with the residents. They set up a wall where information was pasted daily and residents were invited to write comments and contribute to it. Planting and drawing workshops as well as baking events were organised to test their success and failures. All the information was compiled to set the brief. In the design collaboration phase, the foyer residence continued, after having the brief posted on the foyer wall for a week, for comments. Annotated flags were used to open up the debate about the location of various functions in a first platform for discussion. In a second platform about aesthetics, landscape design images were used. It was felt that the architect was seen as an expert rather than as a facilitator, and the architect's presence somehow inhibited the conversation. How to address aesthetic questions is still an open question. However, the narratives were translated into ad hoc models and collages, flags on models, and 1:1 drawings of the final proposal on-site, communicating the spatial and the functional brief, as well as the elements of the project, for more effective communication with the residents. The new proposed landscape is an infrastructure in which social programmes will be run. A community art strategy of residences with open briefs is being set up to take place after the physical proposals are built. Educational and cultural links with existing local cultural institutions' outreach programme will take place. Their overall aim is to create a space which works socially, culturally and spatially, becoming a space 'owned' by the residents (www.publicworksgroup.net).

School of Architecture at the University of Sheffield

The Sheffield School of Architecture is one of very few in the UK which has participation embedded into its curriculum. Very present within the school is the concern with the development of social skills, with students learning how to communicate well with clients and users, as well as the promotion of participation. The School also introduced 'Live Projects', which embed students into the whole process of participation, design and production.

In the 'Live Projects Programme' architecture, which has run since 1999, students work in groups on Live Projects with a range of real clients including local community groups, charities, health organisations and regional authorities. In some cases the projects involve actual building, while other designs involve urban masterplans and/or consultation exercises.

An overall critical educational approach permeates the whole course, but a stronger focus on participation takes place during the diploma years or MArch (RIBA accreditation Part 2), when students are considered to be mature enough for this kind of work.

During the Live Projects, teaching on communications and creative techniques in participation are delivered via communication and brief-building workshops, as well as via seminars on consultation and participatory techniques. The module 'Management and Practice 1' also supports the process, as it encourages students to reflect on the nature of architectural practice based on a critical self-appraisal of their own experience in their year out and in the Live Projects developed in the studio.

For more information about participation within the University of Sheffield School of Architecture and examples of Live Projects see Chapter 7 (www.shef.ac.uk and www.liveprojects.org).

Social Housing Foundation

Modelled on the UK and Dutch housing association movements, the South African Social Housing Foundation is a non-profit company set up in 1997 in collaboration with the South African Department of Housing in accordance with the Housing Amendment Act of 1999. Its aim is to develop a sustainable social housing sector for South Africa, creating credible social housing institutions (SHIs), and developing housing capacity. It provides expertise, products and services, aiming to benefit the subsidised housing market and low-to-moderate income families, encouraging:

- consistently well-managed housing;
- affordable quality living environments;
- integrated, empowered communities;
- collective ownership and secure tenure;
- inner-city regeneration and urban area densification;
- wider consumer choice.

(www.shf.org.za).

Urban Homesteading Assistance Board

The Urban Homesteading Assistance Board (U-HAB) in New York was created in 1974 by architects inspired by squatters in Latin America and Asia. It provided technical assistance to gang members and ex-offenders, promoting self-help labour, and facilitating the rehabilitation of abandoned houses by their own inhabitants. With time, the provision of technical assistance for rehabilitation became part of a much larger process of cooperative ownership of affordable housing in Manhattan. By 2002 U-HAB had turned into New York City's largest non-profit developer of affordable housing co-ops, supporting co-op organisation, development, management training, technical assistance and emergency support programmes (www.uhab.org).

Notes

1 The EDAW consortium comprises mainly EDAW PLC (urban planning and landscape architectural activities), Buro Happold, Foreign Office Architects, HOK Sport and Allies & Morrison.
2 See   www.mind.org.uk/NR/rdonlyres/71469E1E-552E-4A14–8E50–4158695850AD/0/Improv-
   inghealthcarereportweb.pdf.
3 See www.peabody.org.uk.
4 Information from the website (www.publicworksgroup.net), informal communication and
   unpublished documents made available to the authors (May 2008).
5 Unpublished document made available to the authors (May 2008).

Appendix III

Bibliographic resources

The following are texts which are of relevance to social wider participation in architecture, some but not all of which are used in the book and hence are not necessarily in the Reference section. This bibliography is presented here as a resource.

Abrams, F. (2007, 30 October) 'Building Up a Surplus', *Guardian*. Available at: www.guardian.co.uk/education/2007/oct/30/schools.newschools (accessed 9 March 2009).

Al-Kodmany, K. (1999) 'Using Visualization Techniques for Enhancing Public Participation in Planning and Design: Process, Implementation, and Evaluation'. *Landscape and Urban Planning*, 45: 37–45.

Albrecht, J. (1988) 'Towards a Theory of Participation in Architecture: An Examination of Humanistic Planning Theories', *Journal of Architectural Education*, 42 (1): 24–31.

Alexander, C. (1979) *Timeless Way of Building*, New York: Oxford University Press.

Alexander, C., Ishikawa, S. and Silverstein, M. (1977) *A Pattern Language: Towns, Buildings, Construction*, New York: Oxford University Press.

Aranoff, S. and Kaplan, A. G. (1995) *Total Workplace Performance*, Ontario: WDL Publications.

Arnstein, S. (1969) 'A Ladder of Citizen Participation', *Journal of the American Institute of Planners*, 35: 216–224.

Bailey, N., Haworth, A., Manzi, T. and Roberts, M. (2007) *Creating and Sustaining Mixed Income Communities in Scotland. A Good Practice Guide*, York: Chartered Institute of Housing & Joseph Rowntree Foundation.

Becker, F. (1990) *The Total Workplace: Facilities Management and the Elastic Organization*, New York: Van Nostrand Reinhold.

Beisi, J. (1995) 'Adaptable Housing or Adaptable People?: Experience in Switzerland Gives a New Answer to Questions of Housing Adaptability', *Architecture & Behaviour*, 11 (2): 139–162.

Bell, B. (ed.) (2004) *Good Deeds, Good Design: Community Service Through Architecture*, New York: Princeton Architectural Press.

Blackman, T. (1987) *Community-based Planning and Development: Recent Initiatives in Architecture, Planning, Health Care and Economic Development*, Belfast, Queen's University of Belfast and University of Ulster: Policy Research Institute.

Blundell-Jones, P., Petrescu, D. and Till, J. (2005) *Architecture and Participation*, New York: Spon Press.

Brauer, R. L. (1992) *Facilities Planning: The User Requirements Method*, New York: American Management Association.

Brown, R. and Jackson, G. (1997) 'Personalisation Made Easy: Use of Computer to Facilitate

Personalisation by the Individual User in User-participatory Design', *Open House International*, 22 (1): 24–29.

Campbell, I. and Flint, J. (2004) *A Good Practice Framework for Tenant Participation in Scotland* (Report), Edinburgh: Communities Scotland.

Carley, M., Jenkins, P. and Smith, H. (eds) (2001) *Urban Development and Civil Society: the Role of Communities in Sustainable Cities*, London: Earthscan.

Carlson, N. F. (2006) *UHAB Comes of Age. Thirty Years of Self-help Housing in New York City*. Article commissioned for the 30th anniversary of UHAB. Available at: www.uhab.org/index. cfm?fuseaction=document.showDocumentByID&nodeID=1&DocumentID=161 (accessed 9 March 2009).

Chambers, R. (1997) *Whose Reality Counts? Putting the First Last*, London: Intermediate Technology.

Chiles, P. (2003) 'Classrooms for the Future: An Adventure in Design & Research', *Architecture & Design Quarterly*, 7 (3/4): 245–261.

Cohen, J. (2003) 'Participatory Design with the Internet', *Architectural Record*, 191 (8 August): 157–158.

Comerio, M. (1987) 'Design & Empowerment: 20 Years of Community Architecture', *Built Environment*, 13 (1): 15–28.

Cooper, C. and Hawtin, M. (1998) *Resident Involvement and Community Action: Theory to Practice*, Coventry: Chartered Institute of Housing.

Cowan, R. (1988) 'Belfast's Bid to be Miles Better', *Architects' Journal*, 187 (7): 17.

Cowan, R. (1988) 'There's no Money in Community Technical Aid', *Architects' Journal*, 187 (7): 17.

Craig, T., Abbott, L., Laing, R. and Edge, M. (2005) 'Assessing the Acceptability of Alternative Cladding Materials in Housing: Theoretical and Methodological Challenges', in R. Garcia-Mira, D. L. Uzzell, J. E. Real and J. Romay (eds) *Housing, Space and Quality of Life*, London: Ashgate, pp. 59–70.

Crayton, T. (2001) 'The Design Implications of Mass Customisation', *Architectural Design*, 71 (2): 74–81.

Cropley, A. (2001) *Creativity in Education and Learning, A Guide for Teachers and Educators*, London: Kogan Page.

Cullingworth, J. B. (1999) *British Planning: 50 Years of Urban and Regional Planning*, London and New Brunswick, NJ: Athlone Press.

Cunningham, A. (2005) *Designs on My Learning ... A Guide to Involving Young People in School Design*, Glasgow: The Lighthouse.

Danko, S., Meneely, M. S. and Portillo, M. (2006) 'Humanizing Design through Narrative Inquiry', *Journal of Interior Design*, 31 (2): 10–28.

Davidoff, P. (1995) 'Advocacy and Pluralism in Planning', in J. M. Stein (ed.) *Classic Readings in Urban Planning*, London: McGraw-Hill.

Davidson, S. (1998) 'Spinning the Wheel of Empowerment', *Planning*, 1262: 14–15.

Davidson, C., Johnson, C., Lizarralde, G., Dikmen, N. and Sliwinski, A. (2007) 'Truths and Myths about Community Participation in Post-disaster Housing Projects', *Habitat International*, 31 (1): 100–115.

Davis, H. (2006) *The Culture of Building*, New York: Oxford University Press.

Demetrios, M. (1994) 'Residents Play a Part in Making Hulme Habitable', *Architects' Journal*, 199 (16): 16–17.

Douglas, M. and Friedmann, P. (1998) *Cities for Citizens – Planning and the Rise of Civil Society in a Global Age*, Chichester: John Wiley & Sons.

Edge, M., Conniff, A., Laing, R., Webster, R., Davies, A. M. and Spicker, P. (2003) *Mapping Survey of Non-technical Research on the Social Value and Benefits of Good Architectural Design – Education Department Research Findings 1*. Robert Gordon University, Aberdeen:

Scottish Executive. Available at: www.scotland.gov.uk/Publications/2003/11/18470/28670 (accessed 9 March 2009).

Ellin, N. (2000) 'Participatory Architecture on the Parisian Periphery: Lucien Kroll's Vignes Blanches', *Journal of Architectural Education*, 53 (3): 178–183.

Engler, M. (1999) 'A Living Memorial: Commemorating Yitzhak Rabin at the Tel Aviv Square [Speaking of Places]', *Places*, 12 (2): 4–11.

Faga, B. (2006) *Designing Public Consensus: The Civic Theater of Community Participation for Architects, Landscape Architects, Planners, and Urban Designers*, Hoboken, NJ: John Wiley & Sons, Inc.

Falanga, M. (1987) 'Start Making Sense: Designing with User Participation', *Design Methods and Theories*, 21 (4): 732–739.

Fenby, E., Bain, M. and Cunningham, A. (2004) *From Consultation to Design. Designing for Learning: 21st Century Schools*, Glasgow: The Lighthouse.

Forester, J. (1985) 'Designing: Making Sense Together in Practical Conversations', *Journal of Architectural Education*, 38 (3): 119–133.

Forester, J. (1999) *The Deliberative Practitioner: Encouraging Participatory Planning Process*, Cambridge, MA, and London: MIT Press.

Forsyth, W. L. (1987) 'Technical Assistance for Community Groups: Funding and Controlling the Services. The Experience of Comtechsa in Liverpool', *Built Environment*, 13 (1): 29–37.

Forsyth, W. L. (1988) 'The Community Technical Services Agency (Comtechsa) Limited', *Town Planning Review*, 59 (1): 7–17.

Forsyth, W. L. (1988) 'User-controlled Community Technical Aid: A Symposium-Introduction & Conclusion', *Town Planning Review*, 59 (1): 5–7.

Francis, M. (1999) 'Proactive Practice: Visionary Thought and Participatory Action in Environmental Design', *Places*, 12 (2): 61–69.

Frey, H. (1999) *Designing the City: Towards a More Sustainable Urban Form*, London: E&FN Spon.

Friedmann, J. (1988) *Life Space and Economic Space*, New Brunswick: Transaction Books.

Gallie, J. (2006) 'Transformable Architecture for the Homeless', *Architectural Design*, 70 (4): 34–39.

Gesler, W., Bell, M., Curtis, S., Hubbard, P. and Francis, S. (2004) 'Therapy by Design: Evaluating the UK Hospital Building Programme', *Health and Place*, 10 (2): 117–128.

Gibson, J. J. (1979) *The Ecological Approach to Visual Perception*, Boston, MA: Houghton Mifflin.

Gibson, T. (1996) *The Power in our Hands. Neighbourhood-based World-shaking*, Charlbury: Jon Carpenter Publishing.

Gibson, T. (1998) *The Do-ers Guide to Planning for Real Exercises*, Telford: Neighbourhood Initiatives Foundation.

Gifford, R. (1980) 'Environmental Dispositions and the Evaluation of Architectural Interiors', *Journal of Research in Personality*, 14: 386–399.

Gifford, R., Hine, D. W., Muller-Clemm, W. and Shaw, K. T. (2002) 'Why Architects and Laypersons Judge Buildings Differently: Cognitive and Physical Bases', *Journal of Architectural and Planning Research*, 19: 131–147.

Godschalk, D. R. and Paterson, R. G. (1999) 'Collaborative Conflict Management Comes of Age', *Journal of Architectural and Planning Research*, 16 (2): 91–95.

Gorgolewski, M. (2005) 'Learning How Buildings Work', *Canadian Architect*, 50 (9): 65–66.

Groat, L. (1988) 'Contextual Compatibility in Architecture: An Issue of Personal Taste?', in J. Nasar (ed.) *The Visual Quality of the Environment: Theory, Research and Application*, Cambridge: Cambridge University Press, pp. 228–253.

Groat, L. (1988) 'Contexual Compatibility in Architecture', in D. Canter, M. Krampen and D. Stea (eds) *Ethnoscapes: Transactional Studies in Action and Place*, Aldershot; England: Gower Publishing, pp. 215–229.

Groat, L. and Wang, D. (2002) *Architectural Research*, New York: John Wiley & Sons.

Hague, C. and Jenkins, P. (2005) *Place Identity, Participation and Planning*, London: Routledge.

Hamdi, N. (1991) *Housing with Houses: Participation, Flexibility, Enablement*, New York: Van Nostrand Reinhold.

Hamdi, N. and Goethert, R. (1997) *Action Planning for Cities: A Guide to Community Practice*, Chichester: John Wiley & Sons.

Hannay, P. (1988) 'Work Towards Tomorrow', *Architects' Journal*, 187 (1 January): 18–21.

Hansen, G. K. and Knudsen, W. (2006) 'Usability – A Matter of Perspective? The Case of Nord Trondelag University College', paper presented at the sixth European Conference on e-government, Philipps Universitat Marburg, Germany.

Hatch, C. R. (1984) *The Scope of Social Architecture*, New York: Van Nostrand Reinhold.

Healey, P. (1997) *Collaborative Planning: Shaping Places in Fragmented Societies*, London: Macmillan.

Hester, R. T. (1999) 'A Refrain with a View', *Places*, 12 (2): 12–25.

Hollis, E. (2007) *Thinking Inside the Box*, London: Middlesex University Press.

Hou, J., Francis, M. and Brightbill, N. (2005) '(Re) Constructing Communities: Design Participation in the Face of Change', paper presented at the Fifth Pacific Rim Conference on Participatory Community Design. Davis, CA: Center for Design Research, University of California.

Hubbard, P. J. (1994) 'Professional vs. Lay Tastes in Design Control: An Empirical Investigation', *Planning Practice and Research*, 9: 271–287.

Jenkins, P. (2005) 'Creation and Conservation of the Built Environment in the Later 20th Century', in *Edinburgh: The Making of a Capital City*, Edinburgh: Edinburgh University Press.

Jenkins, P., Forsyth, L. and Smith, H. (2004) *Balancing Three Dimensions in Architectural Research: Depth, Breadth and Length. An Institutional Analysis of Research in Architecture in the UK Higher Education Sector*, Edinburgh: Edinburgh College of Art.

Jenkins, P., Kirk, K. and Smith, H. (2002) *Getting Involved in Planning: Perceptions of the Wider Public*, Edinburgh: Scottish Executive. Available at: www.scotland.gov.uk/Publications/2002/10/15632/12118 (accessed: 30 September 2008).

Jenkins, P., Smith, H. and Garcia Ferrari, S. (2005) *Architectural Research and the Profession in Scotland*, Edinburgh: RIAS.

Joiner, D. and Ellis, P. (1989) 'Making POE Work in an Organization', in W. F. E. Preiser (ed.) *Building Evaluation*, New York: Van Nostrand Reinhold.

Katz, P. (1994) *The Urbanism: Towards and Architecture of Community*, New York: McGraw-Hill.

Kellett, P. and Bishop, W. (2006) 'Reinforcing Traditional Values: Social, Spatial and Economic Interactions in an Indonesian Kampung', *Open House International*, 31 (4): 58–66.

Kellettt, P. and Yildiz, H. T. (2006) 'Editorial: Understanding and Researching Traditional Environments', *Open House International*, 31 (4): 4–5.

Kernohan, D., Gray, J., Daish, J. and Joiner, D. (1992) *User Participation in Building Design and Management: A Generic Approach to Building Management*, Oxford: Butterworth-Heinemann.

Klein, S. M. (1999) 'Response: Five Proposals for Participation [Participation with a View – Response]', *Places*, 12 (2): 40–59.

Landman, K. and Liebermann, S. (2005) 'Planning Against Crime: Preventing Crime with People not Barriers', *SA Crime Quarterly*, 8: 21–26.

Larkin, C. (1998) 'Man of the People [Ralph Erskine]', *Architects' Journal*, 207 (15): 24–25.

Lawrence, R. J. (1987) 'Basic Principles for Public Participation in House Planning', *Design Studies*, 8 (2): 102–108.

Lister, S., Perry, J. and Thornley, M. (2007) *Community Engagement in Housing-led Regeneration: A Good Practice Guide*, London: The Chartered Institute of Housing.

Lozano, E. (1993) *Community Design and the Culture of Cities: The Crossroads and the Wall*, Cambridge: Cambridge University Press.

Lynch, K. (1960) *The Image of the City*, Cambridge, MA: MIT Press.

Macmillan, S. (2004) *Designing Better Buildings: Quality and Value in the Built Environment*, London: Spon Press.

Mahtab-uz-Zaman, Q. M. and Lau, S. S. Y. (2002) 'Difficulties in Achieving Open Building in the Mass Housing in Hong Kong and Implication of User Participation', *Architectural Science Review*, 45: 175–181.

Malpass, P. (1979) 'A Reappraisal of Byker. Magic, Myth and the Architect', *Architects' Journal*, 169: 961–969; 1011–1021.

Martens, B. and Keul, A. G. (2004) 'Evaluation in Progress: Strategies for Environmental Research & Implementation', paper presented at the IAPS 18 Conference, Vienna, July.

Matheou, D. (1994) 'Working in Scotland: Project Round-up', *Architects' Journal*: 16–21.

Matrix. (1984) *Making Space: Women and the Manmade Environment*, London: Pluto Press.

Mayo, E., Thake, S. and Gibson, T. (1998) *Taking Power. An Agenda for Community Economic Renewal*, London: New Economics Foundation.

McGregor, W. and Shiem-Shin Then, D. (1999) *Facilities Management and the Business of Space*, London: Arnold.

McNally, M. (1999) 'Drafting a Regional Blueprint for Sustainability [Participation with a View]', *Places*, 12 (2): 26–29.

Mitchell, W. (1972) 'Experiments with Participation-oriented Systems', in N. Cross (ed.) *Design Participation*, London: Academy Editions.

Nasar, J. L. (1988) *Environmental Aesthetics: Theory, Research and Application*, Cambridge: Cambridge University Press.

Noguchi, M. (2007) 'A Renewable Experience of PV Mass Custom Housing in Canada', in B. Dimitrijevic (ed.) *CBE News*, Glasgow: The Centre for the Built Environment, pp. 8–9.

ODPM (2003) *Participatory Planning for Sustainable Communities: International Experience of Mediation, Negotiation and Engagement in Making Plans*, London: ODPM.

Oliver, P. (2006) 'Necessity and Continuity: The Challenge of the Impending Crisis', *Open House International*, 31 (4): 15–19.

Ornstein, S. W. (1987) 'Post Occupancy Evaluation Performed in Elementary & High Schools of Greater Sao Paulo, Brazil: The Occupants & the Quality of the School Environment', *Environment and Behavior*, 29 (2): 236–263.

Ospina, J. (1987) *Housing Ourselves*, London: Hilary Shipman.

Owens, P. E. (2000) 'That Same Old Participation?', *Places*, 13 (1): 34–36.

Pearce, M. and Toy, M. (eds) (1995) *Educating Architects*, New York: John Wiley & Sons.

Pilling, D. N. S. (2000) *Changing Architectural Education: Towards a New Professionalism*, London: Spon Press.

Preiser, W. F. E., Rabinowitz, H. Z. and White, E. T. (1988) *Post-occupancy Evaluation*, New York: Van Nostrand Reinhold.

Pretty, J. N., Guijit, I., Scoones, I. and Thompson, J. (1995) *A Trainers Guide for Participatory Learning and Action*, London: IIED.

Qudsi, A. (2006) 'Old Aleppo: Upgrading an Historic Residential Environment', *Open House International*, 13 (4): 90–94.

Rapoport, A. (2006) 'Traditional Environments, Culture and Preservation', *Open House International*, 31 (4): 7–99.

Richardson, B. (1998) 'Understanding the Whole Story', *Architects' Journal*: 48–49.

Romice, O. R. and Frey, H. W. (2003) *Communities in Action. The Handbook*, Glasgow: Scottish Arts Council & University of Strathclyde.

Romice, O. and Uzzell, D. (2005) 'Community Design Studio: A Collaboration of Architects and Psychologists', *CEBE Transactions*, 2 (1): 73–88.

Saarilumoma, P. and Maattola, I. (2003) 'Stumbling Blocks in Novice Building Design', *Journal of Architectural and Planning Research*, 20 (4): 344–354.

Sandercock, L. (1998) 'The Death of Modernist Planning', in M. D. P. Friedmann (ed.) *Cities for Citizens – Planning and the Rise of Civil Society in a Global Age*, Chichester: John Wiley & Sons.

Sanoff, H. (1985) 'User Needs Programme for a Research Facility', *Design Studies*, 6 (4): 187–195.

Sanoff, H. (1985) 'Organizational Self Assessment', *Design Studies*, 6 (4): 181–186.

Sanoff, H. (1985) 'Attitudes Towards an Open Plan Office', *Design Studies*, 6 (4): 196–202.

Sanoff, H. (1985) 'Human Responses to the Office Work Environment', *Design Studies*, 6 (4): 203–208.

Sanoff, H. (1985) 'The New Work Station', *Design Studies*, 6 (4): 209–212.

Sanoff, H. (1985) 'Modular Laboratories for Instructional Use', *Design Studies*, 6 (4): 213–217.

Sanoff, H. (1985) 'Factory Work Groups', *Design Studies*, 6 (4): 218–222.

Sanoff, H. (1985) 'Workforce Participation in the Design of a Warehouse', *Design Studies*, 6 (4): 223–229.

Sanoff, H. (1985) 'Action Factory', *Design Studies*, 6 (4): 230–234.

Sanoff, H. (1985) 'The Application of Participatory Methods in Design and Evaluation', *Design Studies*, 6 (4): 178–234.

Sanoff, H. (1991) *Visual Methods in Design*, New York: Van Nostrand Reinhold.

Sanoff, H. (2000) *Community Participation Methods in Design and Planning*, New York: John Wiley & Sons.

Sanoff, H. (2000) *Participatory Design: Theory and Techniques*, North Carolina: North Carolina State University.

Sanoff, H. (2003) *Three Decades of Design and Community*, Raleigh, NC: North Carolina State University Office of the Vice Chancellor for Extension and Engagement and the College of Design.

Sanoff, H. (2006) 'Multiple Views of Participatory Design', *METU JFA 2006/2*, 23 (2): 131–143.

Sanoff, H. (2007) 'Editorial: Special Issue on Participatory Design', *Design Studies*, 28 (3): 213–215.

Scottish Government (2007) *Performance Standard: GS2.2 Tenant Participation – Useful References*. Available at: www.scottishhousingregulator.gov.uk/stellent/groups/public/document/webpages/shr_gs2.2tenantparticipation-u.hcsp (accessed 15 July 2008).

Scott, J., Deveci, G. and Brogden, B. (2007) 'The Development of Index 21 Housing Layout Tool: The Assessment of Non-monetary Environmental Benefits', paper presented at the International Conference on Whole Life Urban Sustainability and its Assessment, Glasgow Caledonian University, Glasgow, June.

Sharp, R. (2006) 'View from the Crew', *Architects' Journal*, 221 (11 March): 16–17.

Sharples, S. and Woolley, T. (1987) *The Nature of Community Technical Aid & The Contribution Made to it by DOE's Special Grants Programme*, University of Strathclyde: Housing & Rehabilitation Research Unit, Department of Architecture.

Sim, D. (1993) *British Housing Design*, Coventry: Institute of Housing.

Slessor, C. (1995) 'Mbazwane Resources Centre – Mbazwane Rural Resources Center in KwaZulu, South Africa – Narrow Margins', *Architecture Review*, 3.

Stamps, A. E. (2000) *Psychology and the Aesthetics of the Built Environment*, Norwell, MA: Kluwer Academic.

Steinbach, N. P. C. (1987) *Corrective Capitalism: The Rise of America's Community Development Organizations*, New York: The Ford Foundation.

Stern, A. L., Macrae, S., Gerteis, M., Harrison, T., Fowler, E. and Edgman-Levitan, S. (2003) 'Understanding the Consumer Perspective to Improve Design Quality', *Journal of Architectural and Planning Research*, 20 (1): 16–28.

Stone, S. and Brooker, G. (2005) *Re-readings: The Design Principles of Remodelling Existing Buildings*, London: RIBA Enterprises.

Towers, G. (1995) *Building Democracy: Community Architecture in the Inner Cities*, London: Routledge.

Van der Voordt, T. J. M. and Van Wegen, H. B. R. (2005) *Architecture in Use: An Introduction to the Programming, Design and Evaluation of Buildings*, Bussum: THOTH.

Various (1987) 'Special Issue: Community Architecture', *Built Environment*, 13 (1): 5–60.

Various (2005) 'Special Issue. People', *Lotus*, 124 (June): 4–133.

Various (2006) *Open House International*, 31: 99.

Various (2007) 'Special Issue. Participer [Participation]', *Architecture D'Aujourdhui*, 368 (January/February): 40–109.

Various (2007) 'Special Issue on Participatory Design', *Design Studies*, 28 (3).

Vischer, W. F. E. P. J. C. (2005) *Assessing Building Performance*, Oxford: Elsevier.

Wang, H-M. and Shieh, L. L. (2006) 'Encouraging Communities in Taiwan to Define Historic Preservation', *Open House International*, 31 (4): 77–85.

Wates, N. and Knevitt, C. (1987) *Community Architecture: How People are Making Their Own Environment*, London: Penguin Books.

Wates, N. (1996) *Action Planning. How to Use Planning Weekends and Urban Design Action Teams to Improve your Environment*, London: The Prince of Wales's Institute of Architecture.

Wates, N. (2000) *The Community Planning Handbook. How People Can Shape Their Cities, Town and Villages in any Part of the World*, London: Earthscan Publications.

Watts, J. and Hirst, M. (1982) 'User Participation in the Early Stages of Building Design', *Design Studies*, 3 (1): 11–18.

Wilson, M. A. (1996) 'The Socialization of Architectural Preference', *Journal of Environmental Psychology*, 16: 33–44.

Winograd, T., Bennett, J., Young, L. D. and Hartfield, E. (1996) *Bringing Design to Software*, Reading, MA: ACM Press.

Woolley, T. (1985) *The Characteristics of Community Architecture and Community Technical Aid*, Glasgow: University of Strathclyde, Department of Architecture & Building Science.

Wright, R. P. K. (1999) 'Sandy Vista Regroups and Rebuilds', *Places*, 12 (2): 30–39.

Yildiz, P. K. Y. H. (2006) 'Understanding and Researching Traditional Environments', *Open House International*, 31 (4): 4–5.

Zeisel, J. (2006) *Inquiry by Design: Environment/Behavior/Neuroscience in Architecture, Interiors, Landscape and Planning*, New York: Norton.

References

10th Venice Biennale (2006) *Cities: People, Society, Architecture*, New York: Rizzoli International Publications.

Abrams, F. (2007, 30 October) 'Building Up a Surplus', *Guardian*. Available at: www.guardian.co.uk/education/2007/oct/30/schools.newschools (accessed 9 March 2009).

Al-Kodmany, K. (1999) 'Using Visualization Techniques for Enhancing Public Participation in Planning and Design: Process, Implementation, and Evaluation'. *Landscape and Urban Planning*, 45: 37–45.

Alexander, C. (1979) *Timeless Way of Building*, New York: Oxford University Press.

Alexander, C., Ishikawa, S. and Silverstein, M. (1977) *A Pattern Language: Towns, Buildings, Construction*, New York: Oxford University Press.

Anning, N. *et al.* (1980) *Squatting: The Real Story*, London: Bay Leaf Books.

Arantes, P. F. (2004) 'Reinventing the Building Site', in E. Andreoli and A. Forty (eds) *Brazil's Modern Architecture*, New York: Phandon.

Arnstein, S. (1969) 'A Ladder of Citizen Participation', *Journal of the American Institute of Planners*, 35: 216–224.

Ballerine, F. (2002) 'Sistemas interativos digitais e processos participativos de projeto. Um estudo de caso: Mutirão São Gabriel', unpublished Master's dissertation, Escola de Arquitetura da Universidade Federal de Minas Gerais, Brazil.

Baltazar dos Santos, A. P. and Malard, M. L. (2006) 'RSV – Residencial Serra Verde – Participative Design Process and Self-Management of Low-income Housing Construction in Belo Horizonte, Brazil – A Model for Future Government Loan Programs', in Association of Collegiate Schools of Architecture and Fannie Mae Foundation (eds) *Affordable Design: Convening the Conversation – Final Report*, Washington: Fannie Mae Foundation, pp. 35–46. Available at: www.arquitetura.ufmg.br/eva/docs/art016.pdf (accessed 1 May 2008).

Becker, F. (1990) *The Total Workplace: Facilities Management and the Elastic Organization*, New York: Van Nostrand Reinhold.

Bell, B. (ed.) (2004) *Good Deeds, Good Design: Community Service Through Architecture*, New York: Princeton Architectural Press.

Beni, L. and Callaghan, S. (1997) 'Social Architecture: The New Context for Design', *KwaZulu Natal Institute of Architects' Journal*, 4: 0–1.

Blake, S. (2003) 'Community Design Centers: An Alternative Practice', in D. Watson (ed.) *Timesaver Standards for Urban Design*, Maidenhead, Berkshire: McGraw-Hill Professional.

Blundell-Jones, P., Petrescu, D. and Till, J. (2005) *Architecture and Participation*, New York: Spon Press.

Bødker, S. (2000) 'Scenarios in User-centred Design – Setting the Stage for Reflection and Action', *Interacting with Computers*, 13 (1): 61–75.

Bonduki, N. (1992) *Habitação e autogestão – Construindo territórios de utopia*, Rio de Janeiro: Fase.

Bonnes, M., Uzzell, D., Carrus, G. and Kelay, T. (2007) 'Inhabitants' and Experts' Assessments of Environmental Quality for Urban Sustainability', *Journal of Social Issues*, 63 (1): 59–78.

References

Breakwell, G. M. (1986) *Coping with Threatened Identities*, London: Methuen.

Burdett, R. and Sudijc, D. (2008) *The Endless City*, London: Phaidon Press.

Burgess, R. (1978) 'Petty Commodity Housing or Dweller Control?', *World Development*, 6 (9): 1105–1133.

Burgess, R. (1982) 'Self-help Housing Advocacy: A Curious Form of Radicalism', in P. M. Ward (ed.) *Self-help Housing: A Critique*, London: Mansell.

Burgess, R. (1985) 'The Limits to State Self-help Housing Programmes', *Development & Change*, 16: 271–331.

Burgess, R. (1987) 'A Lot of Noise and No Nuts: A Reply to Alan Gilbert and Jan van der Linden', *Development & Change*, 18 (1): 137–146.

Burgess, R. (1992) 'Helping Some to Help Themselves: Third World Housing Policies and Development Strategies', in K. Mathey (ed.) *Beyond Self-help Housing*, London: Mansell.

CABE (2006) *Better Public Building*. Prime Minister's Award. 6 July 2006. Available at: www.cabe.org.uk/publications/better-public-building-shortlist-2006 (accessed 15 March 2009).

Carley, M., Jenkins, P. and Smith, H. (eds) (2001) *Urban Development and Civil Society: The Role of Communities in Sustainable Cities*, London: Earthscan.

Carlson, N. F. (2006) *UHAB Comes of Age. Thirty Years of Self-help Housing in New York City*. Commissioned for the 30th anniversary of UHAB. Available at: www.uhab.org/indexcfm?fuseaction =document.showDocumentByID&nodeID=1&DocumentID=161 (accessed 9 March 2009).

Carroll, J. M. (1995) *Scenario-based Design: Envisioning Work and Technology in System Development*, New York: John Wiley & Sons.

Carroll, J. M. (2000) *Making Use: Scenario-based Design of Human–Computer Interactions*, Cambridge, MA: MIT Press.

Carroll, J. M. and Rosson, M. B. (2007) 'Participatory Design in Community Informatics', *Design Studies*, 28: 243–261.

Chambers, R. and Conway, G. (1992) 'Sustainable Rural Livelihoods: Practical Concepts for the 21st Century', *IDS Discussion Paper*, 296, Brighton.

Chawla, L. and Heft, H. (2002) 'Children's Competence and the Ecology of Communities: A Functional Approach to the Evaluation of Participation', *Journal of Environmental Psychology*, 22: 201–216.

Chiles, P. (2005) 'What if.... A Narrative Process for Re-imagining the City', in P. Blundell-Jones, D. Petrescu and J. Till (eds) *Architecture and Participation*, Oxford: Spon Press.

Comerio, M. C. (1984) 'Community Design: Idealism and Entrepreneurship', *Journal of Architecture and Planning Research*, 1: 227–243.

Comerio, M. C. (1987) 'Design & Empowerment: 20 Years of Community Architecture', *Built Environment*, 13 (1): 15–28.

Communities Scotland (2005) *Evaluation of Kincardine O'Neil Innovative Rural Housing Design Project: Canmore Place*. Available at: www.scr.communitiesscotland.gov.uk/stellent/groups/public/documents/webpages/cs_009004.pdf (accessed 9 March 2009).

Conti, A. (1999) 'A experiência da autogestão em Ipatinga: uma busca pelo conceito', Master's dissertation, Escola de Arquitetura, Universidade Federal de Minas Gerais, Brazil.

Cooper, A. (1999) *The Inmates are Running the Asylum: Why High Tech Products Drive Us Crazy and How To Restore The Sanity*, London: Macmillan.

Coppola, C. (1995) 'Folweni Adult Learning Centre in KwaZulu Natal', *Institute of Architects' Journal*, 1: 8–1.

Cunningham, A. (ed.) (2005) *Designs on my Learning.... A Guide to Involving Young People in School Design*, Glasgow: The Lighthouse.

Cunningham, A., Kenyon, K., Sim, M. and Cassels, S. (2008) *Senses of Place: Building Excellence – The Toolkit and Outcomes*, Glasgow: The Lighthouse.

Curry, R. (2000) 'History of Community Design', in J. M. Cary Jr. (ed.) *The ACSA Sourcebook of Community Design Programs at Schools of Architecture in North America*, Washington, DC: ACSA Press, pp. 38–43.

Curry, R. (2004) 'Community Design Centres', in B. Bell (ed.) *Good Deeds, Good Design: Community Service Through Architecture*, New York: Princeton Architectural Press.

Davidoff, P. (1995) 'Advocacy and Pluralism in Planning', in J. M. Stein (ed.) *Classic Readings in Urban Planning*, London: McGraw-Hill.

Davidson, S. (1998) 'Spinning the Wheel of Empowerment', *Planning*, 1262: 14–15.

Davies, C. (2005) *The Prefabricated Home*, London: Reaktion Books.

Davis, H. (2006) *The Culture of Building*, New York: Oxford University Press.

Deckler, T., Graupner, A. and Rasmuss, H. (2006) *Contemporary South African Architecture in a Landscape of Transition*, Cape Town: Double Storey Books.

Department for Education and Skills (2004) Schools for the Future: Transforming Schools: An Inspirational Guide to Remodelling Secondary Schools. Available at: http://publications.teachernet.gov.uk/default.aspx?PageFunction=productdetails&PageMode=publications&ProductId=DfES%201140/2004& (accessed 9 March 2009).

Docherty, I., Goodlad, R. and Paddison, R. (2001) 'Civic Culture, Community and Citizen Participation in Contrasting Neighbourhoods', *Urban Studies*, 38 (12): 2225–2250.

Duivesteijn, A. (1996) *De Verborgen Opgave: Thuis in de Stad = The Hidden Assignment: At Home in the City*, Rotterdam: NAI Publishers.

Edge, H. M. and Pearson, R. (2001) 'Vernacular Architectural Form and the Planning Paradox: A Study of Actual and Perceived Rural Building Tradition', *Journal of Architecture and Planning Research*, 18 (2): 156–177.

Falke, I. and Balatti, J. (2004) 'Identities of Place: Their Power and Consequences for VET', paper presented at the seventh Australian VET Research Association Conference – The Heart of the Matter, Canberra, Australia, March.

Fenby, J., Bain, M. and Cuningham, A. (eds) (2004) *From Consultation to Design – Design for Learning: 21st Century Schools*, Glasgow: The Lighthouse.

Forester, J. (1999) *The Deliberative Practitioner: Encouraging Participatory Planning Processes*, Cambridge, MA, & London: MIT Press.

Freire, P. (1970) *The Pedagogy of the Oppressed*, New York: Continuum.

Friedmann, J. (1987) *Planning in the Public Domain*, Princeton, NJ: Princeton University Press.

Gesler, W., Bell, M., Curtis, S., Hubbard, P. and Francis, S. (2004) 'Therapy by Design: Evaluating the UK Hospital Building Programme', *Health and Place*, 10 (2): 117–128.

Gibson, J. J. (1979) *The Ecological Approach to Visual Perception*, Boston, MA: Houghton Mifflin.

Gifford, R. (1980) 'Environmental Dispositions and the Evaluation of Architectural Interiors', *Journal of Research in Personality*, 14: 386–399.

Gifford, R., Hine, D. W., Muller-Clemm, W. and Shaw, K. T. (2002) 'Why Architects and Laypersons Judge Buildings Differently: Cognitive and Physical Bases', *Journal of Architectural and Planning Research*, 19: 131–147.

Glendinning, M. (2008) *Modern Architect: The Life and Times of Robert Matthew*, London: RIBA Publishing.

Groat, L. (1988) 'Contextual Compatibility in Architecture: An Issue of Personal Taste?', in J. Nasar (ed.) *The Visual Quality of the Environment: Theory, Research and Application*, Cambridge: Cambridge University Press, pp. 228–253.

Groat, L. and Wang, D. (2002) *Architectural Research Methods*, Oxford: John Wiley & Sons.

Grudin, J. and Pruitt, J. (2002). 'Personas, Participatory Design and Product Development: An Infrastructure for Engagement', in *Proc. PDC 2002*: 144–161. Available at: http://research.microsoft.com/users/jgrudin/publications/personas/Grudin-Pruitt.pdf (accessed 24 July 2008).

Habraken, N. J. (1972) *Supports: An Alternative to Mass Housing*, London: Architectural Press.

Hackos, J. and Redish, J. (1998) *User and Task Analysis for Interface Design*, New York: John Wiley & Sons.

Hague, C. and Jenkins, P. (2004) *Place Identity, Participation and Planning*, London: Routledge – RTPI Library Series.

References

Hamdi, N. (2004) *Small Change: About the Art of Practice and the Limits of Planning*, Sterling, VA: Earthscan.

Harris, S. and Berke, D. (1997) *The Architecture of the Everyday*, Princeton: Princeton Architectural Press.

Healey, P. (1997) *Collaborative Planning: Shaping Places in Fragmented Societies*, London: Macmilllan.

Hillier, B. (1996) *Space is the Machine*, Cambridge: Cambridge University Press.

Hillier, B. and Hanson, J. (1984) *The Social Logic of Space*, Cambridge: Cambridge University Press.

Horelli, L. (1997) 'A Methodological Approach to Children's Participation in Urban Planning', *Scandinavian Housing and Planning Research*, 14 (3): 105–116.

Horelli, L. and Kaaja, M. (2002) 'Opportunities and Constraints of "Internet-assisted Urban Planning" with Young People', *Journal of Environmental Psychology*, 22: 191–200.

Hubbard, P. J. (1994) 'Professional vs. Lay Tastes in Design Control: An Empirical Investigation', *Planning Practice and Research*, 9: 271–287.

Huchzemeyer, M. and Karam, A. (eds) (2006) *A Perpetual Challenge? Informal Settlements at the Local and Policy Level*, Cape Town: University of Cape Town Press.

Jenkins, P. (2008) 'Research and Knowledge Development in Architecture: Reflections on Academic, Professional and Wider Social Approaches', paper presented at EAAE/ARCC Conference Changes paradigms of the basic understanding of architectural research, Copenhagen, July. http://www.eaae.be/eaaez/documents/Transactions/42/Vol_2.pdf pp. 254–267.

Jenkins, P. (2009) 'Architectural Modernism, Modernisation and Modernity in Lusophone Countries: Brazil, Angola and Mozambique', paper presented at DOCOMOMO Symposium, 'Modernist Urbanism in the Southern Hemisphere: Past, Present, Future', Edinburgh School of Architecture, Edinburgh, January.

Jenkins, P. and McLachlan, F. (forthcoming 2009) 'Is There a Role for Architects in Mainstream Private Sector House Building?', *The Journal of Architecture*.

Jenkins, P., Smith, H. and Garcia Ferrari, S. (2005) *Architecture Research and the Profession in Scotland: A Research Study for the Royal Incorporation of Architects in Scotland*, Edinburgh: RIAS.

Jenkins, P., Smith, H. and Wang, Y. P. (2006) *Planning and Housing in a Rapidly Urbanising World*, London: Routledge.

Joiner, D. and Ellis, P. (1989) 'Making POE Work in an Organization', in W. F. E. Preiser (ed.) *Building Evaluation*, New York: Van Nostrand Reinhold.

Kadushin, R. (2008) *Open Design*. Available at: www.ronenkadushin.com/Open_Design.asp (accessed 6 May 2008).

Kapor, M. (2006) 'A Software Design Manifesto', in T. Winograd (ed.) *Bringing Design to Software*, New York: ACM Press.

Kensing, F. and Madsen, K. H. (1991) 'Generating Visions: Future Workshops and Metaphorical Design', in J. Greenbaum and M. Kyng (eds) *Design at Work: Cooperative Design of Computer Systems*, Hillsdale, NJ: Lawrence Erlbaum, pp. 155–168.

Kernohan, D., Gray, J., Daish, J. and Joiner, D. (1992) *User Participation in Building Design and Management: A Generic Approach to Building Management*, Oxford: Butterworth-Heinemann.

Landman, K. and Liebermann, S. (2005) 'Planning Against Crime: Preventing Crime with People not Barriers', *SA Crime Quarterly*, 8: 21–26.

Law-Viljoen, B. (2006) *Light on a Hill: Building the Constitutional Court of South Africa*, Johannesburg: David Krut Publishing.

Lewis, O. (1961) *The Children of Sanchez*, New York: Random House.

LMU Department of Architecture and Spatial Design (n.d.) *Undergraduate Courses*. Available at: www.londonmet.ac.uk/ug-prospectus/academic-departments/department-of-architecture-and-spatial-design.cfm (accessed 9 March 2009).

Low, I. (1998) 'Building and Self-reliance', in H. Judin and I. Vladislavic (eds) *Blank: Architecture, Apartheid and After*, Cape Town: David Philip Publishers.

Lyons, M. and Smuts, C. (1999) 'Community Agency in the New South Africa: A Comparative Approach', *Urban Studies*, 36 (122): 2151–2166.

Malard, M. L., Baltazar dos Santos, A. P. and Pontes, M. M. (2006) 'Autogestão habitacional e gestão de projetos: conflitos e possibilidades', in *ENTAC 2006 – a construção do futuro – XI Encontro Nacional de Tecnologia do Ambiente Construído*, Florianópolis, Brazil. CD-ROM. Available at: www.arquitetura.ufmg.br/eva/docs/art008.pdf (accessed 1 May 2008).

Mangin, W. (ed.) (1970) *Peasants in Cities: Readings in the Anthropology of Urbanization*, Boston: Houghton Mifflin.

Maricato, E. (1979) 'Autocontruçao: a Arquitetura possivel', in E.A. Maricato (ed.) *A produçao capitalista da casa (e da vidade) no Brasil industrial*, Sao Paolo: Alfa-Omega.

Maricato, E. (1994) *Política habitacional no regime militar – Do milagre brasileiro à crise econômica*, Petrópolis: Vozes.

Maricato, E. (1997) *Habitaçao e Cidade*, Sao Paolo: Atual.

Marschall, S. (2000) 'Community Participation', in S. Marschall and B. Kearney (eds) *Architecture in the New South Africa: Opportunities for Relevance*, Pretoria: University of South Africa.

Marschall, S. and Kearney, B. (eds) (2000) *Architecture in the New South Africa: Opportunities for Relevance*, Pretoria: University of South Africa.

Mathey, K. (ed.) (1992) *Beyond Self-help Housing*, London: Mansell.

MEARU (2007) *Report on the Charrette Process at Tornagrain*, Glasgow: The Glasgow School of Art.

Mikkelson, N. and Lee, W. O. (2000) 'Incorporating User Archetypes into Scenario-based Design', 9th Annual Usability Professionals' Association (UPA) Conference, Asheville, North Carolina, August.

Morojele, M. (1998) 'Towards an Architecture of Empowerment', in H. Judin and I. Vladislavic (eds) *Blank: Architecture, Apartheid and After*, Cape Town: David Philip Publishers.

Mull, R. and Markey, A. (2005) 'Editorial', *ASD Projects Newsletter*, 1 (Autumn): 1.

Murray, N. (2006) 'Re-framing the Contemporary, Architecture and the Postcolony', in T. Deckler, A. Graupner and H. Rasmuss (eds) *Contemporary South African Architecture in a Landscape of Transition*, Cape Town: Double Storey Books.

Nasar, J. L. (1988) *Environmental Aesthetics: Theory, Research, and Applications*, Cambridge: Cambridge University Press.

Netherlands Architecture Institute (2007) *Visionary Power: Producing the Contemporary City*, Rotterdam: NAI.

Nicol, D. and Pilling, S. (2000) 'Architectural Education and the Profession: Preparing for the Future', in D. Nicol and S. Pilling (eds) *Changing Architectural Education: Towards a Neto Professionalism*, London: Spon.

Noguchi, M. (2007) 'A Renewable Experience of PV Mass Custom Housing in Canada', in B. Dimitrijevic (ed.) *CBE News*, Glasgow: The Centre for the Built Environment, pp. 8–9.

Noguchi, M. (2008) *PV Zero-energy Mass Custom Home Mission to Japan 2008*. Available at: http://mass-customization.blogs.com/mc_home-mission.pdf (accessed 18 July 2008).

O'Sullivan, B. P. (1988) 'Community Participation in Urban Development: The Role of the Community Architecture Movement', unpublished M.Phil. thesis, Department of Urban Design & Regional Planning, University of Edinburgh.

Office of the Prime Minister (2004) *Building Schools for the Future Factsheet*. Available at: www.number10.gov.uk/Page5801 (accessed 9 March 2009).

Oliver, P. (1987) *Dwellings: The House Across the World*, London: Phaidon.

Ospina, J. (1987) *Housing Ourselves*, London: Hilary Shipman.

Pateman, C. (1970) *Participation and Democratic Theory*, Cambridge: Cambridge University Press.

Pereira, M.A. (2001) 'Designing Collaboration', paper presented at the ECER2001 European Conference on Educational Research, Symposium on Networked Learning in Higher Education,

Lille, France, September. Available at: http://caad.arch.ethz.ch/info/pdf/PereiraECER2001.pdf (accessed 21 July 2008).

Perlman, J. E. (1976) *Myths of Marginality: The Urban Squatter in Brazil*, Berkeley: University of California Press.

Preiser, W. F. E., Rabinowitz, H. Z. and White, E. T. (1988) *Post-occupancy Evaluation*, New York: Van Nostrand Reinhold.

Proshansky, H. M., Fabian, A. K. and Kaminof, R. (1983) 'Place Identity: Physical World Socialization of the Self', *Journal of Environmental Psychology*, 3: 57–83.

Rios, M. (2004) 'Timely Tactics: the Strategic Role of Participation in Community Design', in B. Bell (ed.) *Good Deeds, Good Design: Community Service Through Architecture*, New York: Princeton Architectural Press.

Sachner, P. M. (1983) 'Still Planning with the Poor: Community Design Centers Keep Up the Good Works', *Architectural Record*, June: 126–131.

SAIA (2005/6) 'Negotiating Extremes – Global Condition, Local Context', *Digest of South African Architecture*, Cape Town: South African Institute of Architects.

Saint, A. (1985) *The Image of the Architect*, New Haven, CT: Yale University Press.

Sandercock, L. (1998) 'The Death of Modernist Planning: Radical Praxis or a Postmodern Age', in M. Douglass and J. Friedmann (eds) *Cities for Citizens*, London: Wiley.

Sanoff, H. (2000) *Community Participation Methods in Design and Planning*, New York: John Wiley & Sons.

Schneider, T. and Till, J. (2007) *Flexible Housing*, London: Architectural Press.

ScotMARK/gm+ad (2007) *Research into Architecture Practice. A Pilot Study of Capturing Experiential Knowledge*, Edinburgh: ScotMARK/eca.

Scottish Executive (2006) *Public Attitudes to Design in Scotland*. Available at: www.scotland.gov.uk/Publications/2007/01/04085321/0 (accessed 9 March 2009).

Scottish Government (2001) A Policy on Architecture for Scotland. Available at: www.scotland.gov.uk/Publications/2001/10/10129/File-1 (accessed 9 March 2009).

Scottish Government (2007) *Building Our Legacy. Statement on Scotland's Architecture Policy 2007*. Available at: www.scotland.gov.uk/Publications/2007/02/19145552/0 (accessed 9 March 2009).

Scottish Government Social Research (2007) *Design at the Heart of House Building*, Edinburgh: Education Information and Analytical Services. Available at: www.scotland.gov.uk/Resource/Doc/202545/0054006.pdf (accessed 9 March 2009).

Scottish Government Social Research (2008) *Public Value and Participation: a Literature Review for the Scottish Government*, Edinburgh: The Work Foundation.

Sim, D. (1993) *British Housing Design*, London: Longman.

Slessor, C. (1995) 'Mbazwane Resources Centre – Mbazwane Rural Resources Center in KwaZulu, South Africa – Narrow Margins', *Architecture Review*, 3.

Stamps, A. E. (2000) *Psychology and the Aesthetics of the Built Environment*, Norwell, MA: Kluwer Academic.

Stevens, G. (2002) *The Favoured Circle: The Social Foundations of Architectural Distinction*, Cambridge, MA: MIT Press.

Tahir, M. F. (1997) 'Who's On the Other Side of Your Software: Creating User Profiles Through Contextual Inquiry', paper presented at Usability Professionals' Association (UPA) Conference, Monterey, August.

Teachernet (2007) *About BSF*. Available at: www.teachernet.gov.uk/management/resourcesfinanceandbuilding/bsf/aboutbsf/ (accessed 9 March 2009).

Tenants Information Service (TIS) and University of Glasgow Department of Urban Studies (2004) *A Good Practice Framework for Tenant Participation in Scotland*, Edinburgh: Communities Scotland.

Till, J. (2005) 'The Negotiation of Hope', in P. Blundell-Jones, D. Petrescu and J. Till (eds) *Architecure & Participation*, London: Spon Press.

Toker, Z. (2007) 'Recent Trends in Community Design: The Eminence of Participation', *Design Studies*, 28: 243–261.

Toker, Z. and Toker, U. (2006) 'Community Design in its Pragmatist Age – Increasing Popularity and Changing Outcomes', *Journal of the Faculty of Architecture, Middle East Technical University*, 23 (2): 155–166.

Towers, G. (1995) *Building Democracy: Community Architecture in the Inner Cities*, London: Routledge.

Turner, B. (1988) *Building Community*, London: Building Community Books.

Turner, J. F. C. (1963) 'Dwelling Resources in South America', *Architectural Design*, August: 360–393.

Turner, J. F. C. (1968) 'The Squatter Settlement: An Architecture that Works', *Architectural Design*, October: 355–360.

Turner, J. F. C. (1976) *Housing by People*, London: Marion Boyars.

Turner, J. F. C. (1978) 'Housing in Three Dimensions: Terms of Reference for the Housing Question Redefined', *World Development*, 6 (9/10).

Turner, J. F. C. (1982) 'Issues in Self-help and Self-managed Housing', in P. M. Ward (ed.) *Self-help Housing: A Critique*, London: Mansell.

Turner, J. F. C. (1986) 'Future Directions in Housing Policies', *Habitat International*, 10 (3): 7–26.

Turner, J. F. C. (1988) 'Introduction' and 'Conclusions', in B. Turner (ed.) *Building Community*, London: Building Community Books.

Turner, J. F. C. (1992) 'Beyond Self-help Housing: Foreword', in K. Mathey (ed.) *Beyond Self-Help Housing*, London: Mansell.

Turner, J. F. C. and Fichter, R. (eds) (1972) *Freedom to Build: Dweller Control of the Housing Process*, New York: Macmillan.

Twigger-Ross, C. L., Bonaiuto, M. and Breakwell, G. M. (2003) 'Identity Theories and Environmental Psychology', in M. Bonnes, T. Lee and M. Bonaiuto (eds) *Psychological Theories for Environmental Issues*, Aldershot: Ashgate Publishing.

University of Sheffield School of Architecture (n.d.a) *MArch in Architecture (RIBA Part 2)*. Available at: www.shef.ac.uk/architecture/prospectivepg/part2courses/march.html (accessed 9 March 2009).

University of Sheffield School of Architecture (n.d.b) *Live Projects Student Guide*. Available at: www.liveprojects.org/ (accessed 9 March 2009).

University of Sheffield School of Architecture (2007) *MArch in Architecture Course Handbook 2007–2008*. Available at http://sheffield.ac.uk/content/1/c6/06/41/00/mastershb.pdf (accessed 15 March 2009).

Uzzell, D. L., Pol, E. and Badenas, D. (2002) 'Place Identification, Social Cohesion and Environmental Sustainability', *Environment and Behavior*, 34 (26): 26–53.

Valadares, L. (1978) *Passa-se uma casa*, Rio de Janeiro: Zahar.

Valadares, L. (ed.) (1980) *Habitação em questão*, Rio de Janeiro: Zahar.

Wates, N. (2000) *The Community Planning Handbook. How People can Shape their Cities, Towns and Villages in any Part of the World*, London: Earthscan Publications.

Wates, N. and Knevitt, C. (1987) *Community Architecture: How People are Creating Their Own Environment*, London: Penguin Books.

Ward, C. (1976) *Housing – an Anarchist Approach*, London: Freedom Press.

Wilson, M. A. (1996) 'The Socialization of Architectural Preference', *Journal of Environmental Psychology*, 16: 33–44.

Wulz, F. (1986) 'The Concept of Participation', *Design Studies*, 7 (3): 153–162.

Index

eBooks – at www.eBookstore.tandf.co.uk

A library at your fingertips!

eBooks are electronic versions of printed books. You can store them on your PC/laptop or browse them online.

They have advantages for anyone needing rapid access to a wide variety of published, copyright information.

eBooks can help your research by enabling you to bookmark chapters, annotate text and use instant searches to find specific words or phrases. Several eBook files would fit on even a small laptop or PDA.

NEW: Save money by eSubscribing: cheap, online access to any eBook for as long as you need it.

Annual subscription packages

We now offer special low-cost bulk subscriptions to packages of eBooks in certain subject areas. These are available to libraries or to individuals.

For more information please contact webmaster.ebooks@tandf.co.uk

We're continually developing the eBook concept, so keep up to date by visiting the website.

www.eBookstore.tandf.co.uk